Linguistic Contact and Language Change

Linguistic contact is a reality of everyday life, as speakers of different languages come into contact with one another, often causing language change. This undergraduate textbook provides a means by which these processes, both modern and historical, can be analysed, based on cutting-edge theoretical and methodological practices. Chapters cover language death, the development of pidgins and creoles, linguistic convergence and new variety formation. Each chapter is subdivided into key themes, which are supported by diverse and real-world case studies. Student learning is bolstered by illustrative maps, exercises, research tasks, further reading suggestions and a glossary. Ancillary resources are available, including additional exercises and research tasks, further discussion of central arguments and recordings of many of the language varieties covered. Written primarily for undergraduate students of linguistics, it provides a balanced, historically grounded and up-to-date introduction to linguistic contact and language change.

Robert McColl Millar is Professor in Linguistics and Scottish Language at the University of Aberdeen, Scotland. He has a particular interest in the ways in which history, economics and ideology interact with language use, now and in the past. His recent publications include *A Sociolinguistic History of Scotland* (2020), *Trask's Historical Linguistics,* 4th edition (2023) and *A History of the Scots Language* (2023).

'Robert McColl Millar has achieved something often aimed at but rarely attained: a textbook that is at once personal and reader-friendly, while not shying away from tackling challenging material and controversial ideas. Readers at all levels will learn a lot from it, and will find themselves reconsidering what they took to be accepted wisdom, guided by the suggested readings. Beginners are enabled to take part in this discussion, too. I particularly welcome the combined linguistic and sociohistorical approach: Millar shows us how language contact is embedded in a broad sweep of social changes over centuries and across continents.'

Paul Kerswill, University of York

'Historical linguistics and language contact studies are vibrant fields today but their intersection, crucial to both, has lacked this kind of integrated treatment. The prose is accessible, and the author makes engaging connections to his own experience. His rich, detailed case studies give readers some real understanding of the settings discussed. The volume will work well as a class textbook or independent reading for those with limited background in linguistics.'

Joseph Salmons, University of Wisconsin–Madison

'*Linguistic Contact and Language Change* is a compelling exploration of how languages evolve through interaction. The book expertly blends theory with case studies, making it an essential read for students, and useful for anyone interested in the complex nature of language change. This is a thought-provoking, original and insightful contribution to the field – highly recommended.'

Daniel Schreier, University of Zurich

'Professor Millar's book is a comprehensive and very readable introduction to various scenarios of language contact and change, and to some of the theoretical controversies in the field. Each chapter has clear illustrative examples, exercises for students, and suggestions for further reading, making it an ideal introductory textbook.'

Jeff Siegel, University of New England

Linguistic Contact and Language Change

An Introduction

Robert McColl Millar
University of Aberdeen

Shaftesbury Road, Cambridge CB2 8EA, United Kingdom

One Liberty Plaza, 20th Floor, New York, NY 10006, USA

477 Williamstown Road, Port Melbourne, VIC 3207, Australia

314–321, 3rd Floor, Plot 3, Splendor Forum, Jasola District Centre,
New Delhi – 110025, India

103 Penang Road, #05-06/07, Visioncrest Commercial, Singapore 238467

Cambridge University Press is part of Cambridge University Press & Assessment,
a department of the University of Cambridge.

We share the University's mission to contribute to society through the pursuit of
education, learning and research at the highest international levels of excellence.

www.cambridge.org
Information on this title: www.cambridge.org/highereducation/isbn/9781316512739

DOI: 10.1017/9781009071093

© Robert McColl Millar 2025

This publication is in copyright. Subject to statutory exception and to the provisions
of relevant collective licensing agreements, no reproduction of any part may take
place without the written permission of Cambridge University Press & Assessment.

When citing this work, please include a reference to the DOI 10.1017/9781009071093

First published 2025

Printed in the United Kingdom by CPI Group Ltd, Croydon CR0 4YY

A catalogue record for this publication is available from the British Library

A Cataloging-in-Publication data record for this book is available from the Library of Congress

ISBN 978-1-316-51273-9 Hardback
ISBN 978-1-009-06909-0 Paperback

Additional resources for this publication at www.cambridge.org/Millar

Cambridge University Press & Assessment has no responsibility for the persistence
or accuracy of URLs for external or third-party internet websites referred to in this
publication and does not guarantee that any content on such websites is, or will remain,
accurate or appropriate.

Contents

Acknowledgements		*page* viii
For the Teacher		ix
For the Student		xiii

1 Introduction — 1
  1.1 Vignettes of Linguistic Contact: Gaelic Influences — 1
  1.2 Linguistic Contact: An Introduction — 4
  1.3 Multilingualism Is a Reality; It Has Linguistic Repercussions — 5
  1.4 An Example: Multilingualism across Time — 6
  1.5 Central Theories of Linguistic Contact — 9
    1.5.1 Social Position of Speakers of Languages — 10
    1.5.2 Levels of Contact — 12
    1.5.3 *Integration*: Winford (2003) — 23
  1.6 Borrowing and Interference — 25
  Case Study 1 Estonian Halbdeutsch — 26
  1.7 A Very Brief Conclusion — 28
  Exercises — 29
  Suggested Reading — 29

2 Language Death, Language Attrition and Language Contact — 30
  Introduction — 30
  2.1 A Linguistic Palimpsest: Names on the Landscape — 30
  2.2 The Process of Language Shift and Its Connection to Language Death: Theory and Reality — 32
  2.3 An Example of Language Shift: Gaelic in East Sutherland — 35
  2.4 Autochthonous versus Immigrant Language Shift — 38
  2.5 Language Attrition and Linguistic Change — 40
  2.6 External and Internal Influence on the 'Dying' Language — 41
  2.7 L1 Influence on L2? — 45
  Case Study 2 Shetland Norn and Shetland Scots — 45
  2.8 Conclusion — 52
  Exercises — 53
  Suggested Reading — 53

3 Pidgins and Creoles — 55
  Introduction — 55
  3.1 What Do We Mean by Pidgins and Creoles? — 55
    3.1.1 The Study of Pidgins and Creoles: A Few Words of Contextualisation and Warning — 56

		3.1.2	'Simplification'	57
	3.2	Pidgins and Creoles: Some Initial Analysis		59
		3.2.1	Examples of Pidgins and Creoles	59
		3.2.2	Pacific Varieties	60
		3.2.3	Atlantic–Caribbean Varieties	65
		3.2.4	Analysis and Discussion	69
	3.3	Where Are Pidgins and Creoles Spoken?		70
	3.4	Suggestions for the Origins and Development of Pidgins		71
		3.4.1	A Sociolinguistic Discussion of the Development of Pidgins	72
		3.4.2	Linguistic Origin of Pidgins	74
	3.5	Creole Genesis and Development		79
		3.5.1	Creole Origin in Pidgins?	80
		3.5.2	The Quarrel at the Heart of the Matter	81
		3.5.3	Post-Bickerton Interpretations	91
	3.6	Discussion		96
	Case Study 3 The Suriname Creoles			98
	3.7	Conclusion		104
	Exercises			104
	Suggested Reading			105
4	**Semi-creoles: Varieties with Creole-like Features Which Are Not Creoles**			**106**
	Introduction			106
	4.1	Definition of *Semi-creole*		106
	4.2	Pitkern (and Norf'k)		107
		4.2.1	The Linguistic Variety Which Developed	107
		4.2.2	Examples of Pitkern	108
		4.2.3	Discussion	109
	4.3	The English of St Helena		110
		4.3.1	St Helenian Vernacular English: A Brief Description	111
		4.3.2	Comparative Evidence from Tristan da Cunha English	112
	4.4	Afrikaans		113
		4.4.1	What Linguistic State Does Afrikaans Inhabit?	114
		4.4.2	Contrastive Examples	115
		4.4.3	Socio-historical Background	116
		4.4.4	Afrikaans Is Not a Creole	118
	Case Study 4 African American Vernacular English			119
	4.5	Conclusion		125
	Exercises			126
	Suggested Reading			127
5	**Macro-convergence**			**128**
	Introduction			128
	5.1	The Convergence of Distantly Related or Unrelated Languages		128
	5.2	Divergence and the Linguistic Family Tree Model		130

	5.3	Convergence as a Countervailing Force in Linguistic Change: The Balkan Language Area	134
	5.4	Large-Scale Convergence: Beyond the *Sprachbund*	138
		5.4.1 The Uralic Languages	138
		5.4.2 The Altaic Languages	140
	Case Study 5 'Standard Average European'	142
	5.5	Conclusion	144
	Exercises	144
	Suggested Reading	145
6	**Close Variety Convergence and Change: The Koine**	146
	Introduction	146
	6.1	Closely Related Varieties and Convergence	146
	6.2	Koineisation	147
		6.2.1 Koine Glossa	147
		6.2.2 Modern Koines	148
	6.3	Dialect Contact and New Variety Formation: Convergence and Divergence	154
	Case Study 6 The Effects of Contact between Closely Related Languages and Their Outcomes on a Broader Historical Canvas	158
	6.4	Conclusion	165
	Exercises	165
	Suggested Reading	165
7	**Final Thoughts**	167
	Glossary	170
	References	179
	Index	199

Acknowledgements

The research which underlies this book has benefited greatly from discussion of the nature and results of contact with a range of scholars over the years, including Mari Aigro, William Barras, Edit Bugge, Mercedes Durham, Elspeth Edelstein, Anthony Paul Grant, Anna Havinga, Johannes Heim, Raymond Hickey, Paul Kerswill, Nils Langer, Dawn Leslie, Ragnhild Ljosland, Rowan Mackay, Warren Maguire, the late Gunnel Melchers, Alex Nicholls, Jane Roberts, Edgar Schneider, Daniel Schreier, Jeremy Smith, Peter Trudgill, P. Sture Ureland, Nicoline van der Sijs, Ans van Kemenade, Viveka Velupillai and Ilse Wischer. I have learned a great deal from my doctoral students, past and present, who have worked on topics related to those covered in this book. These include Abdullah Al-Awni, Abdullah Alghannam, Sa'ad Alshamrani, Aizhan Amangazina, Ulfatmi Azlan, Beth Cole, Charles-Henri Discry, Ekiyokere Ekiye, Sousen Elbouri, Stig George, Eqbal Ghasemyani, Kerry Karam, Edoardo McKenna, Dian Mukhlisa, Ma'an Omar, Tao Rui, Ashabul Susanto and Zhang Hongwei. Many thanks also go to the students I have taught about these matters at several levels over the last thirty years. I, of course, am sole author of all infelicities and errors.

My thanks go also to Helen Barton, Rowan Groat and Helen Shannon of Cambridge University Press, who saw this project through a rather longer gestation period than was originally intended. Thank you for your patience. Thanks also to Jenny Johnson and Jamie Bowie for the maps included in this work.

Finally, I send words of gratitude and love to Sandra and Mairi, who carry me through. This book is dedicated to them both.

For the Teacher

Aim

This book is intended to provide an up-to-date discussion and analysis of the effects which linguistic contact has on language change and language development. As the discussion at the end of Chapter 1 demonstrates, a considerable number of very good textbooks on language contact have been published over the last thirty years. None of them has such a strong historical linguistics input as this one, however (although all certainly feature elements of such a discussion). Bearing this point in mind, the material presented here has been tried, tested and adapted for at least twenty years.

I have written an advanced textbook on these matters because I would have liked to have had such a resource when I was a student in the 1980s. The linguistic and philological education I received then was excellent. But when asked *why* language changed, my teachers answered by describing *how*: the machine was seen as the cause. This book therefore has its roots in an issue which has troubled me – and many other historical linguists – since the discipline was first put on a fully scientific footing in the middle of the nineteenth century: can the divergence which appears to dominate the process of linguistic change and its analysis truly be the sole model for change of this type? Thoughtful students of the interlocking subjects concerned with language change have always recognised the possibility of features which were not part of the 'genetic' history of a particular language influencing the development of that variety. These variables were often perceived as social in nature (indeed, often as what we would now consider sociolinguistic). Linguistic contact was also recognised as a potential catalyst for change.

Sometimes this latter effect was represented by some scholars as being primarily banal, as is the case with, at least at one level of analysis, the overwhelming amount of French lexis borrowed into English. A number of scholars were willing to consider further and far more profound results of linguistic contact, however. For a long time, these remained something of a minority, perhaps even heretical, view, largely because of the rather mechanistic models of change which came into being in the aftermath of the neogrammarian breakthrough and consecration as the orthodox standpoint.

The growth from the mid twentieth century on in the study of creoles, and of several approaches to language use thrown up by the rise and diversification of sociolinguistics as a discipline, meant that a true contact linguistics came into being. For many of us, this is the beginning of the knitting together of a sociolinguistically informed historical linguistics and an awareness that language contact is a commonplace factor in both change and the catalysts which induce and channel change.

Contact linguistics has grown exponentially in the last sixty years. Subdisciplines have developed which often have limited connection with each other: some scholars work on the processes by which external elements are introduced into everyday language, while others consider the nature of being bilingual and its linguistic repercussions. Some approach contact phenomena from a formal stance, while others retain close connections to sociolinguistic models. This book cannot do justice to all viewpoints, nor has it attempted to do so (to be honest, that way lies madness). What it does provide, I hope, is a discussion, often in some depth, of some of the central themes of the field, designed to be attractive to advanced students of the field, with some new ideas included. I make no apologies for this discussion having a considerable connection to the study of linguistic change and historical linguistics in general. I believe that an understanding of language contact and its products gives us many openings in a quest for an understanding of the mechanisms involved in linguistic evolution.

Structure

This book is split into seven chapters, followed by a glossary with some discussion of central issues aired in the book, as well as a few of some importance which are only touched upon but which can be investigated further if a reader takes a particular interest in a topic. Each of the chapters, with the exception of the last, includes a case study of a particular contact situation and its repercussions. These are intended to provide the reader with an in-depth study of how to relate the ideas found in the chapter (and the book as a whole) to large-scale, real-world issues.

The first chapter is intended to be introductory up to a certain point. It introduces the ideas of a range of scholars and discusses the nature of multilingualism in a language contact situation. Chapter 2 focuses on the effects of language death and language attrition on the natures of both first and second languages, a set of issues which links in with most of what follows in the book.

The third and fourth chapters stand together as a set. Chapter 3 deals directly with the development and nature of pidgins and creoles, while Chapter 4 is concerned with semi-creoles, varieties which share some features with creoles but which do not appear to have gone through as much change away from 'mainstream' varieties of the language which has at the very least supplied most of the lexis used in the variety. At this section's heart is a serious scholarly disagreement between those who believe that creoles are exceptional creations which, in the mind of God, represent new languages and those who consider creoles to be 'natural' developments of a particular language, different from other dialects of that language only in relation to level of change. I have attempted to treat both schools of thought fairly (indeed, I believe that, at some levels, there is truth in both analyses); I am aware, however, that I will not please everyone by this even-handed approach.

Chapters 5 and 6 also form a unit of sorts, since they are both concerned with linguistic convergence. Chapter 5 is particularly concerned with convergence between languages which are, at most, distant relatives. It considers language areas of convergence and discusses the limits of the *Stammbaum* 'family tree' model of divergence across time, paying particular attention to the Uralic and Altaic families. Chapter 6 deals with convergence between dialects of the same language, as well as contact between discrete varieties which are near relatives.

Chapter 7 acts as a conclusion to the discussion, paying particular attention to the themes covered and how these might be developed further.

Exemplification in this book has concentrated largely on English. I make no apology for this: this is the language that all users of this book will know, whether as a first, second or foreign language. It is easier to understand an argument when you understand a language. I have not held back from discussion and exemplification of other languages, however.

Target Audience and Prerequisites

I have been using these materials for some years with students at Scottish Levels 3 and 4 – in other words, an advanced undergraduate level. I have not taught this subject at a taught master's level, but I suspect that this book would be a good choice with students at that stage in their development as well. It could also be used as subsidiary reading for a range of courses.

All of my students who have taken courses of this type have at least a basic understanding of the primary 'building blocks' of linguistic analysis; many will also have some understanding of linguistic change, largely absorbed through a language-heavy History of English course we offer at Aberdeen.

All the course really needs, however, is an enquiring mind. While knowledge of a language other than English might sometimes be helpful, a course based upon this book would not demand this. Most students will quickly work out that they live in an environment which is permeated by linguistic contact.

Pedagogy and Key Features

While each of the chapters (or, perhaps, groups of themes, such as Chapters 3 and 4 or Chapters 5 and 6) can stand as an independent unit, I envisage this book as a course in itself. Material can be added or taken away, but the book is intended to be a whole.

Each of the first six chapters ends with points to be discussed and research tasks to be completed. The book's website (www.cambridge.org/Millar) includes further ideas for activities which might take a somewhat longer time than is available in a class. Each of the chapters also supplies recommendations for central readings. I always encourage my students to use the references at the end of the book to read as widely as possible around the subject they are researching. Such an activity is not only useful in relation to the type of course the book is intended for; it will also help students develop research and bibliographical skills which will be useful for the writing of a dissertation or other extended pieces of work, no matter their subject. Discussions on how to do this fruitfully are available on the book's dedicated website. The website also contains some textual material which, although not included in the final draft, is, I think, of some value. I also include links to examples of many of the language varieties mentioned in the book.

A glossary is provided at the end of the book, which is designed to aid the student in accessing the central features and terminology of the subjects covered and of related fields.

Finally, if you have any questions, comments or suggestions based on your experience, please do get in touch.

For the Student

The way you speak is a product of linguistic contact. No matter where you live, your life will be impacted by contact between different varieties, whether of your native language or of a range of separate languages. In a very real sense, you already know a great deal about the subjects covered in this book. What I hope it will give you are the tools by which you can approach and carry out your own analyses.

This book includes discussion of features from a range of languages. But while it is often useful to have command of a language (or languages) other than your own, you will be able to follow and understand the material if you only know one language. The book does assume some knowledge of the basic ideas and analytical techniques of linguistics. A glossary is available at the end of the book, however, which provides summaries both of central ideas covered in the book and also of some of the more specialised terms which make analysis of the field more straightforward and fruitful.

This book is set up to include a range of themes which will help you develop some of the ideas which are central to the study of linguistic contact in relation to language change. Some of the scholarly debates covered are quite controversial. While taking a critical approach, I have attempted to remain as neutral as possible. There are often good points to be made on both sides of a debate. I encourage you to make up your own mind, based upon the evidence (which should always be paramount). Use the references (and other resources) to read round the subject: your understanding will be deeper.

The exercises and discussion suggestions at the end of each chapter are designed to help you to tease out some of the ideas covered in the chapter. They are not intended to be exhaustive. Please use them creatively. Further issues are represented on the website (www.cambridge.org/Millar).

1 Introduction

1.1 Vignettes of Linguistic Contact: Gaelic Influences

One of my earliest memories is of sitting cross-legged on the carpet of our front room. I am around four years old. One of my grandmother's brothers and two of her sisters are sitting talking to each other in Gaelic. My father is smiling at what they are saying; he is speaking Gaelic as well, although I am aware that his speech is slower than theirs. Then my mother enters the room, bearing teacups, a teapot and the inevitable cake. Everyone switches immediately to their various Scots and English dialects. My mother comes from a Lowlands background, so switching is the polite thing to do (I had already internalised this inequality). My great-aunts and great-uncle appear to have issues distinguishing between /p/ and /b/ and /t/ and /d/ in their second language (for a discussion of Gaelic phonological patterns, see Gillies 1993: 147–66).

In July 2020, in the aftermath of the first wave of the COVID-19 pandemic, we were instructed by our institution, the University of Aberdeen, to record as much of our teaching for the coming semester as possible, since, at most, we would have limited face-to-face contact with our students in the autumn. I spent six weeks doing this. The reason why three courses took so long to record was that the Scottish Parliament (quite rightly) had enacted legislation earlier that year (before COVID-19 hit) which required that all recorded material used in teaching have subtitles, intended in the first place for students with severe hearing impairment or other non-visible disabilities. The software which we used to create captions automatically (it will remain nameless) claimed to have 85–90 per cent accuracy. My experience was that 50 per cent would be a generous estimate (40 per cent might be nearer the mark). Why was there this discrepancy?

In the first instance, there was the subject matter. The software was not designed to reproduce material from a range of languages, modern and ancient. International Phonetic Alphabet symbols could not be represented (at least not readily: you could cut and paste from other documents). Sometimes this lack of specialist knowledge could have unexpected results. The *neogrammarian hypothesis*, a central, if at times controversial, tenet of historical linguistics, became the *New York Romanian hypothesis*, for instance. Secondly, the software was not designed for my pronunciation: it worked better with either the RP (Received Pronunciation – the prestige accent in England) or General American accent. I found that my tap /r/ was regularly interpreted as /t/, for instance. I also have a (very mild) stammer which I generally cope with by placing brief, meaningless vowel segments before, in particular, /p/, /b/, /t/ and /d/. It didn't like that either.

But the final issue was unexpected: I realised what I would analyse as a strong Gaelic influence on my speech, despite having very limited ability in that language. I first noticed this with the word *speakers*, which was normally represented as *because*. There was regular confusion of voiced and voiceless sounds in the transcription. Gaelic *does* have an occasional distinction between voiced and voiceless sounds, but the primary consonantal distinction is between fortis and lenis sounds, the first representing where considerable amounts of breath are released when the consonant is produced, the second where significantly less breath is expressed in pronunciation. In most Germanic languages, the fortis versus lenis distinction is masked by the distinction between voiceless (which is fortis) and voiced (which is lenis). In Gaelic, on the other hand, the distinction between fortis and lenis is essentially independent of voicing. It is possible, for instance, to have a lenited voiceless sound and a fortis voiced sound. To a speaker of English, these all sound voiceless. I think this was what the captioning software was picking up: a prominent feature of West Central Scottish speech, particularly, perhaps, for people who speak Gaelic or have grown up in environments where Gaelic was regularly heard. What I do know is that, while I take a degree of pride in my heritage, on this occasion it made my life significantly more difficult than it might have been.

Let us widen this discussion beyond the personal. I live and work in the North-east of Scotland (for places and regions mentioned here, see Map 1.1). One of the features of the local dialects of Scots (as well as those spoken in Caithness in the far north of the Scottish mainland) most recognisable to both natives and incomers is a change from original /ʍ/ to /f/ in the <wh> words. This can be seen in the pronunciation of the Scots cognate of English *what*, which, to me, is /ʍɪt/ but in the North-east is /fɪt/. The change proposed is not abnormal: similar alternations turn up in the Polynesian languages, although on this occasion the original consonant appears to have been /f/ (Drechsel 2014: 89). But it is unknown elsewhere in the Germanic languages (with the exception of *four*, where the expected *whour was replaced early in the discrete development of the Germanic languages because of distant assimilation with *five*). Why does this change turn up in northern Scotland? (For a discussion of many of the issues covered here, see Millar 1996, 2007, 2009, 2010a, 2016, 2018, 2020, 2023.)

We could just say that this is to do with chance. Things happen. This is not a very satisfactory explanation, however. If we can take this further, I would assume with these types of changes that sociolinguistic and socio-historical forces had been at work in their development. When we have sufficient evidence for the social nature of the place(s) in which change is taking place, sociolinguistic spurs to the change are practically always evident.

Why is the North-east of Scotland different linguistically from the central and southern parts of the country in relation to this change (there are many other linguistic differences as well)? In the latter areas, Gaelic retreated during the Middle Ages, with its presence hardly being felt in the modern era except on the edges of the Gàidhealtachd, the historical Gaelic-speaking area, and, in the case of my family and that of many others, the linguistic residue of migration into the industrial West of Scotland from the nineteenth century on. In the North-east, however, the retreat was far later and slower, with considerable evidence for Gaelic being used even in the coastal strip until the seventeenth century and in less accessible areas until the twentieth century (indeed, the last speaker of the local dialects of Gaelic died as recently as 1984). This implies that it was quite normal for Scots speakers and Gaelic speakers to live side by side (although not necessarily in social relationships associated with equality) until well into the modern age. There are also a considerable number of lexical items borrowed from Gaelic into the local

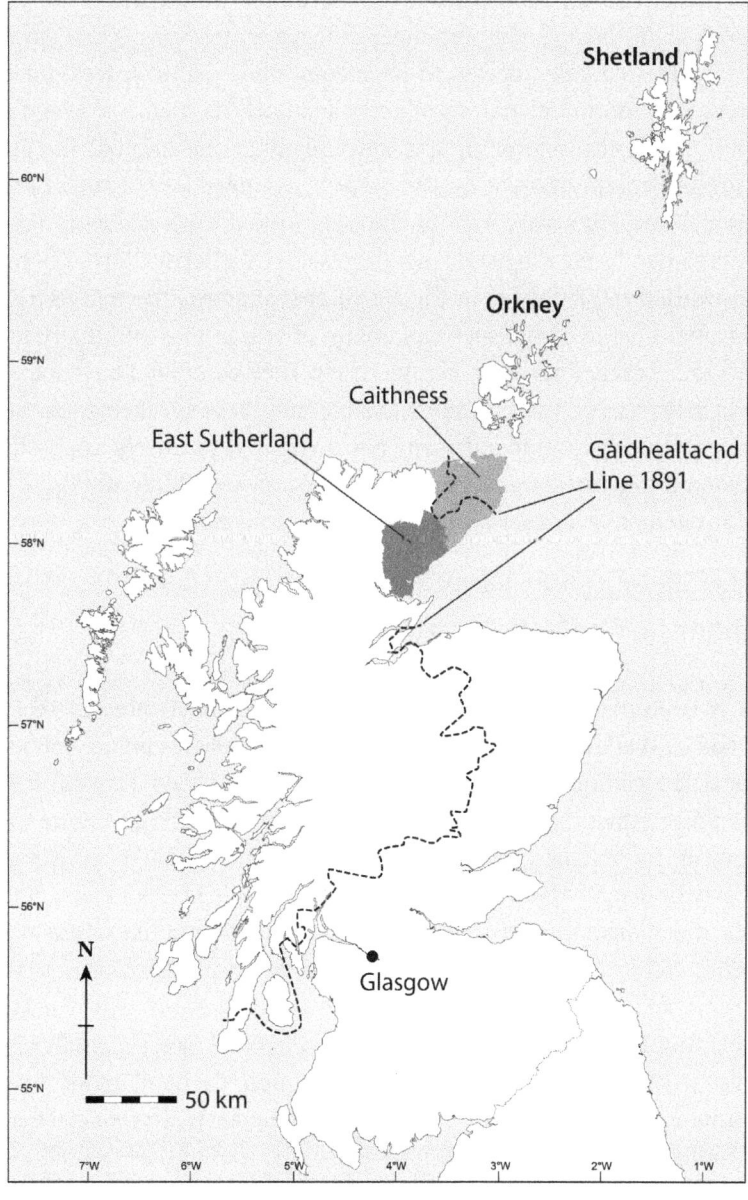

Map 1.1 Places in Scotland mentioned in Chapters 1 and 2.

Scots dialect not found in other varieties. What does this historical reality tell us about this sound change?

A central element to this discussion is that Gaelic does not have either /w/ or /ʍ/ in its phonemic inventory. Historically, words and names with these consonants were nativised in a variety of different ways. Thus *William* is *Uilleam* (occasionally *Liam*, although this often has more Irish associations). The language does, however, have the voiceless bilabial fricative [φ], a sound very similar in articulation to [f] (and /ʍ/, indeed). It is very likely that Gaelic speakers in the North-east of Scotland produced this sound for the <wh> words, where /ʍ/ (in Middle Scots, probably /xw/) was produced by their Scots-speaking neighbours. Similar sound substitutions can be heard with some Irish English speakers. A colleague of mine, from Co. Cork, pronounces *what* as /fat/; the great post-independence writer Seán Ó Faoláin was born John Whelan. This change appears to have some time depth. It was, for instance, evident in the now moribund dialects of Forth and Bargy (a linguistic island in southeast Ireland, apparently representing a descendant of the original English of the medieval English colonisation of Ireland, largely swamped (see Chapter 6) elsewhere by the varieties brought across from England in the sixteenth and early seventeenth centuries), recorded in the nineteenth century (see, e.g., Hickey 2007: 71–9).

The substitution of /f/ for [φ] in the North-east suggests the nativisation of the Gaelic consonant [φ] by Scots speakers, many of whom may originally have been immigrants to the area, forming a 'planter' class. They would not have had the latter sound in their inventory. It is entirely plausible that these speakers took the change to be representative of local identity and approximated as closely as possible to the 'new' consonant (for further analysis and discussion, see Millar 2009).

Linguistic contact, in one form or another, is everywhere.

1.2 Linguistic Contact: An Introduction

This book is concerned with linguistic contact, the central feature of the vignettes discussed above. Whether we are aware of it or not, linguistic contact and its societal and personal associations are an everyday occurrence. When I speak in (Scottish) Standard English rather than my native dialect, I may be making a choice which aids comprehension (for instance, many of my students are not native speakers of either variety). I may be demonstrating politeness towards people I do not know. It may even be a means of demonstrating distance towards people I do not like or am angry with. But the ability to shift in this way is preconditioned by the construction of a continuum between Scots and English over the last three hundred years which has involved considerable transfer of features from one end to the other (see, e.g., Millar 2016: 49–52). In other words, my linguistic 'choice', based upon my imbibing of the sociolinguistic norms for my community from early childhood, is a product of long-term linguistic contact. This contact is nowhere as marked as many we will discuss in this book, but it is contact nonetheless.

This awareness, personal and societal, of both the normal and extraordinary nature of linguistic contact, along with its outcomes, is at the centre of this book. I hope that, in my writing it and your reading it, we will come to a greater understanding of the themes and phenomena covered.

1.3 Multilingualism Is a Reality; It Has Linguistic Repercussions

In order to understand the linguistic outcomes of contact, it is necessary to develop an understanding of the multilingualism – societal and individual – in which it is created.

Most countries have official languages, languages which have a mandated and prescribed function within the state apparatus, in distinction to other varieties used in that polity. This presence is often most strongly felt in education, where linguistic preference (or *diktat*) is particularly overtly expressed. While many countries have more than one official language – South Africa is an outlier in having twelve official languages, but having two, as is the case with Canada, is by no means uncommon – most countries have only one, whether this be de jure, as with French in France, or de facto, as with English in the United States. So central is the French language to the idea of a unitary French state, in fact, that the language's status within the republic is expressed and highlighted at the beginning of the country's constitution.

This official monolingualism (or directed and constrained multilingualism) is useful for ideological purposes (and may save expenditure under certain conditions, although this is debatable) but runs counter to our everyday experience of the world today and, in fact, the reality of human life for millennia. Multilingualism is the norm (for a discussion of a particularly knotty context of this type, see Ewing 2020). France, so monolithically monolingual in the official and public spheres in the present day, was multilingual until very recently, with many parts of the country having very few speakers of French native to their territories. One of the central projects of post-1789 France has been to make French citizens French speakers through the exertion of official power, in compulsory education in particular but also, until very recently, universal male military service. Dutch, once used widely in those parts of Flanders which were included within the Kingdom of France by the Treaty of the Pyrenees of 1659, is now spoken by only a small part of the region's population, many of whom are past child-bearing age. It is quite possible that the linguistic heritage of French Flanders will soon only be carried by place names like *Dunkirk* (Dutch *Duunkerke* 'church in the dunes', French *Dunkerque*; for further discussion, see Ryckeboer 2000).

Yet at the same time as France has become monolingual, the country's imperialist heritage and the forces of globalisation have meant that, in particular in urban areas, previously unattested languages are now regularly heard, if not actually prevalent. The English language, no matter what linguistic arbiters in the French-speaking world might wish, is now omnipresent in many domains, both written and spoken. (For a discussion of why countries become multilingual, see Fasold 1987; this analysis is based on the assumption that countries are naturally monolingual, which might be an example of putting the cart before the horse. Millar 2005: 18–27 provides an analysis of his views, while describing forces which bring about societal monolingualism.)

1.4 An Example: Multilingualism across Time

Let us attempt an analysis of the effects of language contact across a considerable amount of time through evidence from a particular place with considerable time depth. The city of Trier, in the far west of Germany (see Map 1.2), lies on the river Mosel/Moselle (one of the major tributaries of the Rhine). It is named *Trèves* in French. Quite a few German (and Dutch) settlements have additional French

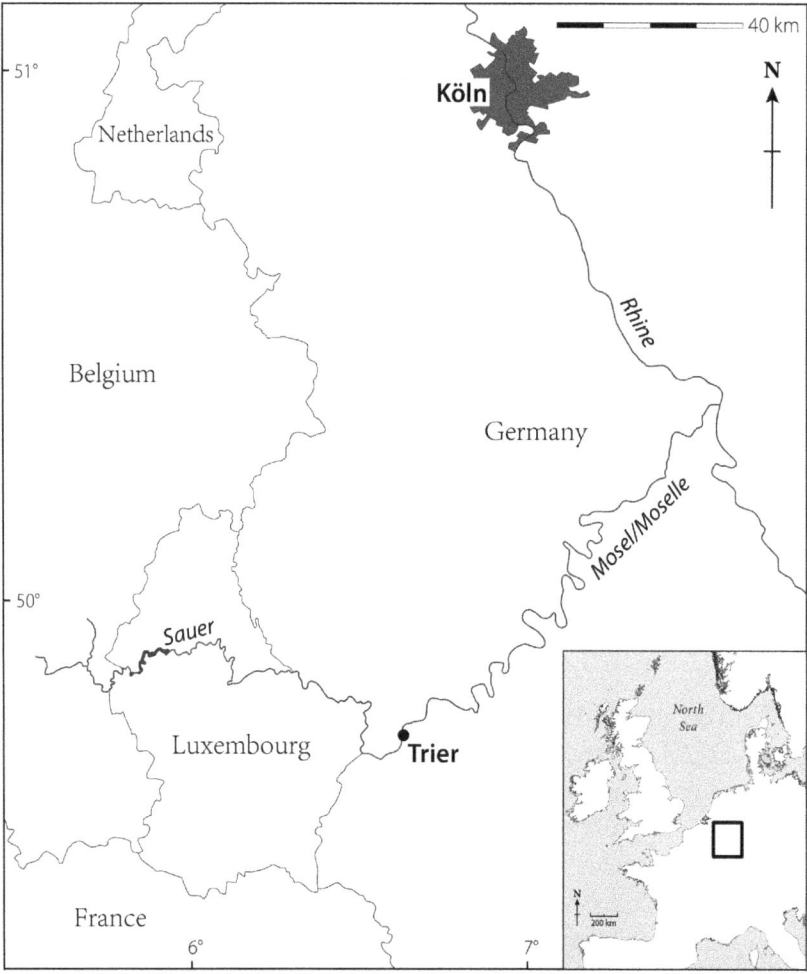

Map 1.2 The lower Mosel Valley and its environs.

names. Mostly these are spelling variants, designed to help French speakers pronounce a German name more 'authentically' (so that *Berlin* is *Berline*) or are translations of the Germanic original, so that *'s-Hertogenbosch* in the Netherlands is *Bois-des-ducs* 'the wood of the dukes'. A range of settlements, mostly on the west bank of the Rhine, display different patterns in the formation of their French and German names, however. A particularly striking example of this is the city of *Köln*, which is known in French (and, by extension, English) as *Cologne*, derived from Latin *Colonia* (*Claudia et Ara Agrippinensium*) 'the Claudian Colony and [the Colony] of the altar of Agrippa and his descendants', a Roman fortified market town established from the first century CE on by the settlement of colonies of discharged soldiers placed there to keep a watch across the Rhine on the inhabitants of 'Free Germany'. The settlement was later Germanised, particularly after the collapse of Roman power on that frontier in the fifth century CE, but the name was maintained. There is evidence that Latin continued to be spoken in the city for some time after this transfer of power, however; this can be seen in the use of that language in quite personal contexts, such as tombstones, which goes beyond the use of stock phrases, such as *requiescat in pace* 'may he/she rest in peace' (Fletcher 1997: 131).

But Trier is in many ways different from settlements like Cologne. The city was particularly Roman (and not merely a frontier post). In the late Roman period, it was the military capital of a large part of the western Roman Empire. One of the few Roman-era buildings still standing roofed is in Trier: the Basilica, a large, self-consciously imposing building, now a church but historically the audience hall where the emperor or his representative dispensed justice and heard petitions.

The name *Trier* is not Latin, however. It commemorates the people who lived in the region before the Romans (and are likely to have been the primary population in the city's hinterland – westwards up the Mosel Valley and northwards up the Sauer Valley – during the Roman period): the *Trēvirī,* a Celtic-speaking nation associated with considerable resistance to the Romans as the latter began to take over the Mosel Valley in the first century BCE (see Hupe 2014). There is some evidence that Celtic speakers remained in the neighbourhood of Trier into at least the third and fourth centuries. Schwindler (2014: 186) reports that there are many more Celtic personal names recorded for Trier than in equivalent cities in southern Gaul. St Jerome, active in the later fourth century, observed that the Celtic language he had heard on a brief visit to Trier in his youth was the same as that he had heard among the Galatians in what is now Turkey (Schwindler 2014: 193). There are, however, reasons for not taking this report entirely at face value. For instance, the amount of time between the third century BCE settlement of central Asia Minor by Celtic migrants and the third century CE seems lengthy for a language to survive in new contexts under constant pressure from a major language such as Greek (although for a contrary viewpoint, see Eska 2006).

It is likely that Roman Trier became highly multilingual, primarily, perhaps, as a result of the diversity of origins soldiers had by the third or fourth century; Greek inscriptions, normally of an official or semi-official nature, are also found

(Schwindler 2014), a sign of growing economic and political power in the eastern Mediterranean basin and the decline of the Latin-speaking former centre in the west, perhaps. The need for service industries to supply the governmental and military apparatus would have encouraged traders from all over the empire to settle in the city. This analysis does not include the large enslaved population, whose origins, again, could have been in any part of the empire and many areas beyond its frontiers, but whom history has left largely nameless and faceless (for a discussion of multilingualism in ancient Rome, see Elder 2020).

Many of the languages spoken in Roman and post-Roman Trier, such as Hunnish (probably a Turkic language) or Sarmatian (an Iranian language), were ephemeral in the region; they had little or no effect on local language use at the time or later. But one language – German, in its Frankish form – eventually became the dominant language of the Mosel Valley up into Lorraine, in what is now France. The Roman linguistic background in Trier was never entirely displaced, however, even if the city relatively quickly ceased to have large-scale strategic importance (see, e.g., Clemens 2014). There is some evidence, in fact, that there were local native speakers of French in the city in the nineteenth century. It is likely, however, that these citizens were descended from modern migrants, some of whom were fleeing from religious persecution. Local varieties of Romance did continue to be spoken into at least the twelfth century, however (Barme 2008: 16).

For the last century or so, Trier has welcomed speakers of many languages. Certainly, since the early 1950s, these have been largely from Turkey and southern Europe, but people from North and sub-Saharan Africa, as well as parts of Asia, have also been drawn to Germany for a variety of reasons. What linguistic effect these contacts have had on the other languages spoken in the city is difficult to say, although it is likely that the primary influence would be from German onto the languages of recent immigration, as well as in the nature of the German produced by speakers of the latter languages. Overall, it is probable that the primary influence from languages of recent immigration upon the local dominant variety will have been lexical, in particular in relation to words describing the incoming culture and its artefacts – the cuisine of that group being particularly likely to encourage lexical borrowing, so that words like *kebap* 'kebab' or *kief* 'sifted material taken from cannabis flowers; by extension, cannabis as a whole' are now commonplace. But it is, in fact, another language – English – which has had particular effects on all these languages, even when the person using the English words and phrases has little or no ability in speaking that language personally.

All of this leaves out a presiding linguistic contact (and conflict in many ways) found in Trier and in many other places: interaction between the national standard variety and the local vernacular. Only very occasionally is Trier dialect represented (semi-)officially in writing. From my own experience, the local variety is certainly heard in the city. I have, however, rarely been aware of its being used in shops or other businesses, at least when people are serving customers. Locally accented Standard German would be the norm.

This is in marked contrast to what happens in the Grand Duchy of Luxembourg, whose border lies no more than fifteen kilometres west of Trier. In the Grand Duchy, the dominant language was, at least until recently, French, although practically all citizens speak Luxembourgish, a Rhine–Mosel variety of German (taken in its broadest sense) similar to the dialect of Trier, as their primary language (for recent discussion, see Gilles 2023). For a number of reasons, this variety has achieved considerable importance as a marker of national identity over the last two centuries; it is now one of the three official languages (along with French and German) of the country. While it is quite normal to be addressed in French when entering an up-market boutique in Luxembourg City, this may primarily be a matter of prestige signalling (many French and Belgian people also commute into the city for work; given the sociolinguistic realities, they may never learn much of the local language). In northern Luxembourg, the part of the country I know best, most businesses (indeed, most people) will assume that you are a native speaker of Luxembourgish and act accordingly.

In some ways, however, the neighbouring German and Luxembourgish contexts are similar. Both places have a language of prestige which, at least until recently, dominated the local language variety. The difference is that, in the case of Trier, the two competing varieties are closely related, while this is not the case between French and Luxembourgish.

French *has* influenced Luxembourgish, but this is generally through the intense level of lexical borrowing from the former to the latter (there is some apparent phonological influence as well). In Trier, however, native speakers will often move between varieties not just situationally but also in the middle of an utterance, in a form of **code-switching** (the use of elements of one language variety alongside another in the same discourse; for a brilliant, but controversial, analysis of this phenomenon, see Myers-Scotton 2002). The change does not always appear to have a meaningful purpose. I suspect that speakers do not often recognise that they are shifting. The effects of this type of linguistic behaviour may encourage the blending of the two varieties, an issue to which we will return on a number of occasions in this book. Indeed, most of the patterns described earlier will be developed further in Section 1.5. In that section and Section 1.6, we will consider means by which we can analyse degrees and levels of language contact, and we will look at different ways in which the effects of contact can be realised.

1.5 Central Theories of Linguistic Contact

In this section we will consider some of the central theories which underlie the analysis of linguistic contact. The first of these is, perhaps, the oldest and most straightforward means of analysing the nature of contact: through its social direction. The second (associated with the work of Thomason) considers the level of contact phenomena found in particular languages. The third, associated with the work of Winford, considers contact phenomena in relation to the impact of interacting sociolinguistic forces. Each of these analyses has many virtues and advantages; none explains all forms of contact and their outcomes.

1.5.1 Social Position of Speakers of Languages

In most societies where two (or more) populations speaking two (or more) different linguistic varieties live, there is social asymmetry: one group possesses more economic, cultural, political and social power than does the other. Inevitably, this means that linguistic relationships, in particular the nature and direction of contact, are affected by these societal features.

Superstratal influence, where the language of the socially, economically and politically prominent (often, dominant) section of the community affects that of the less powerful, is arguably the most prominent level-based contact (essentially because most reporting is carried out from the viewpoint, and often in the language, of the powerful).

My mother tongue, Scots, spoken and written in a variety of forms, is influenced by (Scottish) Standard English in a pervasive way, essentially because the latter is the primary language of literacy in Scotland (and is also a close relative). For instance, historically the particle which marked comparison was either *nor* or *as*, so that you said *(h)it's caulder the day nor thestreen* 'it's colder today than it was yesterday (evening)'. Now, in my experience, *(h)it's caulder the day (th)an thestreen* would be more common.

A more intense level of superstratal contact (possibly because it is between far less closely related varieties) is that between Norman French and English in the Middle Ages. French influence upon the English language had already begun before the Norman Conquest of England in 1066-7 (*pride*, for instance, appears, according to the *Oxford English Dictionary*, to have been borrowed early in the eleventh century). The profound shift in societal structure which followed those events led to the leaders and holders of land and capital becoming largely French speakers, since their native predecessors had essentially been purged. Eventually, this produced mass importation of Anglo-Norman French lexis into English, although limited phonological (pronunciation) and morphosyntactic (structural) features, which we will analyse in greater depth later in this chapter.

The opposing tendency can also be present: **substratal influence**. The language use of less prestigious groups within a society can affect that of more prestigious groups. Scottish Standard English has been influenced considerably by Scots, although this is confused by the fact that many people, including me, can speak both; this makes this contact not between discrete groups per se – although there are a considerable number of Standard English speakers in Scotland who cannot speak Scots and whose speech and writing are imbued with privilege – but within individuals. These phenomena can also be ongoing for the individual. The borrowings are primarily lexical, although there are a small number of morphosyntactic transfers. Some of these borrowings are, to use Aitken's (1984) term, covert: Scots words like *jigget*, a particular type of pork chop, are used without the speaker necessarily knowing they are not Standard English; others, such as *dreich* 'dreary, dull, endlessly repeated', are used in Scottish Standard English far more consciously as an overt marker of Scottishness, often by people who have no or limited command of the autochthonous vernacular (for further discussion of the historical processes involved, see Dossena 2005).

Substratal influence is regularly the product of the imperialist seizure of power and land in a particular territory. This can often be analysed as the opposite, but companion, of superstratal influence. A well-known development of this type involves lexical change through contact as English speakers expanded around the globe in the modern era. The settlement and proliferation of English speakers in North America from the early seventeenth century on led to a significant level of lexical borrowings (the analysis here is derived largely from the *Oxford English Dictionary*), concerned with local flora and fauna, such as *chipmunk* (from a south-eastern variety of Ojibwa); topography, such as *bayou* (an oxbow lake on the lower Mississippi River; from Choctaw, via French); and cultural items, such as *powwow*, now largely in English meaning an animated conversation, often designed to bring about peace, but originally referring to a shaman or indigenous priest. The *OED* suggests that the word is derived from both Narrangansett and Massachusett, Algonquian languages spoken in New England. Occasionally, turns of phrase appear to have been borrowed in a calqued form, such as, possibly, *in this neck of the woods* 'round about here'. But while there have been, and remain, varieties of English associated with speakers of Native American languages, the influence of these varieties upon mainstream varieties of North American English has been, at most, slight and ephemeral. Given the linguistic diversity of pre-Columbian North America, along with the moribund or entirely extinct state of many native languages, however, this topic is unlikely ever to be discussed fully; Newmark, Walker and Stanford (2016) provide an illuminating recent treatment of some of these features and issues.

Similar patterns can be found practically anywhere where English speakers, bringing their language, colonised and exploited. Māori words have been borrowed into local, New Zealand (and occasionally global) varieties of English, as can be seen with lexical items such as *kiwi*, referring both to the flightless bird and the people of New Zealand, no matter where they or their ancestors came from, while more recent and enlightened times have led to cultural borrowings, such as *kōhanga reo*, literally 'language nest', referring to a Māori language immersion nursery school provision. But despite the fact that New Zealanders of European origin refer to themselves by the Māori term *Pākēha*, New Zealand English is a mainstream Southern Hemisphere variety. Indeed, it could be argued that, beyond a patina of 'exotic' lexis, New Zealand English is, like most 'colonial' varieties dating from the nineteenth century, essentially a direct descendant of colloquial South-East England English varieties, similar to, and in contact with, the norms of Standard English (see Hay, Maclagan and Gordon 2008; see also Chapter 6 in this volume; for Māori English, see Holmes 1997). The Gaelic influence on West Central Scots mentioned at the beginning of the chapter represents a similar phenomenon in the dialect of most speakers.

Although substratal influence on more prestigious varieties must be (indeed, is) very common, it is often difficult to trace. This was particularly true in the past, when ability in writing (and access to materials and an audience) was primarily confined to speakers of the dominant variety, deriving from social backgrounds which were least likely to be influenced by contact with the ruled. Imagination often needs to be used to rebuild these contacts. Sometimes this develops into scholarly over-imagination.

Probably the rarest form of language contact, taken from the point of view of directional influence, is **adstratal**. This contact occurs where two populations speaking different varieties live side by side in a state of equality (or near equality). This is a situation which, sadly, has rarely pertained for long in human history. A good example of this type of contact is that between English and Norse in the north of England during the Viking Age. Although the Norse were normally rulers in these territories, they often ruled by the (tacit) consent of the native English and with an English-speaking chancery (since English speakers were more likely to be literate, at least in Roman script). Most of the population, no matter what language they spoke, worked the land in similar ways and eventually intermarried. Influence between the languages therefore took place in an intimate and essentially egalitarian context. We will return to this contact in Chapter 6.

Another contact of this type can be evinced and analysed in the development of Michif, a language presently spoken by somewhat more than a thousand people in Saskatchewan and Manitoba in Canada and in North Dakota, across the border in the United States (Thomason and Kaufman 1988: esp. 228–33; see also Winford 2003: 183–9). An ethnically mixed group of Cree and French speakers developed their own language, which bears similarities to both source varieties but is of its own type, unintelligible to other French or Cree speakers. It is important to stress how extreme this product of contact is; the fact that the process of creation appears to have been at least semi-conscious may explain this.

This observation is, in fact, what renders this type of analysis problematical. It describes the *nature* of the social relationships between the speakers of different varieties quite well. What the *results* of these relationships are (or were) and what *level* of influence there was cannot be represented by this model. That is the great virtue of the next model to be discussed.

1.5.2 Levels of Contact

Another way of looking at the nature of linguistic contact is through the appraisal of levels of contact. This appears to address many of the criticisms connected to the directional model just discussed. The most distinguished model for this means of viewing contact is that produced by Thomason. Her model conceives of there being four levels of contact, from the essentially banal borrowing of vocabulary, with practically no structural influence evidenced, to a situation where any or all elements of one language can be brought into the other and where the linguistic nature of the borrowing variety is fundamentally changed by the contact. The quality of this proposal does not mean, of course, that Thomason's model (as discussed in a range of places; here based upon Thomason 2001: 70–71) is itself free from problems, however.

Thomason begins her model with stage 1, although it can be assumed that there might be a stage 0, where a linguistic variety has not undergone any contact with other varieties. Although possible, this state is unlikely to be found in any but a highly circumscribed set of languages and, in the past, before the development of the nation state, even less so. Even 'island' languages, such as Icelandic, show considerable evidence of both modern contact and (to a lesser extent, perhaps) similar phenomena in the past (an analysis of this type also ignores the evidence for ancient contacts found in all the Germanic languages, such as Icelandic *vín* 'wine', borrowed through contact between Germanic and Latin speakers during the Roman period, although the word has a more complex and disputed primary origin, and *kirkja* 'church', borrowed from Greek in the early Christian centuries, particularly along the Roman Rhine and Danube frontiers).

1.5.2.1 Thomason Level 1

Thomason Level 1: 'casual contact'

Sociolinguistic context: small number of bilinguals; fluency not needed for borrowing
Lexis: only content words; largely nouns
Structure: practically no borrowing

I have a fair, if somewhat random, knowledge of a range of Slavonic words, built up through many years of reading Russian literature (in translation, sadly) and taking an interest in the history of east central and eastern Europe; this has been added to by personal connections to Belarus in the last few years. In addition, from 2004 on, a considerable number of Polish people moved to Scotland (supplementing a smaller but significant Polish population, exiled since 1945). Polish food products in particular have become highly prized in the host population. This means that I can go from *Narodniki* (the Populists, a rather naive Russian revolutionary group which briefly gained prominence in the 1870s), to *raduga* (a rainbow), to *chleb* (bread). This does not mean that I could hold a conversation in any Slavonic language, however. I have a (rather basic) understanding of aspects of their phonologies, but my knowledge of any of these languages' morphosyntax is, at best, negligible. The effect of these contacts upon my everyday language is banal.

Moving beyond my own experience, the effect Italian has had on English is a striking example of this level of contact. Italian has had lexical influence upon English in essentially two ways, similar to the substratal and superstratal influences discussed earlier in this chapter. In the first instance, this influence is connected to mass immigration into urban areas in the English-speaking world by Italian speakers. The other represents evidence for the migration of a small number of Italian-speaking experts (often in music, art and cuisine) into the English-speaking world from the seventeenth century on. Connected to this is the prominence and prestige given to Italian culture by non-Italians, under the influence of this migration, largely due to indirect communication transference of innovation through the arts.

Large-scale migration of Italian speakers into the English-speaking world was particularly prevalent in the late nineteenth and early twentieth centuries; it has continued, albeit at lower levels, since then (see Gabaccia 2013). While, as was suggested earlier, some of these migrants were associated with prestige occupations, most came from relatively impoverished rural and urban backgrounds, originating in particular in those areas associated with systemic instability and poverty. Illiteracy in their own language was by no means uncommon (for a discussion of relations between the early Italian American community and the host community, as well as within the Italian American community itself, see Scodari 2018). Simplifying somewhat, when and where there were sufficient immigrants speaking the same language, associated with similar geographical and cultural backgrounds (as in the cities of the eastern and central United States in the late nineteenth and early twentieth centuries), 'ethnic' neighbourhoods developed. These were often in direct contact and sometimes confrontation with nearby groups of different origins.

While affluence necessarily attenuated these ties over time through the move away from the original ethnic neighbourhood (this was particularly the case with generational transfer), similar communities in leafier locales – New Jersey, for instance – often demonstrate the continuation of these ties. Italians were, perhaps, particularly given to maintaining cultural connections within defined neighbourhoods because they represented the first large-scale migration into the United States from southern Europe, associated by outsiders with Catholicism and organised criminal activity. They were obvious targets for what has been termed, in the American context, the 'Party of Fear' (see Bennett 1988), associated by the host culture with a series of perceptions, based on ingrained prejudice against the 'other', often caused by panic-based fear of profound changes in the ethnic, cultural, linguistic and social nature of the country.

Inevitably, Italian migrants imported features of their native varieties into their English. The most marked of these in phonological terms, perhaps, was the use of /t/ and /d/ instead of /θ/ and /ð/, in words like *thing* and *though*. This particular pronunciation, combined with similar pronunciations by Irish and Slavonic immigrants, among others, has sometimes also passed into the language of 'native' urban working-class speakers in New York City, Boston and Chicago, possibly as a marker of class and place identity. It was (and is) severely criticised by linguistic and social (particularly educational) mainstream linguistic arbiters (for a discussion of these tendencies, see Lippi-Green 1997). Some elements of Italian lexis from this immigrant source have been borrowed into mainstream English. Many of these, such as *capisc(e)?* (often represented as *capeesh?*), 'Do you understand?', may have come into the latter language through the influence of film, television and other portrayals of Italian American life and culture, no matter how inaccurate. Inevitably, many Italian words for street food have also entered the English language through contact.

Italian also influences English through several kinds of interaction in relatively elevated contexts. This is particularly the case with music. While the terminology of the classical musical tradition is often dominated by Italian terminology in English, whether that be compositional forms, such as *sonata* or *concerto*, or instructions on modes of playing, such as *largo* or *presto*, opera in many ways demonstrates the strongest indebtedness. These instructional conventions that provide advice on stage directions or the use of the voice (most strikingly with terms like *recitativo*, the half-sung, half-spoken 'conversations' between characters, carrying the story between arias) are most predominantly Italian. While it would be possible for English speakers to produce native lexis for any or all of these terms (as is often true with German), sociolinguistic concepts of appropriateness (and elitism) demand that this has been, and is, unlikely to be successful.

Terminology related to other forms of high art in English, including painting and sculpting, is also often Italian, as are words connected to particular types of architecture and construction, such as *stucco* (although this does not imply that borrowings of this type are inevitably high status: in my dialect, for instance, a plaster cast is often termed a *stookie*; to hit someone very hard is to *stookie* them). Cuisine of various sorts has also been profoundly influenced by Italian. As we have seen, many of these terms are likely to have arrived via Italian immigrant groups in English-speaking territories. In my experience, many English speakers attempt to achieve a 'native' pronunciation when ordering from a menu, even though few English speakers have ever studied, never mind achieved any fluency in, Italian. Strikingly, however, this tendency towards 'authenticity' is not always replicated among ethnic Italians in the English-speaking world. I have regularly heard *pizza*, for instance, pronounced by Italian Americans as /ˈpiza/, rather than /ˈpitsa/. It is possible that the first pronunciation is an attempt on the part of the immigrant population to acculturate towards the host culture and language, even as members of the host culture take on the original pronunciation as a marker of 'authenticity'.

1.5.2.2 Thomason Level 2

The next level is as follows:

Thomason Level 2: 'slightly more intensive contact'

Sociolinguistic context: somewhat higher levels of bilingualism; the culture of the speakers of the source language is prestigious among speakers of the target language (alternatively, speakers of the source language may possess political and economic power in relation to target language speakers)
Lexis: some borrowing of function words
Phonology: new phonemes accepted in words borrowed from source language
Morphosyntax: previously unusual or minority construction patterns become more common because of similar constructions in the source

Thomason suggests that, while new phonemes may well be introduced to the borrowing language, these are realised only in words borrowed from the source language. Morphosyntactic features may also be carried over, although this process may be visible primarily in the ways previously rare features in the borrowing language are encouraged while others become 'more restricted', primarily because of the influence of the prominence of these or similar features in the donor language.

Possibly the best-known example of something approaching this level of contact influence can be found in the effects French has had on English. Every history of the English language, no matter how brief and summary (e.g. Leith (1983) 1997), or methodologically and analytically conservative (e.g. Baugh and Cable 2018), recognises the importance of French influence on the nature and appearance of English as it stands today. But French has had only limited influence upon either the phonology (except in relation to the phonemic split between voiced and voiceless fricatives) or structure (except where the impersonal pronoun *one* may be derived from what is now French *on* – although the assumption of a connection between the two is not without problems). The variable word stress which English now exhibits is likely to be due to French influence, primarily through borrowing of lexical items containing stress patterns at variance with native norms. On the lexis of English, on the other hand, French has had an immense impact. Since a language is likely to be seen, by non-specialists, as primarily a collection of words, this means that, for many, this contact is of a particularly powerful kind.

If we analyse the routes by which French words arrived in English, we need to accept the precept that, with the exception of Scots (due to close ties between Scotland and France in the later medieval and early modern periods) and a number of varieties spoken in places like Louisiana in the United States, where English and French are still, or recently have been, in contact through interaction between local people, most French borrowings are shared by *all* English dialects. This implies the percolation of elements of the language of an overclass, relatively evenly spread across a wide territory. Secondly, the period between 1300 and 1450, when the highest proportion of French words entered English (Coleman 1995), represents when the English forms of French were ceasing to be spoken as a first language. As the language use of Chaucer's prioress demonstrates ('For Frenssh of Parys was to hire unknowe'), by the end of the fourteenth century, French in England remained only as a prestigious code of little essential use, in a way similar to that of Latin in English schools in the nineteenth and twentieth centuries.

This process represents an arguably uncommon example supporting Sasse's views (contained in Sasse (1992) 2012a and discussed in Chapter 2) on the influence speakers of an abandoned language have on the now dominant language to which they have switched. We often associate this process with the 'death' of low-status languages and with substratal linguistic influence; it is enlightening to see essentially the same processes at work in connection with a superstratal relationship. There has never been a time between 1000 (in other words, considerably before the Norman Conquest of England in 1066–7) and now when French words, associated with prestigious occupations, pastimes and ideas, have not been borrowed and used by English speakers. The already mentioned effects of the language of the ruling elite on the language of the ruled in the High Middle Ages have regularly been outweighed by the purveyors and promoters of fashion and style (although the two sources do at times coincide).

1.5.2.3 Thomason Level 3
Above this level, according to Thomason, is the following:

Thomason Level 3: 'more intense contact'

Sociolinguistic context: bilingualism common; social attitudes favour borrowing
Lexicon: function words and basic vocabulary (including 'closed class' lexis, such as pronouns) regularly borrowed
Structure: more significant borrowing
Phonology: native phonemes may be lost because they are not found in the source language; stress patterns may change; morphophonemic rules may change
Syntax: element order may change significantly; verbal aspect may be expressed in new ways, in line with the source language
Morphology: borrowed inflectional affixes; borrowed derivational affixes

This stage is characterised by quite intense contact with quite intense results. An example of such intensity can be analysed in the relationships between the Baltic Finnic, Baltic Indo-European, Germanic and Slavonic varieties spoken in north-eastern Europe (and particularly on the eastern and northern littorals of the Baltic Sea; see Map 1.3) These contacts are very ancient indeed (in particular, perhaps, those between the Baltic Finnic and Baltic Indo-European varieties). The most noticeable of these are connected to the borrowing of lexis.

Taking Finnish as an example, we can trace the following sources for generally common lexis. (Finnish has borrowed many lexical items; the language's phonological system does not always make this obvious. For a discussion of the Baltic Indo-European loans in Finnish, here given in their modern forms, rather than the putative form originally borrowed, before it was influenced by Finnish phonology, see Junttila 2012.)

- Proto-Baltic loans: *meri* 'sea'; *heinä* 'hay'; *hanhi* 'goose'; *lohi* 'salmon'; *villa* 'wool'; *heimo* 'clan'; *sisar* 'sister'; *kantele* 'stringed musical instrument'; *perkele* 'devil'
- Ancient Germanic and Old Norse loans: *ranta* 'shore'; *kana* 'hen'; *kattila* 'pan'; *kulta* 'gold'; *keihäs* 'spear'; *joulu* 'Midwinter festival; Christmas'; *kauppa* 'trade'; *tuomita* 'to judge'
- Old Russian loans: *pakana* 'heathen'; *raamattu* 'Bible'; *ikkuna* 'window'; *sirppi* 'sickle'; *pätsi* 'furnace'

There is a temptation to date these influences according to a schema whereby proto-Baltic words predate the Germanic borrowings, which themselves predate the Old Russian ones. There is some logical basis to this: Russian borrowings related to Christianity, for instance, must be quite late (as likely as not from the tenth century at the very earliest). It is difficult to distinguish between the Baltic and Germanic influences, however, in terms of age. The two subfamilies are also relatives, so the

Map 1.3 North-eastern Europe.

same ancestral lexical items may have been borrowed twice. It seems likely that some borrowings, dealing with both the everyday and the elemental, as well as the spiritual, lives of the people, are very early indeed, but this would be very difficult to prove (for further discussion, see Laakso 2001).

What we can say, however, is that the Germanic influences on Finnish must have come from the south-west, from the southern and to an extent central parts of the Scandinavian peninsula. (At the time what we now think of as northern Sweden is likely largely to have been settled sparsely, probably by speakers of Finnic dialects; Lang 2020; see also Dahl 2001. Udolph 1994 is something of an outlier in placing the initial contact between Germanic and Baltic Finnic somewhat to the east and north, in the Åland Islands, south-eastern Finland and Estonia.) Baltic Indo-European influences are likely to have come from the south and east. On this occasion, however, the contact with Finland need not have been direct: considerable numbers of Baltic Finnic speakers lived on the southern shore of the Gulf of Finland; many still do (for further discussion, see Larsson 2001).

At present, only one Baltic Finnic language other than Finnish has official status as a national language: Estonian. A number of other varieties continue to be spoken, however, in the Russian Federation, Estonia and Latvia. None can be said to have

1.5 Central Theories of Linguistic Contact

healthy speaker numbers. One of their number, Livonian, may not have any speakers now (although it was spoken well into living memory; historically its geographical extent included a considerable part of northern Latvia). Although modern linguistic nationalism has severely reduced 'external' place names or place name variants, it would be very surprising if Baltic Finnic speakers had not lived farther south into what we now think of as the Baltic Indo-European heartland; by the same token, we must assume that speakers of the latter language grouping were established in areas dominated by speakers of the former. If this is the case, can linguistic evidence, beyond the lexical, be found for this type of contact?

Attributing a contact-based origin to morphosyntactic change and patterns of distribution is rather more difficult than is the case with lexical borrowing. While structures are sometimes transferred from one language to another, my apprehension is that it is the concept behind the structure which transfers more readily. The Indo-European language Armenian, for instance, appears to have become more like Turkish in its morphosyntactic nature over time; the growing similarity is not expressed by the borrowing of Turkish inflectional morphology, however. The new system in Armenian is based upon native morphemes being used in a manner which is strikingly different from a typological viewpoint (a discussion of typological states can be found in Comrie 1981; an excellent contemporary introduction is Velupillai 2012). Let us compare Old Armenian case inflection with Modern Armenian case inflection (Millar and Trask 2023: 295–6) (Table 1.1).

This represents the norm in terms of case endings for the Indo-European languages. The markers themselves are typologically fusional (functional information is carried in morphology which cannot be entirely or at all broken down into its constituent parts). There are certainly similarities between the various endings, but these are not necessarily wholly transparent. It would be very difficult indeed to say what processes produced *-oc* as the genitive, dative and ablative plural marker, when compared with *-oy* for the same contexts in the singular (Table 1.2).

While there are similarities between the older and newer paradigms (with instrumental singular *-ov*, for instance), they appear to be based on different typological precepts. Modern Armenian inflection has strong agglutinative tendencies (the grammatical information is stored in the endings morphology in such a way that it is possible to peel apart the different levels of functional marking). In Old Armenian, plurality and case were expressed in different ways depending upon the context; the connection was not transparent. This is not the case with Modern

Table 1.1 Case inflections in Old Armenian

cer 'old man'	Singular	Plural
Nominative	cer	cerk'
Accusative, locative	cer	cers
Genitive, dative, ablative	ceroy	ceroc
Instrumental	cerov	cerovk'

Table 1.2 Case inflections in Modern Armenian

cer 'old man'	Singular	Plural
Nominative, accusative	cer	cerer
Genitive, dative	ceri	cereri
Ablative	ceric	cereric
Instrumental	cerov	cererov
Locative	cerum	cererum

Table 1.3 Case inflections in Modern Turkish

ev 'house'	Singular	Plural
Nominative	ev	evler
Accusative	evi	evleri
Genitive	evin	evlerin
Dative	eve	evlere
Ablative	evden	evlerden
Locative	evde	evlerde

Armenian, where the case endings in the singular correspond to endings in the plural; these follow an unchanging syllable *-er-*, which marks plurality. This kind of function marking is not at all common with Indo-European languages, to the extent that we might wonder if contact lies at the heart of the change.

This does seem to be the case, in fact. Until at least the First World War, Armenian speakers had been in regular (often everyday) contact for a little less than a thousand years with speakers of Turkic varieties which eventually coalesced as Turkish and Azeri. Both of these languages are agglutinative in **typology**, as we can see in Table 1.3 with the paradigm of Turkish *ev* 'house'.

As with Modern Armenian, the case marking illustrated here is based upon a transparent ordering of endings expressing case and number, with one (*-ler-*) being invariant and demonstrating plurality. The plural suffix always precedes the case ending, if there is one.

This ordering is, of course, identical conceptually to that found in Modern Armenian, although the 'building blocks' for the Armenian paradigm appear to be derived largely from native sources. While we cannot prove that the changes in the way that Armenian is structured were derived from contact with Turkic varieties, the probability that this is the case must be very high. (It should be noted that Old Armenian did not exist in a vacuum: Meyer 2023 presents evidence for influence on that language from the Iranian languages, its distant cousins.)

Returning to north-eastern Europe, let us consider the grammatical case systems of the Baltic Finnic and Baltic Indo-European languages (see Fritz and Meier-Brügger 2021: 243–7). Both systems are case-rich, in particular in comparison with the Indo-European languages presently found in western Europe, such as

English or French, where grammatical case as a marker of syntactic (and semantic) function is vestigial at most. With Baltic Indo-European, significantly more case inventories are to be found. Some of these derive directly from the inflectional conception and morphology of Proto-Indo-European (Lithuanian in particular is often considered to be the most conservative daughter of that proto-language presently spoken). But both Lithuanian and Latvian contain cases which do not have quite the same syntactic connections as is true for other Indo-European languages. Some appear to be more semantically inspired, acting in similar ways to how prepositions work in English.

Latvian cases appear at first glance to represent a mainstream Indo-European pattern in relation to this. If you look closer, however, there are remnants of the inessive 'being inside' and allative 'being moved to be on top of' cases. Lithuanian demonstrates rather more evidence for the use of apparently 'extra' cases. These are strikingly similar to the systems found in the Baltic Finnic language and include the survival both of allative case and also illative 'taking in' case marking, strikingly non-Indo-European in their semantic nature. As we have seen, Lithuanian in general is more linguistically conservative than Latvian in any event, ignoring linguistic contact for the moment, so more features from the contact may well survive here than in the more northerly variety. At the very least, these survivals demonstrate how far south Baltic Finnic speakers lived in the (probably distant) past.

1.5.2.4 Thomason Level 4

Thomason's fourth level, the highest in her typology, can be expressed this way:

Thomason Level 4: 'intensive contact'

Sociolinguistic context: high level of bilingualism in the borrowing population
Lexicon: heavy borrowing with both content and function words
Structure: 'anything goes'
Phonology: phonemic and phonotactic structures may change utterly
Syntax: all levels are affected and may be changed entirely
Morphology: major typological change; loss and addition of categories and inflectional patterns

This level, it could be argued, is centred upon Thomason's idea that 'anything goes'. The very nature of the language – structurally, phonologically, lexically – can be changed irrevocably, to the extent, perhaps, that the variety's ancestry and original connections can be hidden.

There is considerable temptation at this level to focus on 'mixed' languages, such as Michif (see earlier) or Mednyj (Copper Island) Aleut (spoken on that island in the far east of the Russian Federation; see Thomason 1997b). These fascinating varieties, well covered in the literature, appear to be genuinely mixed languages. But this state may have come about with speakers of the input languages making a (semi-)conscious decision to create a new variety which attributed different syntactic roles to the different inputs, in ways which seem almost impossible to anticipate.

A more mainstream example of level 4 contact can be found in Matras' (1999) discussion of Domari in Jerusalem. Domari is at heart an Indic language, now spoken in pockets across south-west Asia and Iran; like its relative Romani, its lexis (and other parts of its linguistic structure) demonstrates accretions evidencing centuries of movement and contact with speakers of other languages (for further discussion, see Matras 2002: 46–8). The interaction between Arabic and Domari in Jerusalem demonstrates a rather more powerful contact, however, particularly since Domari speakers are a relatively small (although highly visible) minority in a situation where Arabic is omnipresent. Matras provides considerable evidence for the nature of the contact. We will concentrate on two features, however (Matras 1999: 46):

a. baʔdēn   kānat   šara   amake   biddhā   qumnar
   [then]   [was.3sg.f]   say.3sg.imp   me.ben   [wants.3sg.f]   eat.3g.subj
   'then she would say to me that she wants to eat'
   ben = beneficiary

b. na   kildom   bara li' annhā   warsari
   neg went.out.1sg out   [because.3sg.f]   rain.3sg
   'I did not go out because it was raining'

Matras (1999: 46) comments that

> in [(a)], the feminine gender of the subject is not indicated on the Domari verb, nor would a personal pronoun include such indication, but it is marked on the Arabic verb and modal. In [(b)], the complementiser agrees with what in Arabic would be the feminine subject of the verb 'to rain', namely *ad-dunyā* 'the world/nature', which is in turn interpolated into the Domari verb. The two examples suggest that, for a synthesis of inflectional patterns to function, sentence processing must take place simultaneously in Domari and Arabic, applying complementary parameters of cross-reference operations to the sentential constituents.

What we can see here, therefore, is both an intense form of **interference** caused by a bilingualism based on unequal relationships between speakers (in other words, Arabic is in a superstratal relationship with Domari) *and* evidence of what happens to a language from which speakers are beginning to shift, two points to which we will return in Chapter 2.

1.5.2.5 Thomason Levels: Discussion

Thomason's typology of levels of contact is, of course, brilliant. It replaces and supersedes earlier conceptions of the nature of contact-induced change being essentially created by differences in social relationships. These are, as we have seen, vital to our understanding of the process of linguistic contact. But they do not provide an understanding of levels of contact, which Thomason's model presents. There is an abiding problem with Thomason's model, however. It foregrounds linguistic borrowing as a central feature of linguistic contact-induced change, while apparently downplaying interference; it also does not distinguish between the effects of the two forces underlying change through contact.

1.5.3 *Integration*: Winford (2003)

Winford (2003: 11–24) presents a typology of the nature of linguistic contact which connects with both models already presented (explicitly to the work of Thomason, as Winford 2003:12 points out), while adding in factors expressed implicitly in earlier work. Many of these also form part of the analytical framework of this book.

The first major category Winford identifies is language maintenance, the sociolinguistic context where none of the languages in contact is in danger of ceasing to have native speakers. **Borrowing** situations form a major part of these situations (Winford 2003: 11-12). Winford describes these in terms of degree of contact and their linguistic results. In relation to a *casual* degree of contact, he perceives this as being connected to 'lexical borrowing only', giving the example of the French lexis borrowed into English in the last few centuries. A *moderate* degree of contact will involve 'lexical and slight structural borrowing', invoking the influence Latin models had on Early Modern English and Sanskrit had on the Dravidian languages of southern India. An *intense* degree of contact involves 'moderate structural borrowing'. He cites the German influence on Romansh, the Alpine Romance language spoken in south-eastern Switzerland.

As is the case with Thomason's typology, Winford attempts to present a dynamic and differentiated sense of the levels of contact influence, largely based on different types of social dominance by one group over another. The boundaries between the different levels of influence are naturally vague.

Winford's typology contains distinctions which Thomason's does not immediately provide. A striking example of this is that he divides his analysis of *language maintenance* in two, separating borrowing situations from **convergence** situations. On this occasion (Winford 2003: 23–4), he begins by defining types of contact, followed by their linguistic results. Contiguous geographical location produces 'moderate structural diffusion'. He exemplifies this with reference to the Balkan Language Area, to which we will return in Chapter 5. Following this type of contact is *intracommunity multilingualism*, which he perceives producing 'heavy structural diffusion', using the convergence in languages studied in the south-central village of Kupwar, again discussed in greater detail in Chapter 5. A further type of contact, he suggests, is *intense pressure on a minority group*. He suggests that this involves 'heavy structural diffusion', exemplifying this with the Tibetan influence on Wutun, a nearby Chinese dialect, along with Turkish influence on Asia Minor Greek. The final type of contact he proposes is *intense intercommunity contact*, involving trade, exogamy and other intense contacts. This will involve 'heavy lexical and/or structural diffusion', citing the languages of north-west New Britain (a large island to the north-east of New Guinea; see Map 3.1) and of Arnhem Land in northern Australia.

Again, as with borrowing situations, Winford makes a distinction between different levels of contact, ones more associated with differences in social relationship – not necessarily on this occasion based on position in the hierarchy of a society but rather based on the level of intimacy engendered in the contexts where contact takes place. Strikingly, he includes heavy lexical influence only in the most intense contexts. As we will see, there is some logic to this layout, although I would not want to downplay the level of lexical transfer which happened in, for instance, the Balkan Language Area (see Chapter 5), even if the primary scholarly focus is inevitably related to structural change. The model also lacks discussion of languages, like Romani, which appear to have gone through several intense contacts during their geographical spread and transit of speakers.

Winford's second major category relates to linguistic contact phenomena brought about through language shift (Winford 2003: 23–4). On this occasion he identifies three types of shift. The first of these is *rapid and complete shift* by the minority group. This results in little substratal influence on the target language. This can be seen, he suggests, in the language use of immigrants shifting to English in the urban United States (although this is certainly possible, as Winford 2003: 17–18 demonstrates through his use of Thomason and Kaufman's 1988: 40 discussion of the mutual influence felt between Yiddish and American English among speakers of both varieties); we will return to this type of contact in Chapter 2. The second type is *rapid shift by a larger or prestigious minority*, which will result in a 'slight to moderate' substratal interference on the target language. He suggests that this type can be exemplified by the influence of Anglo-Norman French on English as its speakers shifted to the latter language, as discussed earlier in this chapter. Finally, there is shift by the indigenous community to the imported language, causing a 'moderate to heavy' substratal influence, which he illustrates by reference to the shift to English by speakers of Irish, which we discuss in Chapter 2. His categorisation of the development of an intermediate 'creole' (his use of quotation marks) in Barbados as an example of shift of this type is questionable, since, with the exception of the Kalinago people, who were at best sidelined in the new colony, those who contributed to the local dialects were not indigenous: we will return to varieties of this type in Chapters 3 and 4.

What marks off Winford's model from Thomason's is that he adds a discrete typological category related to language creation (*new contact languages*, as he also terms its products). He breaks these down into three types. The first of these are bilingual mixed languages, which, as he suggests, are 'akin to cases of maintenance, involving incorporation of large portions of an external vocabulary into a maintained grammatical frame'. The second are **pidgins**, which he defines as 'highly reduced lingua francas that involve mutual accommodation and simplification; employed in restricted functions such as trade'. Finally, there are **creoles**, which he defines as being 'akin to cases of both maintenance and shift, with grammars shaped by varying degrees of superstrate and substrate influence, and vocabulary drawn mostly from the superstrate source'. We will discuss this categorisation further in Chapters 3 and 4. It must be recognised that, since Winford's book was published, debate has been intense over the categorisation of creoles and pidgins (and the relationship between the two states, if that is the correct term to use); for that reason, this book will apply necessary rigour in their discussion.

Winford's typology is obviously excellent. It has a more 'three-dimensional' feel to it than Thomason's has (indeed, it might be striking that I do not provide such schematics in this book from my own standpoint, instead developing ideas conceptually from his ideas: much of the schematisation has been carried out already). What the present book can add to the mix, however, is the discussion of the 'grey area' between creoles and 'natural' dialects, as well as a conception of linguistic contact as involving intimate contact between closely related varieties, including dialects. In a very real sense, the concept of *koine*, a compromise variety created between different but closely related dialects (see Chapter 6), will be at the heart of a large part of this book.

1.6 Borrowing and Interference

There are, as we have already seen, issues with defining borrowing and interference as processes. Are they entirely separate from each other, or are they essentially the same process, but looked at in different ways and from different viewpoints? Or is there a middle course, a source from which both processes derive? Because of this apparent confusion, many – perhaps most – scholars dealing with evidence of contact tend to concentrate on borrowing. There are, of course, sound reasons for why Thomason and other scholars should choose to do so. If we look at the present lexis of the English language, for instance, it is straightforward to tease out the vocabulary items which have come from other sources. With Modern Armenian, as we have seen, the agglutinative inflectional morphology it now tends towards, in contradistinction to earlier varieties of the language where fusional (otherwise synthetic, a term employed to cover, in many ways, both fusional and agglutinative morphological expression) structures dominated, can be seen as a conceptual borrowing from the Turkic languages spoken in the areas where Armenian is, or until quite recently was, spoken. This could be described as both borrowing and interference, since new categories are introduced through bilingualism (as may well have been the case with the case systems of the Baltic Indo-European languages). They could be said to be straightforward to analyse because their origin in contact is immediately visible.

But other types of interference exist. These fit less easily into the Thomason model. Saying, for instance, that the apparent morphosyntactic 'simplification' which took place within English between around 900 and 1350 CE was at the very least encouraged by contact between speakers of Old English and Old Norse during the Viking period is, as we will see in Chapter 6, eminently possible. On that occasion, transfer of structural material from one language to the other is not prevalent (although it does happen); nor is the transfer of conceptual material central to the development (although, again, there is some evidence for this).

Instead, it is the situation of the contact involving, for a significant part of the population, a degree of bilingualism between varieties which are closely related which causes morphosyntactic 'simplification'. Interference between the two source languages causes alterations in structure. This tension between borrowing and interference will be a central theme of this book. In the following case study, a brief analysis of an example of this type of process is provided.

Case Study 1   Estonian Halbdeutsch

The following text was recorded by Falk in 1881 in Estonia (it is possible that he may have acted at times in a manner more like that of an author than an editor; I suspect that the 'German' he presents here is rather more like Standard German than would have been the case for most varieties of second language German used in Estonia at the time). It is an example of *Halbdeutsch* 'half German', a non-native form of German. Varieties named in this way were spoken in Estonia and Latvia by speakers of Estonian, Latvian and other languages from the Middle Ages until the evacuation of the territories by German speakers in the early 1920s (on a few occasions, the 1940s). From the High Middle Ages on, German speakers were dominant in these territories, both as country landowners (many of the more elevated families descended from members of crusading orders which were secularised during the Protestant Reformation) and townspeople: Riga was strongly German demographically, Reval (Tallinn) only somewhat less so. Generalising somewhat, many of the urban Germans (whose ancestors had often lived in the region for centuries) would have spoken varieties of Low German (although they would have been literate in High German, the language of the Lutheran liturgy and their government), while propertied rural Germans were more likely to speak High German varieties (for a nuanced discussion involving an analysis of native speaker German in the Baltic territories, see Stegmann 1952). These differences stand as evidence of initial migration origins for dominant members of specific communities. As the text demonstrates, many Estonian settlements had a German and an Estonian name (as we have already seen, this was also the case with cities: the great German university city of Dorpat is now Tartu). Socially, German was dominant in the region, in particular in the towns (although it is difficult to know how many rural speakers of Estonian were able to speak more than a few words of German).

"Warrt", tenk' hig mal hin meine Sinn "Willst wahren tog heinmal
Wait   think I   in my mind   (you) will go yet once

Su Wreint nag Hoperpahlen inn!"   Hun jink nu   hin das Tall
To friend in Oberpahlen [Põltsamaa] And went now in the stable

Hun nahm   tas Wuks   mit lange Wans
And took   the reddish brown horse with long tail
(Holm 1988–9: II, 613; text derived from Falck 1881)

The Standard High German equivalent follows, kindly prepared by Dr Sandra Weyland; language in square brackets is less idiomatic:

'Warte', denke ich mir [in meinem Sinne], 'Du gehst jetzt mal [Willst du doch einmal] zu eine Freund in Oberpahlen [fahren], und ging dann in den Stall und nahm das rot-braune Pferd (Fuchs 'fox') mit dem langen Schwanz.

(Before we start our analysis, we should note that, in German orthography, <w> is pronounced /v/ (or related approximants); <z> is /ts/; <j> is /j/; <ch> is /x/.)

An interesting discussion of Halbdeutsch as a system just as German ceased to have great relevance in the lives of Estonians can be found in Stammler (1922). Lehiste (1965) provides a more scholarly analysis, albeit one based wholly on textual analysis.

Most Baltic Finnic languages do not have the sounds /f/ and /x/ (they do have /v/ and /h/ – although see later). Thus German /x/ is represented by <g>: *hig* 'ich 'I' and *nag* 'nach 'towards'. In fact, this <g> may represent /k/: German (along with Dutch and the Slavonic languages) has word-final devoicing. Initial devoicing (again replicating the sound patterns of the Baltic Finnic languages) may also be present: note *tog* 'doch 'though, indeed' and *tas* 'das 'that/the' (although note *das* in the preceding line). *Wreint* is equivalent to Standard German *Freund* (the vowel distinction may be German-internal: the use of <ei> (presumably /ai/ or /ei/, merging with words like *frei* 'free') can be found in Bavarian dialects; it is also the norm in Luxembourgish). There is a general tendency of avoiding initial consonant clusters (the *-ranta* in Finnish *Happuranta* is a borrowing from Germanic: *strand* 'beach, coastline'). Thus we have *su* 'zu/tsu/ 'to', *Tall* 'Stall 'stable' and *Wans* for *Schwanz* 'tail'. Note *Wreint* 'Freund 'friend', however, where an initial consonant cluster is maintained. With *Wreint*, *Wuchs* 'Fuchs 'fox, reddish brown fox' and *wahren* 'fahren 'to go, travel', we see the replacement of German /f/ by something like /v/. A particularly striking feature is the use of <h> before an initial vowel, as with *hig* 'ich 'I', *hin*, 'in 'in' and *hun* 'und 'and'. This may be an example of the phonemicisation of the German glottal 'rough onset'; on the other hand, initial /h/ use can be variable in Estonian (it is my understanding that Livonian, a close relative to Estonian formerly spoken in north-west Latvia, did not realise ancestral initial /h/ at all). Finally, the text realises largely High German phonology (such as *tas*, equivalent to High German *das*, whose English cognate is *that*); *jink* is Low German in form, with the change of /g/ > /j/, however.

The Baltic Finnic languages do not have **grammatical gender**, although they do have a fully functioning **grammatical case** system (several of these cases are semantic rather than syntactic in nature; see Mäkinen 1999-2004; Karlsson 2018: 76-7). German has grammatical gender; it also has grammatical case, although based on somewhat different precepts from its Baltic Finnic equivalents. The latter languages do not express definiteness (or indefiniteness) through the use of articles.

We can see the levelling out of case marking with *hin meine Sinn* where Standard German would have *in meinem Sinne* (although this construction would not be particularly idiomatic in the context) and *mit lange Wans* 'with [the] long tail', compared with *mit dem langen Schwanz*. On both occasions, what might be seen as oblique or prepositional use triggers the *-e*; it is unlikely that this was perceived as 'case' (it is also worth noting that a number of Low German dialects have merged the inherited accusative and dative cases; see, e.g., Berg 2014). Two nouns in the passage appear to be marked explicitly for grammatical gender: *tas Tall* and *tas Wuchs*, *tas* being a variant of the German *das*, the definite article/demonstrative form used with nouns with neuter gender in the nominative and accusative cases. The problem is that both nouns – *Stall* and *Fuchs* – are members of the masculine gender class in mainstream varieties. In these contexts, the accusative singular masculine form *den* would be expected. Might it be suggested that *tas* here is being used as a pure demonstrative (there is an equivalent paradigm in Estonian) rather than as a definite article proper? Something similar appears to have happened in English (see Millar 2000). Certainly, this rather brief passage does not seem to realise any forms where a definite (or indefinite) article would be the norm in German (the examples of *das* appear largely to have a demonstrative function); again, this would be in line with issues which Estonian speakers would have when using German.

What are we to make of this text and the variety which underlies it? It suggests, of course, considerable bilingualism, probably of an unequal sort. Was this a rural variety, spoken by people who had intermittent interactions with German speakers? Does this represent only a form of 'foreigner talk'? Such a conclusion might lead to the assumption that, in more urban areas, Estonian speakers who aspired to greater things would speak German in a more native manner (some of these – or other descendants – becoming German-dominant speakers, perhaps)? Alternatively, was this a variety which had become the norm in interaction between Estonian speakers and German speakers? If that was the case, would Halbdeutsch have affected the German of the smaller farmers within a district, where direct interaction between speakers of the two varieties must have been the everyday norm? Would the regular use of Halbdeutsch have affected the German of native speakers? Sadly, we cannot really make decisions of this sort based upon such small amounts of evidence. Very few – if any – people will now be able to remember what interactions of this type were like before 1917 (or even 1939).

1.7 A Very Brief Conclusion

All of the theoretical and analytical points made in this chapter will be returned to in the following chapters. Even though phenomena of a particular type in a particular context will inevitably be distinguished from other phenomena in other contexts, it is necessary to accept that the same universal processes and states underlie *all* contact phenomena.

Exercises

1. Find an example of one of the following (other than those mentioned in this chapter): a (a) superstratal, (b) substratal or (c) adstratal contact phenomenon.
2. Research the *sociolinguistic* history of a language which has been formed through contact – Luxembourgish, Copper Island Aleut and Tok Pisin are good examples, but feel free to look further. What are the linguistic results of this history?

Suggested Reading

For the last twenty years I have used Thomason (2001) as the primary text for courses I have taught on linguistic contact. It has many advantages (not least its discussion of indigenous language contact in North America, a specialism of the author). Its brevity means that certain subjects I consider of some importance, such as dialect contact, are barely treated. I have always found the book easy to use and well written; in recent years a number of students have said that they find it difficult to navigate (which surprises me). It is perhaps becoming dated, in particular in relation to issues concerned with the development and nature of pidgins and creoles.

Matras (2010) is somewhat more advanced than Thomason (2001). It is a brilliant collation of ideas about contact, often dealing with less well-covered languages spoken in south-west Asia. Its discussion of bilingualism is particularly revealing. It is not always a straightforward read, however. This may be a mark of honesty (the subject is not always straightforward, after all). It does mean that specific points and discussions of analyses may have to be read more than once to be processed.

A further worthwhile introduction is Winford (2003). I particularly recommend the first chapters, where, as I have attempted to dissect in this chapter, an elegant typology of the ecologies and outcomes of linguistic contact is presented.

Hickey (2020) provides a useful overview of cutting-edge research on the subject.

2 Language Death, Language Attrition and Language Contact

Introduction

This chapter will consider the effects which **language death**, the movement by individuals and groups from the use of one language to another, has both on the now preferred language and, in particular, the language which is ceasing to be spoken. These processes will be considered for both speakers of autochthonous languages (varieties which are native to the 'soil' where they are spoken) and speakers of languages of recent immigration. Do the linguistic effects which language shift has upon threatened languages differ, depending on the status – as 'native' or 'immigrant' – of the speakers? Can we identify language **attrition**, the systematic breakdown in transfer of the 'correct' form of language across communities, but also within an individual's lifetime, as a central process within the changes involved? Firstly, however, we will consider the historical reality of language death and the evidence it leaves behind.

2.1 A Linguistic Palimpsest: Names on the Landscape

Apart from regions like Antarctica, where any human presence has been recent and historically fleeting, place names can act as a palimpsest of past linguistic use and behaviour, with layers of linguistic history lying underneath the modern 'reality'. We do not see all this evidence completely or directly, but we do 'feel' its existence. This is likely to be the case because, even though which languages are used in particular places as everyday spoken varieties changes across time, many place names remain as fixed points of (prior) settlement and orientation. *Moscow*, for instance, is a Baltic, not Slavonic, place name, commemorating a time when a contact zone existed in the upper Volga region between speakers of local Baltic and Finnic varieties (Miller 2007: 250–51). *New York* commemorates a transfer in European control over that city and its hinterland in the seventeenth century, while *Manhattan* provides evidence for a pre-colonial reality (it probably derives from a phrase meaning something like 'the place where we harvest wood for bows' in the local Munsee language).

Let us consider names for neighbourhoods and streets in the city in which I work, Aberdeen (for places and regions mentioned here, see Map 1.1). Some of these names are outliers: products of social realities at a particular time. The names of streets in the West End, the leafy part of the city laid out in the late nineteenth century, for instance, appear to be focussed primarily on the names of Queen Victoria and her children (Balmoral Castle, bought by Victoria and her husband, Prince Albert, is up the river Dee from Aberdeen; the royal family remain regular visitors). It is likely to have been in the city's interests to remind Victoria and her descendants of its loyalty and need for patronage.

Most local names in Aberdeen are steeped in local linguistic history, however. A thousand years ago, people in the area would largely have spoken Pictish, a P-Celtic language closely related to the ancestor of Modern Welsh. *Aberdeen* 'mouth of the (river) Don' itself derives from this source. Gaelic, the language which replaced Pictish in the early years of the second Christian millennium, is evidenced everywhere within the city (perhaps most in the names of areas which were urbanised in the last two hundred years). One example of this is *Tillydrone* 'knoll with thorn trees growing on it', now a council estate ten minutes' walk from my office. This strong Gaelic influence stands in contrast to the fact that that language has not been spoken by many people local to Aberdeen for hundreds of years.

Given the language's status as the primary vernacular of the city, it is unsurprising that Scots names are also very common, such as *The Kirkgate* in the City Centre (with Old Norse *gata* '(urban) street'; *kirk* 'church' is also a Norse borrowing). *Dubford*, known by most Aberdonians primarily as the northern terminus of a major bus route through the city, is indeed based around a *ford* across the river Don (one of the last before the river empties into the North Sea), but one that is muddy (*dubs* is a Scots word for watery mud, often blended with other unpleasant substances; alternatively, *dub* could be from a Gaelic word for 'dark' or 'brown', although the two potential origins may have bled into each other, with later Scots speakers reinterpreting an earlier Gaelic name). There are also, of course, many English names, although it is interesting that *Castle Street*, at the tougher end of Union Street, historically the main shopping thoroughfare of the city, is normally called *The Castlegate* by local people.

This type of historical mixture is relatively easy to untangle when, as with the North-east of Scotland, local literacy has been present for centuries (and before this the region was commented on by literate people from elsewhere; indeed, the river *Deva* 'goddess', the present *Dee*, is first mentioned in Ptolemy's *Geography*, written in Alexandria in the second century CE, but probably based on earlier sources). This means that we have some records of a period when particular languages were spoken in a territory before they ceased to have speakers anywhere or retreated from a particular place or region. It is a fundamental truth that there are many place names across the world which cannot be explained by reference to the present distribution of languages.

From evidence like this, we can strengthen an awareness many of us have already developed: which languages are spoken in which place alters over time. Once thriving languages are often no longer spoken anywhere. In relation to the place names of Aberdeen, we can say that this is the case for Pictish, which probably has not been spoken anywhere since the twelfth century; Gaelic is still spoken in parts of Scotland and Canada but can hardly be said to have a healthy number of speakers.

While this process has been accelerated by political centralisation, imperialism and globalisation over the last five centuries, the potential for shift has always been present, practically since humans first developed the ability to produce language. The results of language shift and language death can often be seen in a language as it is abandoned by most but still has some native speakers; they can also be seen, however, in the languages which have replaced it. If we had more historical evidence, spread more evenly, we would be able to find evidence of these phenomena practically everywhere.

2.2 The Process of Language Shift and Its Connection to Language Death: Theory and Reality

The terms *language shift* and *language death* are often used interchangeably, in particular, perhaps, by scholars who are not concerned especially with the processes involved as their primary research focus. The two concepts are, indeed, nearly synonymous.

Language shift might be taken as referring in essence to the process by which individuals and members of a community move from one language to another across generations, but also within the lifetimes of individuals. The focus of research certainly does not ignore the linguistic effects of these changes but is primarily sociolinguistic in its analysis (indeed, it can even be reactive and proactive, as is the case with Fishman's 1991 classic treatment). *Language death*, it could be argued, refers more to the actual linguistic processes which affect a variety as shift takes place.

For many scholars, of course, using the word *death* in these contexts is contentious: just because a language is ceasing, or has ceased, to have native speakers does not mean that it is necessarily 'dead'. Manx (the Q-Celtic language of the Isle of Man in the Irish Sea) ceased to have native speakers when Ned Maddrell died in 1974. The language continued to be used by a number of activists and enthusiasts who learned the language from Mr Maddrell, however. A small number of what can only be categorised as native speakers are now present among the next generations: their parents spoke Manx to them in their early years.

Moreover, sociolinguistic and linguistic factors can rarely be fully distinguished from each other in these situations in any context where shift is taking place, past or present. Bousquette and Putnam (2019: 190) observe that

> language death refers to the usage of a particular language in various sociolinguistic domains within the community. Language death refers to the elimination of a given language or vernacular due to the death of remaining speakers, or to the complete shift of the L1 from one generation to the next.

Finally, analyses of either phenomenon can cover both autochthonous languages (languages which are native to a particular place and, to reify somewhat, are under threat from languages of wider communication) and languages of recent immigration, where the dominant language is native to the place in which speakers undergoing language shift from an immigrant language find themselves. These contexts are certainly similar but, as we will see, may have both different linguistic and sociolinguistic effects.

Generally, elements of our understanding of both the sociolinguistic and linguistic effects of language death through language contact have helped form our theoretical understanding of the phenomenon's processes and effects. But it needs to be recognised that an overarching theoretical analysis and representation of the process at both sociolinguistic and linguistic levels still largely eludes us. The closest we have to such provision can be found in a paper by Sasse ((1992) 2012b) which is now more than thirty years old. Despite its age, it remains of considerable importance, however.

Sasse defines language shift and its linguistic and social consequences in relation to three contexts present within any speech community: external setting; the social, economic, political and cultural forces which work on both the speech behaviour of the community (largely in terms of which language varieties are used, and by whom, in a community); and the structural consequences which come about through the forces deployed. The first category is undoubtedly sociolinguistic, while the last is inherently linguistic. The intermediate category contains elements of both.

A central point made regularly in this book is that most relationships between speakers of different languages within the same territory are unequal; this implies that use of these languages or language varieties will also be unequal. I, for instance, do not expect people who do not come from Scotland to understand my dialect; people from other social and geographical backgrounds may expect (indeed, assume) my understanding of theirs, however. Sasse suggests that when two groups associated with two discrete languages occupy the same or nearby territories, the history of the relationships between the two groups, as well as present socioeconomic realities, will mean that the variety associated with lesser control on power in the wider region will increasingly only be used in certain domains and in relation only to certain themes, largely associated with domestic, or at least group-specific, topics.

In his 1970s work on users of Slovenian, spoken as a first language by a minority of inhabitants of the German-dominant Austrian province of Carinthia, for instance, Gumperz (1982: chaps. 2 and 3) found that speakers of Slovenian practically solely used German rather than their mother tongue when discussing politics and local matters external to their own experience and community. Partly, he suggested, this was because, as a minority in a province which has seldom had particularly liberal governments, it might have been politic to discuss these matters in such a way that the people around you could follow and gauge what you were saying.

Partly, the Slovenian speakers may not have wished to seem impolite or exclusionary in a mixed-language context (although this did not stop them using Slovenian when discussing other matters). Partly they may have been demonstrating their lack of connection with what was then socialist Yugoslavia to their south and the Slovenian speakers who were represented in considerable numbers there. But it is also quite possible that they did not have the vocabulary in their own language to discuss (Austrian) politics. Unlike what is now the Republic of Slovenia, where a political vocabulary had developed in an official register in the local language, this had not happened in Carinthia, where the German vocabulary for the concepts involved inevitably encouraged the use of German in the surrounding phrases. But *not* having a terminology – perhaps even a register – for discussing certain topics has inevitable results for the use and retention of the home language.

After a particular point, Sasse suggests, it may become functionally impossible to use the variety associated with the less powerful community and its 'home' domains. In particular, perhaps, those domains associated with events and relationships which are formal or official and are associated with domains external to the family, and the immediate community will increasingly not be used in these public spheres. The external variety becomes the *T* (target) language, associated with overt prestige. *A*, however, the language which is being (or will be) abandoned, begins to be associated only with certain, generally not overtly prestigious domains. Since it is not used in domains associated now with T, the speakers' ability to use (or even know) lexis and phrases previously used in those contexts become increasingly threatened. As part of a vicious circle, this means that A may begin to be perceived as 'unworthy'.

The situation then, Sasse ((1992) 2012b) suggests, becomes increasingly unstable. This is unlike **diglossia**, whether in its classic (Ferguson 1959) or extended (Fishman 1967) form, where the assignment of roles in terms of topic and acceptable place for use of the variety is time honoured and essentially static. Because of the restriction of linguistic domains in which A can be spoken in a language shift situation, that variety's use becomes stigmatised by some members of its own speech community (a discussion of how diglossia and linguistic contact interact with each other can be found in Sayahi 2014; Millar 2005: 1–8 provides a brief discussion of how diglossia breaks down).

Those who choose (or at least feel impelled) to make this type of shift are likely often to be aspirational people (identifiable with elements of the middle classes, if such a designation is not too out of place for particular contexts). Their children will not normally acquire A in its fullest form directly from their parents, since the parents will generally encourage the speaking of T in home domains. These children are nevertheless likely to pick up A, but in less 'natural' ways: when their parents do not think they are listening, through conversation with older relatives who do not have full command of T and, predominantly, from age mates who maintain use of A as their primary code. The A which these non-traditional learners take on will be different from that which their parents' generation speaks (for examples of this phenomenon, see Schmidt 1985). It will be much more notably influenced by T and may be considered partly or entirely 'ungrammatical'. Its novel and apparently simplified nature will make it take on illicit associations, which are likely to make it attractive to some younger speakers but condemnable by the 'elders' (for a discussion of how the T of members of the A community might affect the A of monolingual speakers of the same language, see Baladzhaeva and Laufer 2018: 128). This last point may mean that a move away from A towards T becomes increasingly attractive, particularly since the perceived unworthiness of the new variety will lessen further the number of domains in which it is used. Central family events, for instance, such as marriages, often associated with A culture and tradition, will increasingly be carried out in T.

At this point, Sasse suggests, a large part of the community will have abandoned A for T in most contexts. Those who continue to speak A in most domains will tend to be older and, in some contexts, research suggests, female, as seen in our discussion of Dorian's findings later on. Semi-speakers remain, displaying an only partial ability in A. Over time, even these abilities will fade. While the primary linguistic contact effects will be either direct transfer from T to A or a general simplification of A by semi-speakers based largely on the use of pre-existing majority constructions in A, a T_A dialect will also develop, where A features – in particular but not solely phonological – are carried over to the T spoken by members of the A community. On occasion at least, elements of these A-based features will be carried across to speakers of T who have never spoken A (or are not members of a community which has spoken or speaks A). Certain features of North American English, and of simple past for the present perfect constructions normal in British English (*did you eat?* vs. *have you eaten?*), may represent this type of phenomenon, under the influence of German, Yiddish and Dutch, all languages regularly spoken by immigrants to these territories (on this occasion, the influence may be of a reverse nature, with speakers avoiding a structural development not shared with T). A specifically Yiddish example would be the use of phrases like *enough, already!* (a not always scholarly debate exists on matters like this: see Mermin Feinsilver 1962; a more recent treatment can be found in Steinmetz 2001).

What is striking about Sasse's model, however, is that, although he envisages an 'end of regular communication in A', that does not mean that the language itself will be entirely forgotten by the A community, even when they habitually only use T. Sasse suggests a continued 'use of residue knowledge for specialized purposes = ritual, group identification, joke[,] secret language'. Not all A varieties are lost without regret, particularly if elements of a culture are contained within that language. We will return to this point in our discussion of Shetland Norn and the Scots dialect which replaced it in Case Study 2.

2.3 An Example of Language Shift: Gaelic in East Sutherland

Perhaps the best-known early research on language death can be found in the work of Nancy Dorian on the decline in use of Gaelic over the last two centuries within the fishing communities in East Sutherland in northern Scotland (see Map 1.1).

Elements of this research can be found in her 1981 book; much astute linguistic observation is also present in her articles of 1977 and 1978.

East Sutherland is a particularly interesting place to carry out linguistic research. Most of the county of Sutherland is practically deserted (although this was not always the case, as we will see). The eastern side of the county, facing onto the North Sea, is very different, however: a highly fertile strip of raised beach, often of no more than five kilometres in breadth. Road and rail routes from central Scotland pass through it on their way to the one-time major fishing and whaling ports of Wick and Thurso in Caithness. The main settlement is Dornoch, but other population centres are present along the coast. None of these settlements is large (all have fewer than 1,500 inhabitants, according to the most recent estimates), but they are of considerable economic and social importance for their hinterlands.

At the end of the eighteenth century, however, the Duke of Sutherland (for whom the county was essentially a personal fiefdom) cleared central Sutherland of its inhabitants in order to develop profit-creating forms of animal husbandry (for further discussion, see Devine 2018; see also Hunter 2015). Although many of these new migrants moved to the developing industrial cities and towns of central Scotland and others emigrated, with different levels of volition, to Canada in particular, some former residents arrived on the eastern coastal strip, where they were told that they were to become fishermen, despite little or no previous experience.

On the coastal strip, the relatively cold waters of the North Sea made the sea particularly bountiful. Although fish and other sea creatures had been a central part of the locals' diet since prehistory, it had not been commercially exploited until the Sutherland interest invested in harbours and produced a new fishing population from those they had cleared from the central regions of the county.

Before the Clearances, East Sutherland had what might be described as a typical post-medieval northern Scottish (socio)linguistic ecology. Those who worked the land generally spoke Gaelic as their first language, while those who lived in settlements like Dornoch would have spoken Scots or English (or, most likely, an ongoing and variable continuum between the two varieties). There would have been some bilingualism, although this is likely to have been skewed: native Gaelic speakers would have been more likely to speak Scots/English than would the speakers of the latter have been likely to have known much Gaelic.

The new cleared population, on the other hand, would practically all have had Gaelic as their dominant language; many would have spoken only this language with any confidence (this might have particularly been the case with women). As an essentially indigent people, there is considerable evidence that they were looked down upon by the original residents of the coastal strip.

Following fishing as a primary occupation has practically always, anywhere in the world, placed a barrier between the landward and seaward populations. Certainly, the new settlers were not made particularly welcome in the cultural institutions – primarily related to church activities – already present in East Sutherland. As was the case all along the eastern coast of Scotland in the course of the nineteenth century, the fishing community moved towards evangelical forms of Christianity otherwise rarely seen in the country, such as Methodism and the (Plymouth) Brethren. The barriers between seaward and landward became increasingly impermeable ('the corn an the cod dinna mix', as they say on the other side of the Moray Firth); intermarriage was very rare (for discussion on these matters, see Thompson 1983: esp. 202–24; see also Dickson 2002: 307; Hutchinson and Wolffe 2012: chap. 1).

This separation had a strong linguistic dimension. By the end of the nineteenth century, Gaelic in East Sutherland was essentially confined to the fishing communities, with the originally Gaelic-speaking peasantry switching over to English, at least in part expressing their identity as 'locals' rather than 'incomers'. Conversely, the fishing community used Gaelic as an internal code, perhaps particularly when deals of particular types had to be discussed in the hearing of outsiders, but generally as a marker of identity.

Later sociolinguistic change in the area was dictated by the breakdown of these barriers and the cultural issues which underlay them. As the twentieth century moved forward, the fishing became increasingly marginal to the economic life of the coastal strip. New technologies, such as steam and, later, oil propulsion, spread across the industry, meaning that larger boats became the norm. The small harbours of East Sutherland could not compete. Moreover, consumers of fish in the large urban centres to the south began to prefer fresh fish to cured. Our communities were generally too small and undercapitalised to invest in the new refrigeration technologies. They were also distant from the main population centres. More global economic and ecological changes further encouraged the retreat of the industry from the region. As the incoming fisher population became less distinctive, it was inevitable that, by the middle of the twentieth century, close connections with the other members of the local population, including intermarriage, became increasingly commonplace. Religious distinctions gradually became less important for most of the inhabitants. Gaelic use among the fishing community went into decline.

By the time Dorian began to research language use in East Sutherland in the late 1960s, she found that, while a part of the fishing community habitually used Gaelic as their everyday language, this group was most strongly represented among older people (in particular, perhaps, among women). Many members of the community were what she termed **semi-speakers** (a term which is now used generally among scholars working in this and related fields). Semi-speakers in East Sutherland normally had a good passive understanding of Gaelic but seemed unable to produce the language 'correctly' when prompted. Their learning of that language was, Dorian suggested, partial and associated often with older members (often female) of the community, many of whom were no longer alive. Within a community where families regularly lived close to each other, if not in multi-generational shared residences, older women often carried multiple roles for a number of children, while mothers were more directly connected to the family business. Naturally, these 'aunties' and 'grannies' were, as I have already suggested, less likely to have been fully bilingual in English than many other members of their communities.

Dorian pointed out, moreover, that there was a continuum of ability in Gaelic among semi-speakers: some were, in Sasse's ((1992) 2012a: 61) terms, *forgetters* (although *rememberers* might serve equally well):

> These persons mostly develop from former fluent speakers who were on their way to becoming full speakers, but never reached that degree of competence, due to a lack of regular communication in the language. These individuals cannot be reckoned among the semi-speakers proper; they are simply 'forgetters'. Lise Menn coined the term 'rusty speakers'. (Sasse (1992) 2012a: 59)

He goes on (Sasse (1992) 2012a: 59; cf. Menn 1989) to suggest that

> the other type of semi-speaker is a person whose command of the language is from the outset imperfect to a pathological degree. This is what we call the semi-speaker proper, the producer of the pathological speech forms we are examining here. The term "pathological" is chosen deliberately to express the similarity of this type of distorted speech to certain types of aphasic speech such as agrammatism.

The varieties used by semi-speakers, he suggests, 'result from the interruption of language transmission', noting that, in his own fieldwork on Arvantika (Albanian) speakers in rural Greece, all of these 'learned the language just by listening to older fluent speakers'. Dorian noticed this first: 'Most of the semi-speakers maintain close ties with older Gaelic-speaking kin. Social discontinuity is, then, not the explanation here for linguistic discontinuity' (Dorian 1978: 605, emphasis original). Similar points can be made about another seminal study on the linguistic results of shift, that of Gal (1979), concerned with Hungarian speakers in eastern Austria. The difference between Dorian's and Gal's findings is that it is younger Hungarian women who led the shift in Austria, through a desire among many to marry workers (most of whom were German speakers) with a regular (and predictable) wage packet, rather than the variable income normal in their own peasant community.

Dorian's work demonstrates how social pressures on a minority can lead both to language support through community specialisation and, eventually, movement towards the locally dominant language as these social pressures lessen and the communities as a whole change orientation.

2.4 Autochthonous versus Immigrant Language Shift

As has already been noted, there are essentially two means by which language shift can affect language use. As well as shift away from autochthonous languages towards a dominant, often originally non-local, language, it has become increasingly common for the dominant local language to become the replacement, in a variety of different ways, of languages of recent immigration, whether in the first or the following generations of migration. Although movement of individuals, groups and peoples has, of course, been a feature of human life from its very beginnings, imperialism (and its aftermaths), industrialisation and globalisation over the last five centuries have accelerated this process and allowed migration to take place across much greater distances than was previously the case. While much of this migration has been voluntary (although often with powerful social, political and economic forces encouraging, even necessitating, the choice to move), a great part of the linguistic development and change we will discuss in Chapters 3 and 4 was caused by forced movement brought about by mass abduction and slavery, often given longevity by racist ideology.

What is striking, however, is how little analysis was carried out on immigrant language use until well into the twentieth century (except, as we will see in Chapter 3, in terms of the radical development of pidgins and creoles; even here, however, notions of 'corruption' tied in well with the racist assumptions so prevalent in this period). The Romantic focus on 'authenticity', which dialectology and its related subjects have inherited from their nineteenth-century forebears, is likely to have made language contact and change caused by migration seem somehow less 'vital' and essentially less 'genuine' than were similar situations involved with autochthonous dialects (for discussion of how these views still affect our understanding of language use, see Bucholtz 2003).

In many ways, however, the sociolinguistic experiences of autochthonous minorities and immigrants are quite similar. Over time, as part of the 'modernisation' project, a prestigious language takes over an increasing number of linguistic domains from the minority or disparaged, but local, language, leading eventually to shift for most, often all, residual speakers of the latter. In most economically developed polities, the prestige, normally official, language is associated with mass education, high-status employment and a 'patriotism' spread from the centre (for a description of the process, see Anderson 2006). Naturally, this is framed according to the interests of the more powerful members of the majority (or those who are dominant, if the two are not the same) culture and language. The experience of someone whose peasant family has always lived in the lower Rhone Valley in France, and whose ancestors for generations have spoken Occitan, but who has been taught from an early age that French is the national language and the only route to a better life is not that different from the experience of a Quechua-speaking peasant in Peru or Bolivia who moves to a big city and quickly learns that, while many people speak their native language, only the (largely monolingual) knowledge and use of Spanish will lift them out of poverty and into the economic mainstream.

In other ways, however, the two experiences, while running in tandem, do not necessarily follow exactly the same paths in terms of shift. There is some evidence for autochthonous minority languages, connected to 'the land' and 'the ancestors', holding on rather better across generations than their immigrant equivalents. Indeed, it is this type of community to which Sasse primarily refers in his model discussed earlier. Generally, the chances of multigenerational perpetuation of a language of recent immigration in a particular 'foreign' setting, while not impossible, are hindered by the necessity, felt in particular by the first native generation, to compete in the new linguistic marketplace. For many immigrants, it is impossible to create anything like a simulacrum of 'home' for more than a generation.

In the aftermath of the traumatic Irish Potato Famine of the 1840s, many Irish speakers found themselves internal or in particular external migrants, suddenly having to cope with the use of English in these contexts (the classic, although now venerable, study of the linguistic and cultural outcomes of this catastrophe is De Fréine 1965). But this type of sudden switch is unusual. Speakers of non-prestigious autochthonous languages are more likely to maintain family connections within their communities which remain vital and, in a sense, natural. You are very likely to know your extended family across a range of generations. Language use in environments of this sort can often involve perpetuation of some degree of knowledge of a language due to close proximity with people, with whom you are emotionally close, who may prefer to speak the local language. Semi-speaker status is, it would appear, an ongoing and evolving phenomenon. At its heart, therefore, we can descry a distinction between the catalysts for the linguistic outcomes of language shift and of language attrition across a large range of circumstances and domains.

2.5 Language Attrition and Linguistic Change

Over the last twenty years, the study of language attrition has come to the fore as a major field for research in both psycholinguistics and **sociolinguistics**. Essentially, the term can be defined as referring to

> changes in a native language that has either fallen into disuse or is used alongside an environmental one. In accordance with this definition, attrition is a process that is driven by two factors: (a) the presence, development and regular use of a second linguistic system, leading to crosslinguistic interference (CLI), competition and other effects associated with bilingualism and (b) a decreased use of the attriting language, potentially leading to access problems. (Schmid and Jarvis 2014: 729–30)

The field therefore studies and analyses how individuals gradually 'lose' their native language in favour of an environmental one, which would regularly be the dominant one in the place they now live. Of particular interest to our study, of course, is what this attrition means in terms of the forms of language used by these individuals. At a deeper analytical level, Opitz (2019: 53) remarks that

> attrition is thus 'negative' or inverse language growth, which become noticeable in the absence of conditions which would normally support the acquisition or maintenance of a language, such as input in that language. As a result of the interconnectedness of the components of the language system, adaptations to environmental or internal changes in one part of the system potentially have consequences in other parts and at whole-system level.

As can be seen readily through the use of terms like *environmental*, the study of linguistic attrition is essentially focussed on the language use of immigrants. Thus

Schmid's work is primarily concerned with attrition in first language use across a lifetime by individuals who have lived for considerable periods elsewhere. This can throw up some interesting contrasts. In her work on German-speaking people of Jewish background living along the West Coast of the United States and Canada, Schmid (2002, 2011) found that personal experience could affect the level of first language retention and the level to which second language norms (at all linguistic levels) affected those of the first language. Jewish Germans whose families left Germany before the full effects of the Nazi regime were felt inevitably had stronger positive feelings about German culture than someone of the same age who had remained in Germany until the late 1930s and whose immediate family had been murdered in the Holocaust. What is striking in Schmid's work is the level to which these experiences and attitudes affected individuals' knowledge and use of German lexis and structure.

Evidence of this type should not be taken to say, however, that attrition studies and fields related to it do not throw up interesting points about group behaviour in terms of the maintenance of immigrant languages. Clyne's work on immigrant varieties used primarily in Australia (discussed in greatest detail in Clyne 2003) demonstrates that desire to fit in to their new environment, treatment by the host community and adherence to culture-specific norms and practices can certainly all affect individual linguistic behaviour. Clyne's work shows, however, that the group behaviour to which these individuals contribute can be analysed as exhibiting similar traits with similar motivations.

2.6 External and Internal Influence on the 'Dying' Language

A marked feature of divergence between the results of linguistic attrition and language shift is that the former regularly demonstrates transfer of features from L2 (second language) to L1 (first language), while the latter often does not allow it; this is a major feature of the contact between T and A. Why should this be the case?

In relation to attrition, Riehl (2019: 315) observes that

> second-generation speakers, who often acquire the system of their parents' language completely, are more prone to transfer items or structures from their dominant language into the home language and they are also more prone to feed back contact-induced changes to their parents' speech.

She presents a number of potential reasons for this transfer, including that

> concrete material or structural patterns can be transferred from Language B and into the language system of Language A or vice versa. This viewpoint is also in line with more recent approaches to multilingualism, such as the multi-perspective, which considers the different languages a person speaks as one connected system. This, in turn, means that in one bilingual or multilingual mind there is always mutual influence between the L1 and L2 (or the third language (L3)). (Riehl 2019: 316)

The **critical period hypothesis**, the popular view that children up to the ages of between around nine and twelve have a considerable ability to learn other languages more rapidly than do older children and adults, appears also to affect the nature of L2 influence upon L1 capability (for full analysis of the issues involved, see Pallier 2007). In relation to subjects who had Turkish as their first language and English as their second, Schmid and Karayayla (2020: 84) observe that

> the first language Turkish speakers who learned English after age 10 resembled monolingual Turks in Turkey [in their use of English]. In contrast, the speakers who were younger when they started learning English showed a much broader range in proficiency in Turkish.

The level to which English linguistic patterns influenced first language use also appears to be affected by the age of acquisition of the former.

This is not the whole story, however. In the same study, Schmid and Karayayla (2020: 84) note that 'how often a speaker used their first language also correlated with how they learned English'. Schmid and Jarvis (2014: 730; see also Schmid 2007) observe that 'the more migrants use the L1 at work, the less L1 attrition they exhibit'.

A fundamental issue therefore underlies any appreciation of potential differences in terms of linguistic consequences between language shift and language attrition. The former is concerned primarily with immigrant language contact, where multi-generational linguistic example and support is not so strong (if it exists at all). The latter points out that, when discussing the linguistic consequences of language death, as Sasse ((1992) 2012a: 59–60) observes,

> if we condict [sic] a linguistic investigation in a speech community where only semi-speakers are left, we must be aware of the possibility that most, if not all, of the elicited material will be distorted speech that has undergone certain processes of reduction with the result that the original grammatical system of the former full speakers of the language under investigation will be accessible only by way of reconstruction.

A number of scholars have made the point that most of the reduction which takes place with languages which are increasingly moribund is not a matter of borrowing from the now dominant language (for a particularly strong phrasing of this view, see Cook 1995: 226). Dorian (1978: 607) discusses the possibility of some functional borrowing from English in East Sutherland Gaelic but also observes (Dorian 1977: 24) that

> any language which continues to be spoken by only a very few people will exhibit a much reduced form as compared with the same language in vigorous use by a rich linguistic community. Exceptions will certainly be found in those cases where a language dies with extraordinary rapidity and without replacement by another language. … But on the whole the assumption that the reduced use of a language will lead to a reduced form of that language seems realistic.

Cook (1995: 227) claims that 'the process of simplification and decay in language death is due to semi-speakers' impeded and prematurely terminated learning process', rather than being due to transfer of features from the dominant language. Following her argument, in fact, it could be claimed that these reduction-related features are part of a general **drift** within the languages as a whole, even when a particular variety is not itself under threat (something Cook 1995: 277 demonstrates with a set of examples of particular phonological features). On occasion, however, this association with drift can actually mask radical change caused by contact, as we will discuss in Case Study 2.

Scholars working on immigrant and heritage languages are more likely to suggest influence from the second language on the first (Cook 2003 is a particularly interesting and coherent introduction), however. Bousquette and Putnam (2019: 190) observe, following Bayram et al. (2019), that, with languages of recent immigration,

- previously acquired linguistic representations are altered in a way that is commensurate with exposure to the sociolinguistically dominant L2 (convergence towards L2);
- features/attributes of the L2 begin to affect the representations of the heritage L1; promotion an alteration or reconfiguration of information previous [*sic*] acquired. Language contact motivates changes in the heritage L1 without including convergence towards or impositions from the L2.

Why should this apparent divergence between the results of language shift with autochthonous and immigrant languages exist? Is it due to their status in being autochthonous rather than immigrant (and vice versa)? Might it have something to do with levels of literacy in the community which speaks the threatened language? Would the perceived hegemonic – as well as omnipresent – status of the T language, 'environmental', as we have seen some scholars term it, help to peripheralise the use of A among native speakers of that language?

A striking example of this type of phenomenon can be found in examples such as the following, produced by a second generation German-Australian (Clyne 2003):

Wir haben   gegangen   zu Schule in Tarrington
we   AUX+have go+PAST.PT to school in Tarrington
(where AUX = 'auxiliary function' and PAST.PT stands for 'past participle'),

The Standard German equivalent would be as follows:

Wir sind   in Tarrington zur   Schule gegangen
we   AUX+be in Tarrington to-the school go+Past.PT

There are a number of striking differences between the Australian German phrase and its standard equivalent. In the first instance, the use of *be* with certain verbs to express perfect aspectual meaning in the latter is apparently replaced by the equivalent to English *have*. With a small number of exceptions, English lost the use of the *be* + past participle perfect construction several centuries ago. Moreover, the archetypal German *Satzklamme* 'sentence brace', where the lexical part of the verb is transferred to the end of the clause if an auxiliary verb is also present, is not found in the Australian example, which closely follows the English clause structure model. In addition, the standard *zur*, where the preposition *zu* 'to' is combined with the dative singular feminine definer *der*, is equivalent to Australian German *zu*, which both comes close to the English equivalent *to school*, the norm in most varieties of that language, and also means that grammatical gender and case marking can be ignored. Most of the grammatical issues found with the Australian German example are, from experience, precisely those found in the German of learners.

Another way of looking at immigrant varieties can be found in the study of heritage languages. These are varieties continued in families where the dominant language in the place they live has eventually become the main family language. We tend to associate this phenomenon with languages other than English, primarily, although not necessarily solely, in migrant contexts. Phenomena of this type can occur with heritage English speakers, however, as the following examples from Polinsky (2018: 38-9) demonstrate. On both occasions, the speaker, who is in their teens, has been asked to describe in their own words what has happened in a cartoon they have just watched. The first speaker is obviously more fluent in English than the latter; this is not the point being made, however:

> So there's a sort of wolf who's walking in the street and he he take out a cigarette ... and he smokes but a drop of water goes on the cigarette after his nose, he look upward and he see a rabbit who's putting water on his flowers and he imagines the rabbit in a plate. So he sees clothes who are attached at the rope. (heritage English in a French-speaking environment)

> The second time, he eh almost catched it ... catched him, in this, he done like he's eh his ... him a goat and then, he took oh the ... costume ... of the goat and then he run after him. (heritage English in an Israeli (Hebrew-speaking) environment)

Which features in the preceding examples would be unusual in a fully first language environment? Can all of these be ascribed to interference from the dominant language? Polinsky (2018: 9) comments that

> their phonetics is native-like, but as these short paragraphs attest, they make a number of errors, including regularized or partially regularized forms of irregular verbs (*catched* [...]), lack of agreement, wrong use of tense, numerous hesitations, semantic mismatches.

Of course, a number of these 'errors' are found in varieties of fully 'native' English. I say *catchit* quite regularly, for instance. The point here, however, is that most of the abnormal (if that is the right way to put this) language here appears to be the result of attrition on structures which are less common or, as in the use of plural (or base) forms in singular contexts in the present tense, represent the occasional jettisoning of a feature which is also carried by the subject (the Scandinavian languages, for instance, as we will see in Chapter 6, have all lost this feature). While both informants' usage may occasionally be influenced by the dominant language (as with *he sees clothes who are attached at the rope*, where French *qui*, standing for both animate and inanimate heads of relative clauses, and the meaning of French *à* dominate in comparison to the equivalent meanings of English *to* and *on*), interference within the speaker (and, to a degree, the speech community) has created what often seems like a rationalised form of the target language (this bears some resemblance to ideas about the nature of 'natural morphology'; Dressler 1983, 1985).

Thus we can say that a profound difference in terms of interference phenomena appears to exist between immigrant or heritage varieties and autochthonous language as they go through language shift. The former types are far more affected by the dominant language, while, with the latter, breakdown appears to be represented by language-internal processes. As these final examples demonstrate, however, internal interference is not confined to autochthonous contexts.

2.7   L1 Influence on L2?

Up to now, we have been primarily concerned with the influence of a second language on the first language. If the use of the first language is declining markedly, however, more long-lasting influence might be said to be exerted from the first language on the second language: T_A, as described by Sasse, discussed earlier. It could be claimed, as Riehl (2019: 316) suggests, that the potential for change is always inherent in language contact contexts. As we will see throughout this book, however, under certain circumstances, this potential is more likely to be activated than it is in others.

We have already touched upon a number of examples of this type. Each of these derives from its own particular linguistic, cultural and political ecology. One which ties in well with this discussion since it returns us to northern Scotland is Highland and Islands English (for a recent treatment, see Clayton 2018), where Gaelic phonological features are carried across to the speaker's native- or near-native-level English. Structural features, such as the use of the *-ing* progressive with stative verbs, which are likely to be of Gaelic origin (for instance, *I am thinking it will rain tomorrow*), are also present in the variety. It is immediately comprehensible nonetheless for all English speakers, unlike earlier Gaelic-influenced varieties of Scots (Millar 1996). Interestingly, Highland and Islands English is also employed by people from the Highlands and Islands who do not have Gaelic, quite possibly as a regional identity marker.

Case Study 2   Shetland Norn and Shetland Scots

Let us consider how we can analyse the linguistic effects of language shift and linguistic contact across several centuries in a relatively isolated island environment.

Shetland dialect is arguably the most distinctive of the dialects of Scots; even for Scots speakers from elsewhere, it may be quite opaque at times. This is true at all linguistic levels. Phonologically, a rounded front vowel is present in words like Scots *schuil* 'school': /skyl/ (in my West Central dialect, the equivalent is /skɪl/; where I work, it is /skwil/). In parts of southern Shetland, <kw> and <wh> at /ʍ/, so that *what* and *quit* are /ʍɪt/, while in the northern parts of the archipelago, <kw> and <wh> merge at /kw/. Most markedly, initial and medial /θ/ and /ð/ in mainstream varieties of Scots are realised as /t/ and /d/ in Shetland dialect. Although it shares most of the lexis held in common by the various Scots dialects, it also has many words, largely of Norse origin, which are either unique to that territory or shared with Orkney varieties. A striking example of this is *solisp* 'to wander dreamily in a manner similar to a sheep grazing'. Structurally, the perfect construction *I am worked here since 1993* is particularly marked. The question, then, is, to what extent can language contact be used as an explanation for developments of this type?

Historical Background

Shetland and its more southerly sister archipelago, Orkney, have strikingly different histories from the rest of Scotland. In fact, until 1469–71, when the territories were mortgaged to the Scottish Crown in place of a dowry, the islands were a part of the Kingdom of Norway (later, through a personal and eventually political union, Denmark-Norway) in the same way as the Faeroe Islands and Iceland were. Indeed, the Earldom of Orkney was, in the eleventh and twelfth centuries, a major player in the politics and trade of the North Atlantic world. Locally specific descendants of Old Norse, often termed *Norn* 'northern', were spoken in the islands as the primary vernacular (for further discussion, see Barnes 1998, 2010).

It should be noted, however, that knowledge and use of Scots was spreading among the upper and middle classes well before 1469. This is likely to have been particularly the case in Orkney: it was the centre of power and also easily visible from the Scottish mainland on clear days (while Shetland is on the edge of the European continental shelf; later its rich fishing resources made that archipelago attractive to many people in Scotland, the Netherlands and northern Germany, however). Moreover, the Norse line of earls died out in the thirteenth century, meaning that the position was taken on by Scottish relatives, most of whom would have spoken Scots as their mother tongue. Their chancery was likely to have used that variety in its correspondence (although Danish continued to have status as a written variety for a considerable period).

How long Norn took to 'die' in the archipelagos is difficult to say. The language was essentially used orally only, and, from the early sixteenth century at least, most speakers would have been essentially native speakers of Scots as well. This would have been particularly the case in some parts of the islands where monolingual speakers of Scots moved in the early modern period. Nevertheless, Norn appears to have been maintained in some places at least until the eighteenth century.

The following is a Norn version of the Pater Noster recorded in Shetland towards the end of that century but is likely to have been composed considerably earlier:

Fy vor or er i Chimeri. Halaght vara nam dit. La Konungdum din cumma. La vill din vera guerde i vrildin sindaeri chimeri. Gav vus dagh u dagloght brau. Forgive sindorwara sin vi forgiva gem ao sinda gainst wus. Lia wus ikè o vera tempa, but delivra wus fro adlu idlu. For do i ir Kongungdum, u puri, u glori, Amen.

For comparison, here is an Old Norse version of the same prayer:

Faþer vár es ert í himenríki, verði nafn þitt hæilagt. Til kome ríke þitt, værði vili þin sva a iarðu sem í himnum. Gef oss í dag brauð vort dagligt. Ok fyr gefþu oss synþer órar, sem vér fyr gefom þeim er við oss hafa misgert. Leiðd oss eigi í freistni, heldr leys þv oss frá ollu illu.

Whoever composed the Shetland version would have been most unlikely to have even seen the Norse equivalent, however. It is very likely that they would have known the English version mandated in the Scottish Presbyterian churches (including those in Shetland):

Our father, which art in heaven, hallowed be thy name. Thy kingdom come, thy will be done, on earth as it is in heaven. Give us this day our daily bread. And forgive us our debts, as we forgive our debtors. And lead us not into temptation but deliver us from evil. For thine is the kingdom, the power and the glory. Amen.

This connection can be seen in the apparent transfer of lexis from the version in English to the Norn equivalent, as seen in

For do i ir Kongungdum, u *puri*, u *glori*

in comparison to

For thine is the kingdom, the *power* and the *glory*,

although it should nevertheless be observed that the Norn equivalent to *kingdom* maintains Norse *kong* rather than *king* and that *u* is likely to be the equivalent of Swedish *och* or Norwegian *og* 'and' (at least the latter of which normally being pronounced /oː/). We can therefore see here external influence upon Norn from the dominant languages (spoken Scots and written English). But the language represented is still structurally North Germanic. The phrase *i vrildin* 'on earth; in the world' maintains the enclitic definer which is the norm in those languages (the Norwegian equivalent would be *i varden*). Elements of the case system (which, unlike the Scandinavian languages, is well preserved in Icelandic and Faeroese) can be seen in the dative plural endings in *fro adlu idlu* (Modern Icelandic *frá öllu illu*).

Within a generation or so, however, Norn was moribund. There is no space here to discuss the political, social and economic changes that appear to have triggered the change (see Millar 2007, 2008). But, by the middle of the eighteenth century, most, if not all, Shetlanders had become Scots-dominant; most were monolingual.

(There is a minority viewpoint on this, which I cannot analyse here, that Norn continued to be spoken well into the nineteenth century in some of the more isolated parts of the islands; see, e.g., Rendboe 1984, 1987. While I am dubious about such a view, it is clear that, no matter the time of the final shift, Scots had been dominant in the community for some time before.)

Norn Influence on the Scots Dialects of Shetland

As we have seen, the modern Scots dialects of Shetland are unique at all levels. The Norse linguistic heritage of the islands has led many to suggest that at least some of these discrete features have been brought about through transfer from Norn (an earlier view that Shetland dialect is a Scotticisation of the Norn dialect, prevalent in the late nineteenth and early twentieth centuries, can be ignored, since it is self-evidently incorrect; see Millar 2012a). At a maximal level (here based on Heddle 2010), claims have been made that the following features of Shetland dialect could be seen as being of Norn origin:

1. large-scale borrowing of Scandinavian vocabulary not found with any mainland varieties (with the partial exception of Caithness; see the rather tentative Thorsen 1954)
2. the change of initial and medial /θ/ to /t/ and /ð/ to /d/, at present only found in Shetland, although place name and other evidence suggests that it was at one point current in Orkney also
3. the retention of rounded front vowels, realised as [y], [ø] or their variants, depending on location
4. the use of the verb *be* in perfective constructions, such as *I'm worked here twinty year*; as with (2), this usage is presently largely confined to Shetland but appears to have been present regularly in Orcadian speech until quite recently
5. the survival of North Germanic second person singular familiar forms *thoo* (Orkney) and *du* (Shetland)
6. the survival of 'grammatical gender' in both archipelagos in the use of *he* or *she* to refer to beings, objects and concepts (such as the weather), in ways which go well beyond the occasional (and idiosyncratic) Standard English use of *she* for cars and ships

Category (1) is very likely to be a correct assignment. There are many words of Norse origin used in both or either of the Northern Isles dialects which are not found in other varieties of Scots. Words of Norse origin found only in Shetland or along with Orkney, according to *Dictionaries of the Scots Language*, include *snug* 'to strike, push, try to prod with the horns' and *moorit* 'reddish brown, describing one of the traditional colours of a Shetland sheep or wool' (for analysis and further exemplification, see Millar 2007: 99–102; Millar 2023: 163–6).

Category (2) is also likely to illustrate direct transfers of phonological features from Norn to the Scots spoken in Shetland in the early modern period. In the Scandinavian languages, words originally pronounced with /θ/ and /ð/ did begin to be pronounced /t/ and /d/ in the course of the Middle Ages, so that Old Norse *þing* 'thing, assembly' is

Modern Norwegian *ting*. Old Norse *höfuð* 'head' is Modern Swedish *huvud*. There is some evidence that a different type of change and outcome affected Faeroese when it lost the two dental fricatives (for a discussion of these and related matters, see Árnason 2011: chap. 2; Icelandic has retained the sounds). At the very least, however, when Scots words with the dental fricatives were learned by Norn speakers, it is likely that /t/ and /d/ would have been the most obvious replacements.

It is after this point that the proposed connections between modern Shetland Scots and the Norn variety which it replaced become problematic. It is certainly true that rounded front vowels as phonemes are unusual in Scots (and practically unknown in English). But there is a considerable amount of evidence for all varieties of Scots having /y(:)/ in the seventeenth century (see Millar 2018: 38-9; 2023: 98-100). Moreover, no words which have rounded front vowels in Modern Norwegian have a rounded front vowel in Shetland Scots, and vice versa. Instead, Shetland /y/ is entirely part of what has been termed the Scots BUIT lexical set. Finally, there is some evidence that the last versions of at least Orkney Norn had lost the inherited rounded front vowels. This is in line with Icelandic among the West Norse insular languages (although not Faeroese, which, given the Faeroe Islands' greater geographical proximity to the Northern Isles, might be assumed to be closer to Norn historically). What we appear to have here is, in fact, evidence for coincidence rather than transfer. It is probable, however, that, if Shetland Norn had rounded front vowels, their presence among bilingual speakers would have encouraged their presence and retention in the local forms of Scots.

The *be*-perfect is certainly a striking feature of Shetland Scots syntax. It is also the case that the modern North Germanic languages have preserved the construction considerably more than have either Scots or English (although rather less so than Modern High German does). The connection is not immediately obvious with the Norn predecessor, however. Ljosland (2016) has convincingly explained the origin of the construction. It is not from Norn. In fact, as Yerastov (2010) demonstrates, the construction is found sporadically across a fair part of the English-speaking world.

It *is* true that the preservation of a discrete second person pronoun is unusual in either present-day Scots or English. But it is still found in a number of places - rural Yorkshire and Lancashire, for instance. While it is not used now in Mainland Scotland, its realisation was remembered until recently in relation to the Scots of the Black Isle in the early twentieth century (Millar 2007: 67-8); it was also used in West Central urban dialects, such as that of Paisley, up to at least the early nineteenth century (Millar 2023: 132-3). As with (3), it is very likely that this is a recessive feature, once found in all Scots dialects, which has now retreated into the Northern Isles. With this type of evidence, it might even be claimed that we have evidence here *not* for the influence of Norn but rather for features which make Shetland dialect more 'Scottish' and 'traditional' than other varieties of Scots. This does not rule out the possibility that the continuing use of *du* in Shetland Scots was supported by the use of the same form in Norn and the grammatical and pragmatic distinction which underlies it. Even bearing this in mind, however, it must be noted that the oblique form of the pronoun in Shetland is the West Germanic *dee*, rather than any envisaged North Germanic equivalent.

Northern Isles 'grammatical gender', expressed through the use of third person singular pronouns, is indeed unusual from the point of view of either English or Scots. In other varieties, *she* is often used for ships (particularly by people who are connected to sailing in some way; some people use it for their car, although I am not as aware of this happening as regularly now as it did in the past). The use of *she* with countries, once so common, is, again following my own experience, practically moribund. There have been attempts to connect the use of *he* and *she* with many nouns, as is the case in the Northern Isles with the gender system of Norn. As Ljosland (2013) and Velupillai (2019) point out, however, there is no obvious connection between the two systems. Moreover, while the systems of pronoun attribution hold together consistently well beyond the personal and idiosyncratic, their distributions differ markedly from one archipelago to the other.

Are There Any Other Norn Influences upon Shetland Scots?

It therefore appears as if the Norn influence on the succeeding Scots variety has been relatively small, but not entirely intangible. There are unusual points which need to be made about the 'death' of Norn, however, and how these might have affected the development of local forms of Scots.

One of the latest pieces of 'native speaker' Norn recorded is the 'Hildina Ballad', a poem of some length. The Reverend Mr George Low, Church of Scotland minister of a parish on the Mainland of Orkney (although a native of Kincardineshire in the North-east of Scotland), carried out a tour of Orkney and Shetland in summer 1774. While in the latter archipelago, he visited the island of Foula, one of the most isolated in Shetland. An elderly resident, William Henry, dictated the poem to Low, the process taking a whole day (the fact that Low could not speak any North Germanic variety means that his transcription has been criticised and discussed practically since it was first published in 1805). What is truly remarkable about the process, however, is that Henry could not translate what he was reciting: he could only provide a summary. It would take considerable application and ability to be able to remember and recite a poem of this length when you can understand what is happening word for word. How much labour would be involved in remembering the piece when you do not fully understand what is being said? What does this tell us about Henry's connection to the tongue of his ancestors?

Further evidence for views by Shetlanders on the switch from Norn to Scots can be found in the following rhyme, collected by the Faeroese scholar Jakob Jakobsen in the late nineteenth century:

De vaar e (vera) gooa tee,
"when" sona min "guid to" Kaadanes:
haayn kaayn ca' *russa* "mare",
haayn kaayn ca' *bigg* "bere"
haayn kaayn ca' *eld* "fire"
haayn kaayn ca' *klovandi* "taings"

'That was a good time, when my son went to Caithness: he can call *russa* "mare", he can call *bigg* "bere" [a form of barley], he can call *eld* "fire", he can call *klovandi* "taings" [tongs]' (my translation; on this occasion, Jakobsen uses <" "> to imply that the piece of vocabulary is of Scots rather than Norn origin; strangely, Jakobsen does not include *ca'* 'call' among the former set – it is indeed a North Germanic borrowing, but from a far earlier period than many similar words found in Shetland dialect, and it is found in all varieties of English and Scots).

This rhyme seems to suggest considerable regret on the part of Shetlanders over the loss of the 'native' language, as well as a degree of contempt for aspirational parents' embrace of new ways (after all, using a different word for something does not really change the nature of the task performed with it). Shetlanders have always had to be pragmatic: survival in an often adversarial world demands this. But even though they accepted that Scots (and, by extension, English) was necessary for ongoing well-being (or even its possibility), that did not mean that they welcomed the loss of their own language and its cultural connection.

A further part of this survival can be found in the use up to the present day of Norn words as taboo avoidance strategies on board ship. This type of language use is, of course, common in the fishing trade (and other maritime occupations) across the world: there was (and is) considerable (and often immediate) danger, a situation which tends to breed superstition and ritualised behaviour. In the North-east of Scotland, for instance, a salmon is termed *cold iron*, while a rabbit is a *mappie*. What marks off Shetland is that fact that, by using *grice* for 'pig' (Modern Norwegian *gris*), among many others, Shetlanders have continued to employ a 'dead' language as an ongoing (albeit somewhat marked) part of their everyday language use (given their environment, most Shetlanders would have had at least some connection to the fishing trade, or at least to the use of boats). Knooihuizen (2006, 2007) provides further detail on this issue (see also Fenton 1968–9, 1978). Moving beyond this, Melchers (1980) demonstrated that Shetlanders in the 1970s often knew which parts of their dialect lexis were of Norn origin: a most unlikely survival so many years after the language shift.

Finally, in his fieldwork, Jakobsen recorded several examples of rhymes in Norn, one of which we have already considered. Along with this, he also presented examples of phrases in that language which had been given to him, normally, but not always, on the northern islands of Yell and Unst. One of these follows:

Jarta, bodena komena ro'ntəna Komba 'My heart, the boat has come round "de Kaim" ['the comb', a well-known local rock]'

Rendboe (1984: 129–30) renders this phrase in Nynorsk, the more West Norse standard form of Norwegian, as *Hjarta, båten er komen rundt om Komba*. In a series of arguments, he (Rendboe 1984, 1987) makes the claim that the material Jakobsen recorded provides evidence that Norn had 'died' only a generation or so before Jakobsen visited the islands: the Norn presented in examples like this is just too accurate for another explanation.

If we look closely at the example, however, this supposedly accurate and close connection to the Norwegian equivalent might be called into question. There seem to be too many unstressed syllables, providing a highly regular rhythm, for the phrase to work grammatically. What we have instead, I believe, is an example of a strong but distorted memory of an earlier language state, whose nature is remembered through its prosody (indeed, it is worth remembering that, as a Faeroese and Danish speaker, Jakobsen could parse a phrase of this type, in particular in relation to word division).

In fact, the differing levels of Norn knowledge and use in these reminiscences can be found in a comparison between two versions of the same riddle (probably referring to snowflakes), both recorded in northern Yell (very rough attempt at translation: 'White bird (bird flying) without feathers; out came a handless man, who could also walk without legs, and plucked the white bird without feathers'; features in italics – as annotated by Jakobsen – are Scots rather than Norn in origin):

Version 1:	Version 2:
Flɔkəra flūra *fedderless*,	*White fool fedderless*,
ut kɔm modərə häŋa*less*,	ut kɔm modərə hä'ŋta*less*,
häŋæ beŋæ gōra*less*	otsa gōa bender*less*
	and plucked awa white fool fedderless

One of the variants demonstrates greater proximity to Norn than does the other – despite being recorded in the same period within a relatively small geographical space. Yet even then, the same rhythmic issue is apparent. Moreover, many of the basic structural words are Scots. It may be that this suggests that, by the time this material was recorded, memory of Norn was becoming increasingly confined to lexis. Recollections of the structure of the language had become a matter of rhythm.

I believe that what can be taken from this is that Norn had a 'half-life' within the developing indigenous variety of Scots. This was less a case of direct transfer from one language to the other, although this certainly happened. More potent than this was a sense of disruption, interference, crossover, which lasted, for a variety of sociocultural reasons, for a considerable period after the variety had ceased to have native speakers. Of course, other contacts fed into the nature of Shetland Scots, not least more mainstream forms of that variety brought from elsewhere (as Knooihuizen 2009 points out, albeit overstating somewhat; see also Millar 2008, 2016; Donaldson 1983). But Norn died hard and was a pervasive presence in the linguistic 'pot' which produced a mature version of the new variety.

2.8 Conclusion

Language shift almost inevitably implies language contact. With the exception of cases of genocide and near genocide, the same speakers or their descendants will begin speaking another, normally dominant variety. In relation to autochthonous languages, fundamental mutations in terms of power, economic and political, and culture regularly cause this shift, although the transfer is often hard-fought. Because speakers of languages of recent immigration may find the process of retention rather more difficult to maintain due to the hegemonic force exerted for the dominant language, it is not possible to resist shift through a sense of the native identity of the language. As a norm, autochthonous languages tend to survive longer than do languages of recent immigration.

A distinction can also be made between autochthonous and immigrant languages in relation to the sources for new structures and structural simplification in the A variety. The former variety apparently favours modifications based upon features of that variety, while immigrant varieties appear to be more likely to borrow material from the target language. Whether a view of this type could be taken much further is impossible to say.

Sasse ((1992) 2012a; (1992) 2012b) also theorised, as we saw, that native speakers abandoning their language would inevitably carry material into the target language. This is undoubtedly the case. From a long-term perspective, however, the effects of the transfer may be rather less tangible than might be predicted. It might be suggested that this is because, after a few generations, memory of the former mother tongue becomes severely constrained or lost entirely (although see the discussion of Scottish Highlands and Islands English in Section 2.5). The example of Shetland Scots analysed in Case Study 2 demonstrates, however, that strong ties with the cultural past can lead to a form of 'half-life' for the ostensibly 'dead' variant generations after it ceased to be spoken as a native variety; this 'undead' language would inevitably affect the living variety.

Exercises

1. Find out about the linguistic ecologies of one of the following contact situations: linguistic minorities in German-dominant Austria; Spanish–English contact in Los Angeles; Gaelic in Cape Breton, Nova Scotia, Canada; Finnish in Sweden.
2. In this chapter, arguments were made for differences in the effects of language shift on the varieties spoken by autochthonous groups in distinction to those spoken by recent immigrants. Do you think this distinction can be said to hold entirely?
3. Is the individual responsible for language shift? What about the group?

Suggested Reading

The classic theoretical treatment of the nature and linguistic and sociolinguistic outcomes of language shift is Sasse ((1992) 2012b). Every time I read this essay and consider its arguments, I learn something new or gain a new insight into how to analyse the phenomenon. Some early treatments of the phenomenon in particular places are especially useful in placing the phenomenon in a particular environment. I recommend Dorian (1981) and Gal (1979).

Language attrition and its linguistic repercussions are particularly well covered in Schmid (2011). I would also recommend the essays in Schmid et al. (2007) and Schmid and Köpke (2019). Clyne (2003) is *the* treatment of variation and change in immigrant varieties during the process of language shift.

Riehl (2019) brilliantly sums up a great many of the issues associated with the subjects discussed here in a relatively short space.

3 Pidgins and Creoles

Introduction

This chapter is concerned with the origins and development of pidgins and creoles, language varieties with a limited historicity which seem to appear when the necessity for communication is combined with large-scale multilingualism. While trade is often a primary spur for developments of this sort, manifest inequalities, often involving slavery or at least a major loss of basic personal and group rights and status, have regularly encouraged their development.

Both pidgins and creoles exhibit linguistic **simplification** (although rationalisation might be a better term), where large-scale structural norms within a language may be stressed over smaller-scale patterns, thus making a variety more straightforward to acquire. Some scholars see developments of this sort as representing evidence for how language universals are employed to form a new variety. Other scholars would reject this viewpoint.

The chapter will focus in particular on the ongoing debate between the creole exceptionalist theoretical position, where the development of a pidgin, with no native speakers, to a creole, with native speakers, is seen as supplying evidence for new language formation, perceived as being of a unique sort, and the **uniformitarian** position, where creoles are analysed as being nothing more than dialects of a language which have been put under particular stresses because of the histories of the territories in which they are spoken and the people who have lived there. The chapter ends with the tentative suggestion that there may be a number of interrelated ways in which a creole can develop, meaning that elements of both major theoretical models may be sustainable.

3.1 What Do We Mean by Pidgins and Creoles?

Across all inhabited continents, there is evidence of, and present witness to, linguistic varieties with limited historicity. The historical record for a particular variety is likely to be relatively patchy and short; there seems to have been a time in the not so distant past when the variety itself appears not to have existed. While obviously in some way related to other varieties with greater historicity, they appear to be different in other ways at all linguistic levels from these speech forms due to processes which are often termed 'simplification'. For instance, distinctions between verb **tenses** and **aspects** might not be expressed through the use of inflectional morphology but rather through the use of adverbials or clitics, descended from adverbs, verbs or nouns. On occasion, the same verb form will even be used in all positions, with the hearer reconstructing the necessary information from context. Differences between phonemes in the sound system might be severely curtailed, with, for instance, vowels pronounced in similar but separate places in the mouth in most dialects falling together as one set in these apparently simplified varieties. Words which might have quite specific meanings in these close relatives could possess a much wider and more generalised set of semantic fields.

Some of these 'new' varieties might have native speakers, while others might not. In the conventional vocabulary of the 1960s and 1970s, the latter were termed *pidgins*, while the former were known as *creoles*. Pidgins were seen by many as being the primary source for creoles (although most pidgins remained use languages without native speakers; they were no longer employed when their sociolinguistic purpose faded or ceased). As we will see throughout this chapter and the following, the notions underlying this binary distinction have not survived well in most scholarly analyses, in particular in relation to the view that creoles are at least sometimes (and, for some, always) descended from earlier pidgins. This certainty about the canonical position of a two-part typology, with creoles being analysed as new languages (creole exceptionalism), has since been replaced by a forthright (sometimes emotionally fuelled) debate on whether pidgins and creoles came into being through independent development at all (in its most forthright expression, uniformitarianism). The nature of creole origin has also been, and is likely to continue to be, something of a scholarly battlefield.

Much of this debate has been highly fruitful and thought-provoking. The controversies involved have produced heated discussion which has sometimes become vituperative and personal, however. The positions held by several scholars have become articles of faith for many of their followers. The views expressed do not always help us understand what pidgins and creoles are, however. I take no ideological position in the following. For that reason (I hope) I can give a fair presentation of the many virtues and issues which each school of thought possesses. I encourage you to make your own mind up too.

3.1.1 The Study of Pidgins and Creoles: A Few Words of Contextualisation and Warning

The study of pidgins and creoles has a long, albeit not always illustrious, history, reaching back into the eighteenth century. Many early scholars and other commentators admired the 'rationalised' structures that many creoles (and pidgins) have, along with their occasionally 'poetic' word formation process (this last analysis itself possibly exoticising, perhaps even 'othering', these speech forms when compared to the 'normal' language of the analysts). But a considerable number of scholars, many of them eminent, echoed the lay commentary of the time in considering the nature of these varieties to be evidence for the lower intelligence of their speakers. This was, they would have claimed, also 'proved' by the apparently unsophisticated nature of the languages which many speakers of creoles (or their ancestors) had previously spoken. Again, this was said to demonstrate the speakers' lack of intelligence: colonised peoples were incapable of fully internalising the structure and nature of the languages of the colonisers. The fact that many West African languages have a complex set of meaningful lexical **tones** which adult speakers of most European languages would find very difficult to learn never seems to have been recognised by these 'experts'.

This poisonous analysis, which we are obliged to recognise as linguistic racism, was a product of imperialism and, in particular, the slavery (and bonded labour) which supported it. While views of this type are rarely, if ever, voiced by experts nowadays, their presence in the earliest days of the field has cast a long shadow. Even with later commentators, such as Robert A. Hall Jr., who was active as a creolist in the first two decades after the Second World War, their turn of phrase is unfortunate from our viewpoint, 'othering' the speech and lives of speakers of these varieties. Indeed, much more 'modern' linguists, such as Derek Bickerton, used terms like *debased* for the nature of both pidgins and creoles in the 1980s. Elements of this 'othering' process may survive in the work of some scholars, at least as analysed by their ideological and theoretical opponents. In many ways, the remains of these viewpoints have inflamed the debate between creole exceptionalists and uniformitarianists.

3.1.2 'Simplification'

Connected to this is the question of what scholars actually mean by *simplification*, the process some scholars have seen – and see – in the development of pidgins and inherent in the assumed inception of creoles. Since *simplification* is such a controversial term in the field, I will attempt to provide what I hope is an unbiased definition of the phenomenon (or phenomena). The following is a brief attempt to describe what this word might mean in linguistic contexts.

To many commentators, what simplification signifies is subjective; in very real ways its meaning and analysis are formed in the eye of the beholder (Mufwene, Coupé and Pellegrino 2017; for further discussion, see Siegel 2008a: 18, 50; Bakker 2008). For instance, to a monolingual native speaker of English, the tone systems of the various Chinese dialects are – without a great deal of effort and a personal level of ability – difficult to hear and understand, never mind to learn; to native speakers of Chinese, the tone system is an excellent means of maintaining the semantic integrity of their language. From the viewpoint of a native speaker, this element of the system is *simple*. The same kind of observation can be made about the case system of Finnish and the rules of adjective and quantifier concord which derive from it. English speakers (indeed, speakers of most Western European languages) find the Finnish system extremely complex. Its native speakers, conversely, find the dearth of overt function marking in languages like English or French, never mind the idiomatic use of prepositions (rather than the invariant employment in their own languages of endings referring to specific forms of movement and stasis), complex (further discussions of complexity and simplicity can be found in Kusters 2003; Dahl 2004; Nichols 2009; Trudgill 2011).

Nevertheless, it might be possible to agree on what *simple* implies linguistically, primarily in a typological sense (see Section 1.6 and the Glossary). It could be taken as representing a situation where every word used in an utterance can be readily understood in terms of both meaning and structure in a way which is straightforward for a speaker of another language to learn. If numerals are used in a noun phrase, it might be unnecessary to have plural marking on the noun. If plurality is realised at all, this might be carried by a small number of markers (if not one single inflectional paradigm). Phonological features will emphasise a relatively small number of phonemes. Lexis with highly specific reference might be used in a more general sense with the number of lexical items thereby being reduced (in a way similar to, but not the same as, how a toddler develops an appreciation of semantic relationships). At least at times this could be seen as representing the development of natural morphology, a view of linguistic development highly fashionable in the 1980s, which suggested that there is a natural tendency for languages to move towards a more straightforward form (see, e.g., Dressler 1985; for analysis of the view, see Millar and Trask 2023: 108–12).

Each of these features has been found in a range of languages with 'long histories' (although admittedly not all in the one language). The primary objection to using *simple* and *simplification* in relation to topics covered in this chapter is that the terms might be taken to suggest some kind of relationship between ethnicity and complexity (and simplicity). The largest number of people who have spoken (and speak) pidgins and creoles were and are not of European descent (many of the initial speakers of a considerable number of varieties and their descendants had also been enslaved). Their language varieties were compared by entitled outsiders to the **lexifier**, the variety which provided at least most of the lexis for the new variety (conventionally seen as the standard variety of that language, although the actual contact varieties involved were unlikely to be forms of that particular dialect). They were found to be 'broken' and 'wanting'. This view was developed in tandem with the racist assumption, common in the nineteenth century, that *simplification* and *simple* imply a lack of intellectual ability.

Would *rationalisation* work better? Would we be permitted to see the 'drift' (Sapir 1921) which underlies the processes discussed in this chapter as being related to movement towards a more isolative typology (see the Glossary)? This type of linguistic structure is found most markedly in languages such as Vietnamese, represented by practically a one-to-one relationship between morpheme and word. Syntactic roles are marked solely by position. But if creolisation (or comparable processes) were involved in that language's development, this happened before Vietnamese was recorded; in any event, it is something which would not be accepted without evidence by scholars dealing with this language. It should also be noted that many pidgins and creoles have developed means of expressing morphosyntactic relationships not normally marked in the lexifier, a point to which we will return on a number of occasions in this chapter. Rationalisation therefore has the advantage of describing a process from a positive viewpoint, demonstrating a reworking of an inherited system to produce a variety which is straightforward to learn relatively rapidly. On the other hand, the term is not common in a linguistic context. The primary advantage for *simplification* is that it *is* well known and regularly used in linguistic analysis. With this in mind, it will be the primary term used in this chapter. The ideological baggage the term carries with it, as discussed, must always be borne in mind, however.

Similar apparent simplifications can be found with varieties which have non-European languages as their lexifiers. Fanagalo is a form of isiZulu used in South African mines and involving both locals – of whatever ethnic background – and many workers from farther north in the continent. IsiZulu, as is also the case with many other languages of southern Africa, employs a complex set of phonemic 'clicks', probably in origin borrowed into the local Bantu languages from the indigenous Khoisan languages, such as Nama, spoken now largely in Namibia, and Taa (otherwise !Xóõ, !Khong or !Xoon), now spoken in Namibia and Botswana, as a means of preventing homophony, along with other issues (for further discussion, see Millar and Trask 2023: 292–3). In Fanagalo, however, all clicks are replaced with /k/ (so that the consonantal structure is retained; Heine 1979, cited by Githiora 2002: 165). As predicted, the possibility of homophony is encouraged by this change. This pidgin is of a particularly restricted nature, since it is employed only for work purposes and thus need only employ a relatively small lexical inventory (although, as Mous 2019: 359–60 points out, it is likely to have developed initially in the speech of 'masters' communicating with servants, outside the mines). If that situation had changed, however, with a move towards a more developed and expanded state, it is likely that further phonological (and other) changes would have been employed to facilitate the avoidance of homophony more readily.

3.2 Pidgins and Creoles: Some Initial Analysis

In this section we will consider the nature of a range of representative pidgins and creoles as linguistic entities from which more general principles might be derived.

3.2.1 Examples of Pidgins and Creoles

Let us consider some examples of pidgins and creoles which derive their lexis primarily from the English language. Most of these examples are taken from Holm (1988-9). Some of that work's analysis is undoubtedly dated, but most of its exemplification is highly representative both in geographical and linguistic terms of these speech forms (the orthography employed with each example is based upon Holm's own sources and is therefore inconsistent in terms of the level of linguistic information carried). The choice of 'English' varieties (rather than those connected to other languages) is based primarily on a pragmatic need for clarity in relation to the understanding of the analysis; throughout it should be noted that phenomena of similar sorts can be found in pidgins and creoles with little or no connection to the English language. To redress this balance somewhat, Afrikaans, a variety with some creole-like features, derived from Dutch, will be discussed in Chapter 4.

In addition, as this chapter will demonstrate, all varieties identified as pidgins and creoles cannot readily be analysed as being members of one linguistic type or category. While practically all of the varieties discussed here behave in similar ways, the features displayed are not realised in the same manner or at the same level (saying this does not mean that similarities are not present, however). One final point before we begin the analysis: only relatively brief excerpts can be presented here; we are obliged to accept that several phenomena regularly found in varieties of this type do not occur in these particular pieces; this is, we can assume, largely a matter of chance.

3.2.2 Pacific Varieties

Many pidgins and creoles are found around the Pacific Ocean. The following section offers a representative sample.

3.2.2.1 Early Melanesian Pidgin

The following excerpt derives from the testimony of a labourer to an inquiry by magistrates in 1885 on conditions (in particular in relation to health) on sugar plantations in Queensland, Australia (for further discussion, see Mühlhäusler 1990: 244). At this point in the development of these varieties, *pidgin* might be the best term to use for what is being spoken (as far as we can tell, the variety represented is a use language, rather than one native to him), although the breadth of descriptive ability evidenced might suggest a variety becoming an expanded pidgin (of which more later).

> I am a native of New Ireland [a large island to the north-east of Papua New Guinea [see Map 3.1], of which it now forms a part politically]. I work long Mister Scott. Me know Umba. He make him hand long on neck. Me think him sick. He no go work yesterday. He stop long a house. When bell ring me come home and find Umba sitting up. He dead. He no move, him dead. (Mühlhäusler, Dutton and Romaine 2003: 37; see also Siegel 2008a: 84)

Following Mühlhäusler, Dutton and Romaine's analysis, a number of noteworthy features are apparent. In the first instance, there is considerable variation between pronoun forms present, as in *I* and *me*, the latter apparently being used in subject as well as object contexts. The same is true for *he* and *him*, with the latter also being used in possessive contexts (*He make him hand long on neck*).

Most of the verbs which would take inflections based on number and person in Standard English (distribution may be different in different dialects) are left with the bare 'infinitive' form (the *I am* at the beginning of the passage is apparently anomalous and will be discussed briefly later). There is also one occasion where a copula verb would be expected in Standard English but is not present here: *He dead*. Negative marking is also rather different from that of most dialects of English: *He no go work yesterday*.

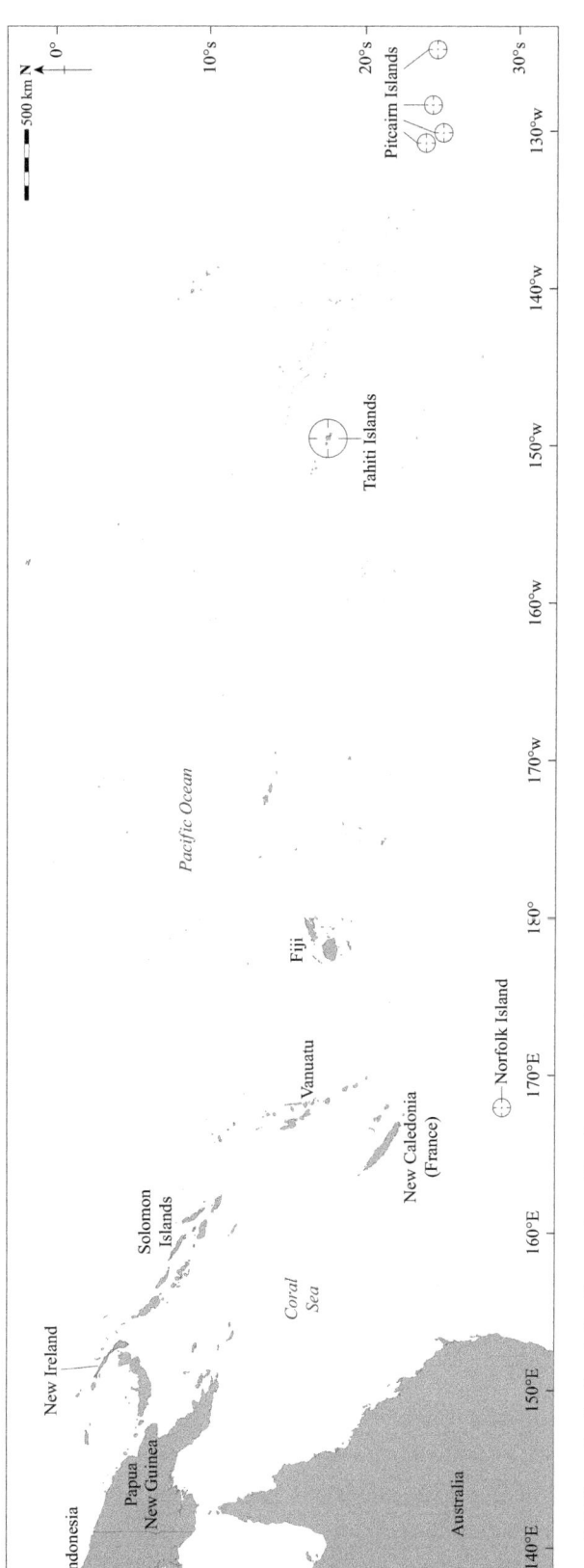

Map 3.1 Places in the South Pacific mentioned in Chapters 3 and 4.

A striking feature of the passage is the use of the preposition *long* in a range of contexts where a number of other prepositions would be expected in more 'mainstream' varieties (so that the *long* in *He stop long a house* might be rendered in Standard English as *inside*, for instance). Mühlhäusler, Dutton and Romaine (2003: 37) comment that '*long* remains the most general preposition in present-day Tok Pisin [a variety spoken (and written) in Papua New Guinea]'. The *-im* transitive marker, so much a feature of present-day Melanesian varieties (and, of course, a structural innovation when compared to most varieties of English), is not used here but is found in other documents from the same period (see Mühlhäusler, Dutton and Romaine 2003: 36–7).

Naturally, as with so many documents of this type, it is difficult to tell how genuine the language is. Usages like *I am* are strikingly different from the lack of copula usage in similar contexts in near proximity. The text, we assume, was produced by an outsider – probably a clerk to the magistrate's inquiry who did not have a full command of this variety spoken. This may explain why limited information on the phonology underlying the text is available: this is a sober attempt to provide information as accurately as possible, not an entertainment or even an illustration. The recorder may have Anglicised the speech; alternatively, although this is less likely, the speaker may have had some understanding of 'mainstream' English and approximated to some extent to that when communicating with outsiders until he felt more relaxed.

3.2.2.2 Pijin (Solomon Islands)

Solomon Islands (the preferred local form of the name) is a former British colony, part of an archipelago which runs east from New Ireland (see Map 3.1). Pijin, a Melanesian variety, is the lingua franca of the country, which may have as many as seventy autochthonous languages spoken by local people. All these languages are Austronesian in origin but are highly diverse, deriving from both the Western Oceanic and Polynesian subfamilies. As is the case for many of the countries in the area, Pijin is the means both for ensuring understanding and maintaining social and national cohesion.

Mitufala jes marit nomoa ia so mitufala no garem eni pikinini iet.
We two just married only   so we didn't   have any children yet
Mi trae had fo fosim haosben blong mi fo mitufala go long sip
I tried hard to force husband of mine for we two go on ship
bat team ia hemi   had tumas fo faendem rum long sip bikos   plende pipol
but time that it-was hard very to find   room on ship because many people
wandem go-go hom fo Krismas   tu
wanted to go home for Christmas too
(Holm 1988–9: II, 538, from a personal communication to him by E. Lee)

It is very likely that most speakers of 'mainstream' dialects of English would not understand this text when spoken, although they might recognise some of the words: in fact, practically all of the lexis is of English origin.

Partly this lack of comprehension is phonological in nature. Many contemporary varieties of English (most of England and Wales, the East Coast of the United States and most Southern Hemisphere varieties) are non-rhotic, in the sense that historical is only pronounced initially or before vowels. This appears to be echoed in this example of Pijin, where 'hard' is *had* and 'force' is *fosim*, with the transitive marker *-im*, mentioned earlier. Let us consider *nomoa ia*, however. This is translated as 'only' by Holm but appears to derive from English *no more here*. In many non-rhotic varieties of English, we would expect /r/ to be present between *moa* and *ia*, to avoid hiatus issues. This does not happen here; *ia* is also non-rhotic, although the apparent loss of /h/, not uncommon in English dialects from England, is not in line with the apparently /h/-bearing pronunciations, like *hom*, found elsewhere in the passage. It may be that *ia* has become grammaticalised, the process by which originally 'free' lexical material is 'bleached' to represent a purely grammatical function, as a discourse marker and is not perceived in the same way as fully lexical *here* would be. Voicing and rhoticisation of the final /t/ in *get* (*garem*) is common in many varieties of English, but it might still act as an inhibitor to comprehension for many speakers of 'mainstream' dialects of English. *Plende* is the halfway house of the change. Finally, the apparent merger of sounds in *tumas* < *too much* masks word origin.

It is with grammatical features that Pijin and English are particularly different. Most marked are the first person plural pronoun *mitufala* ('I/me-two-fellow', the last element apparently a marker of plurality, useful when that feature is not expressed consistently by inflectional morphology) and *-em*, the marker of verb transitivity (this feature is not present in English, demonstrating that the presumed linguistic simplicity of pidgins and creoles is not a straightforward issue). Both features will be discussed later. The word *Fo* < *for* acts as infinitive marker, where West Germanic languages have *to* (and North Germanic *at*); this is a common feature across English-based creoles (we might also compare archaic and dialectal *for to* as a potential source or at least analogue).

In terms of word choice, as has already been said, most words are of English origin, although some, such as *blong* < *belong*, on this occasion becoming a marker of possession, are passing through **grammaticalisation**. The word *pikinini* 'child/children' is, however, of Portuguese origin. It is found in many European language–based pidgins and creoles. Possible reasons for the global presence of this word (and other Portuguese features) will be discussed in Section 3.4.2.1.

3.2.2.3 China Coast Pidgin

China Coast Pidgin (otherwise known as Chinese Pidgin English) appears to be among the oldest pidgin derivatives of English to have come into being in the Pacific basin. Used initially as a means of communication in the Pearl river delta region of China in the eighteenth century (see Map 3.2), it spread alongside Western military force and trade (the two were seldom completely distinguishable) up the great rivers and along the coasts of China in the course of the nineteenth century. It also spread with Chinese migrant communities across the globe during this period (although some commentators, e.g. Kim 2008, make

3 Pidgins and Creoles

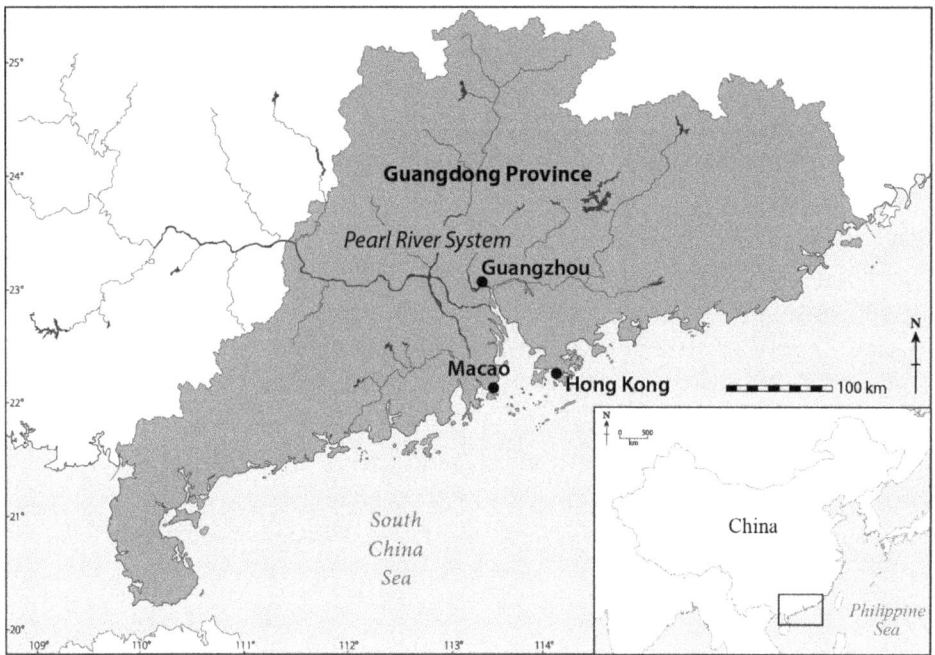

Map 3.2 Southern China

a strong case for some of these varieties, such as Californian Chinese Pidgin English, not necessarily being descended entirely from China Coast Pidgin). China Coast Pidgin may have had considerable influence upon later Pacific varieties; some evidence suggests that pidgin varieties of Portuguese directly influenced the new variety in the earliest stages of its development (for further discussion, see Matthews and Li 2012; Ansaldo, Matthews and Smith 2012; Ansaldo 2009: esp. chap. 8). Because of political developments in China across the twentieth century, involving, at least for a time, a rather more Sinocentric ideology and a degree of officially sponsored xenophobia, along with global shifts in economic power, it is likely that this variety, which never had native speakers, is now moribund, except among the very oldest members of the Chinese diaspora. In China itself, English in any form was considered suspect by many ideologues. When official interest in English grew in the period following the Cultural Revolution, it was Standard English – and only Standard English – which was promoted as an auxiliary language.

Tailor: *máj bʊk blɔŋ tú ólə*
my book is too old
Mistress: *máski,   jú pémi lúk-sí*
Never mind you let me look
Tailor: *máj sǽvi misi nó wɔnči ðis fǽšən. səpós misi kǽn kǽči bʊk*
I know you don't want this kind if   you can get book

	máj kǽn méki.	*Səpós misi no kǽn kǽči bʊk máj nó kǽn dú.*	*Misi*
	I can make [it]	if you cannot get book I cannot do	you
	kǽn kɔ́m tumɔ́lo?		
	Can come tomorrow?		
Mistress:	*tumɔ́lo máj nó kǽn kɔ́m. Máj livi silka ðissajd, səpós máj*		
	tomorrow I cannot come I leave silk here perhaps I'll		
	kɔ́m tumɔ́lo nɛ́ks dé.		
	Come the day after tomorrow		

(Holm 1988–9: II, 517; from a nineteenth-century phrase book, discussed by Hall 1966: 152)

This short text is both particularly useful for analysis and also questionable as a piece of realistic dialogue, since it is designed to be used in a way similar to that found in a phrase book (although this has a degree of situational appropriateness for a form of language intended primarily for trade interaction).

In phonological terms, we can see that divergence from 'mainstream' norms is quite limited, with the exception of some excrescent vowels (*silka* 'silk') and the apparent confusion of /l/ and /r/ (*tumɔ́lo* 'tomorrow'). The second phenomenon represents an almost stereotypical feature of the variety, originally brought into being in the Cantonese-speaking area, where /r/ is at most a marginal feature of the consonant inventory, to the rest of the Chinese-speaking world, where /r/ and /l/ are generally contrastive.

Structurally, many verbs employ a new final syllable (as with *kǽči*) in the infinitive; again, this is a stereotype feature of the variety, although it is also found in other varieties spoken across the Pacific and beyond. Negation is of the NEG + verb type, as is the case with other examples presented here. The word *blɔŋ* may represent an innovative copula (Holm translates it in those terms), although, as already mentioned, *belong* in various localised forms can be found in many English-based pidgins and creoles, in particular around the Pacific, where it acts as a possessive marker. Subject and object are not distinguished in pronouns.

Most lexis in the passage is derived from English. Given the Portuguese influence suggested earlier, it is possible that *pémi* 'allow' has a Romance origin, *permit* being, I suspect, a less likely borrowing in restricted contexts from English in the first instance than *allow*. Holm (1988–9: II, 515) suggests that *máski* 'never mind' is derived from Portuguese *mas que*. Matthews and Li (2012) suggest, however, an origin in Malay, although transmitted into China Coast Pidgin via Portuguese, perhaps particularly through the pidgins spoken at Macao. In either event this nevertheless supplies us with evidence for the level of linguistic diversity of, and multilingual interaction in, early modern South-East and East Asia.

3.2.3 Atlantic-Caribbean Varieties

Let us move to the Atlantic-Caribbean region, a region where the legacy of slavery and its aftermath are still tangible, economically, socially, culturally and linguistically.

3.2.3.1 Saramaccan

As we will discuss further in Case Study 3, Saramaccan is one of the English-lexified creoles spoken as a first language by a considerable number of people in Suriname (see Map 3.3), a country situated in north-east South America. Saramaccan is particularly prevalent in 'up country' areas. Its original speakers were maroons, enslaved people who, whether individually or as parts of groups, escaped from slavery from the seventeenth century on. Its written use lies in origin with the usage and practices of Christian missionaries (particularly the Moravian Brethren) from the nineteenth century on. The following excerpt is derived from a Saramaccan teaching tool, primarily, it can be assumed, intended for a missionary audience (and only secondarily a scholarly one).

Nöö e i   go a matu ...   hën I go a kuun liba.   Tet juba   ta   kai bëtë
Now if you go to woods ... then you go to hill top. When rain HAB fall possibly
i   sa si   pakia. Ma a soompu   ka pina dë.   Nöö fa i   si
you can see peccary but in swamp   where pina palm is. now as you see
...   i dou   a di soompu de   kaa,   nöö e   i   bi abi wan katolsi   fii
... as you arrive at the swamp there already now if you ANT have   a   bullet for-you
bi   ta   mëni u suti fou.
ANT HAB think of shoot bird.

<ö> = /ɔ/; <ë> = /ɛ/; HAB = habitual; ANT = anterior
(Holm 1988–9: II, 441–2; from Rountree and Glock 1982: 182)

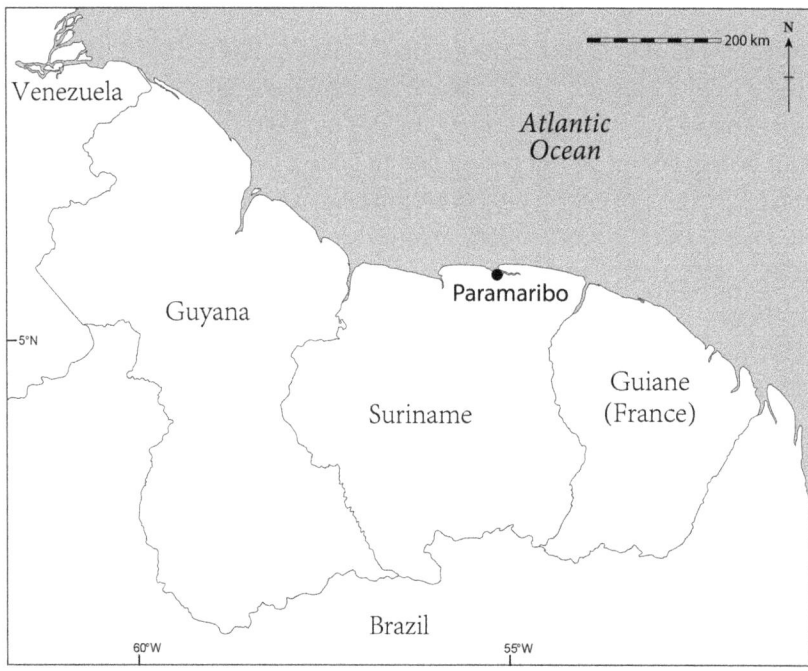

Map 3.3 Suriname and its neighbours.

One look at the text is likely to explain why I felt some trepidation when calling this variety 'English lexified'. Historically, such an identification would certainly be the case with Saramaccan, however. Unlike some varieties discussed here, I would be very surprised, nonetheless, if any native speaker of a 'mainstream' variety of English, except for a small minority with special knowledge, would be able to recognise many of the words here (although other excerpts of Saramaccan might well be more straightforward to analyse and interpret in this way). Many words are of Portuguese (possibly pidgin Portuguese) origin. In the first line of this excerpt alone, four words, *matu*, *kuun*, *liba* and *juba*, are either definitely or possibly from that source. Some others may be borrowed from African (or very occasionally indigenous) languages. Suriname was part of the Dutch overseas empire from the mid seventeenth century until the middle of the twentieth century (with English speakers having limited impact on the day-to-day use of language in the territory from the transfer of power). The country retains Dutch as its official language. Dutch loanwords are therefore likely to be present, possibly carried over from the dominant English-lexified creole of the country, Sranan, rather than transferred directly. Indeed, to me, *mëni* 'think' may not represent a form of English *mean* (which ceased to have the denotation present here, 'think', at its heart centuries ago) but rather its Dutch equivalent, *menen*, which has maintained this association (further discussion of the nature of Saramaccan lexis can be found in Good, n.d., 2009; see Case Study 3).

Phonologically, from the evidence presented here, Saramaccan is not at all close to most varieties of English. *Suti fou*, for instance, appears to represent a merger of /ʃ/ and /s/ at the latter and vocalisation of /l/ in the second word, if this is a form of *fowl* (the latter process is more common than the former in the general history of English). Morphologically, word-final vowels apparently added to the original English root are also commonplace, as with *soompu*. Aspectual information is provided by particles. The overt expression of anterior meaning is not normal in most varieties of English, Irish English and, to some extent, Scottish Highlands and Islands English being exceptions. Both of these 'native' varieties were themselves created under influence from another, typologically distinct, language.

3.2.3.2 Gullah

an dɪ ʌtkwek? yu aks mi if no bʊʊt dɪ ʌtkwek?
and the earthquake? you ask me if I know about the earthquake?
lɒd, haw mʌsɪ! wɛn dɪ ʌtkwek, mɒɪ sʌn, kalwərɪ kʊdn hol dɪ
lord, have mercy! when the earthquake, my son, Calvary couldn't hold the
pipl. yu yɛrɪ dɪ pipl hɒlərɪn ɒl rʊʊn an hʊlə so monfəl
people. you hear the people hollering all around and holler so mournful
"o, lɒd! o, lɒd! dɪ wʌl gwɒɪn tʊ ɛn". sɛ wi də gwɒɪn sa.
"oh lord! oh lord!" the world going to end". [they] say we are going quickly.
(Holm 1988–9: II, 494; taken from Turner 1949: 268, an early academic study of the variety)

Gullah is a Creole English spoken by people of African American ethnicity on the Sea Islands off the Atlantic coasts of South Carolina and Georgia in the United

States. Historically, it was also spoken on the mainland coasts of that region and was associated with large-scale plantation exploitation of enslaved labour connected to the cultivation of rice and indigo. During the eighteenth century, considerable numbers of enslaved people were transferred to this part of North America from the British Caribbean islands.

Even from this brief example, we can see that this variety is not merely an ethnically based variety of (Southern) US English, as many would consider African American Vernacular English to be (as we will discuss further in Case Study 4). Phonological analysis, in particular, demonstrates this divergence. While a lack of full rhoticity is present in Lowcountry South Carolina varieties spoken by all parts of the community (it is also present in most varieties of English, creole or otherwise, spoken in the Caribbean), /t/ and /d/ for /θ/ and /ð/ is less common in the region or elsewhere as a 'mainstream' feature but is not solely a creole marker. It should be noted that the other varieties of English which do demonstrate mergers of /t/ for /θ/ and /d/ for /ð/, such as the vernaculars of New York City and its environs, those of Dublin in Ireland and Liverpool in England, along with Shetland Scots, are often themselves the products of quite intense language contact of one form or another. Gullah pronunciations like *gwɒɪn* 'going' have a Caribbean 'feel' to them. An apparent merger between /w/ and /v/ (*kalwəri*) is presently practically unknown in English outside a small number of creole environments, with the exception of the vernacular of St Helena in the South Atlantic, as discussed in Section 4.2.2, although it appears to have spread and contracted in vernacular South-East England English in the nineteenth century.

Although less evident in this passage, there are some morphosyntactic features which most analysts would consider to be 'creole' in nature, such as *dɪ wʌl gwɒɪn to ɛn*, where no copula is expressed, followed by *wi də gwɒɪn sa*, with the alternative Caribbean English copula *də* (likely to be derived from English *there*) found in both the preceding Saramaccan excerpt and the following Miskito Coast Creole English equivalent.

3.2.3.3 Miskito Coast Creole English

wen   i pik it up   naw i no kom   we a de.   i tel me lay
when   he starts up (drinking) now he doesn't come   where I am. he tells me lies
wen   i kom naw.   da iyvnin   i sey, "mama", i sey,   "a did tayad an neva kom".
when   he comes now. in the evening he says, "mama", he says, "I ANT tired and didn't come".
a say, "yu dam lay.   siy yu ay?   yu mi dringkin;
I say, "you damn liar, see your eye? you ANT drinking
das wai   yu no mi wahn kom ya".
that's why you don't want me to come here"
(ANT = anterior; Holm 1988-9: II, 475, with minor changes; from Holm 1983: 103)

Miskito Coast Creole English is spoken along a considerable length of the Caribbean coasts of Honduras and Nicaragua. The variety has both native speakers and second language users; of the latter, many speak local languages.

Many users now have at least some command of Spanish; some may have it as their first language. The historical reasons for this complexity are inherently connected to ethnic mixture (and who held power) in the region from the seventeenth century on. Most strikingly, English speakers were economically powerful until at least the end of the nineteenth century, even if official control by this group had rarely been fully imposed. But while some of these English speakers possessed considerable prestige, others, such as a considerable number of enslaved people transferred from Jamaica, did not (the history of the region is presented in Holm 2014).

While treating this excerpt as evidence for the variety as a whole is dangerous, particularly in relation to the lack of overt influence from Spanish found there, in contradiction to the evidence discussed by Holm (2014), Miskito Coast Creole English does appear to be fairly mainstream in relation to other Caribbean varieties. In comparison with Saramaccan, for instance, it is likely to be rather more readily comprehensible to speakers of other varieties of English which would not normally be considered 'creoles'. Its structural features, such as the expression of negation or the form of verb–subject concord employed, are similar to those found in the Gullah text. Marking for verb aspect is more readily visible in the Miskito excerpt, as with *a did tayad*, where *did* expresses anterior tense/aspect information. The fact that, as I have already suggested, overt anterior aspect expression is unknown, except in a few 'Celtic' contexts, in all but creole varieties of English must encourage us to reflect on what we mean by 'simplification'.

3.2.4   Analysis and Discussion

These examples were not, of course, chosen at random. While each of the varieties, as illustrated here, has its own particularities, each also shares much with all the other varieties in terms of structure, phonological development and lexis. Most interestingly, perhaps, there is indicative evidence for groupings within the whole. In a sense, these could be (and have been) described as Atlantic and Pacific, with lines of descent and relationship enabled, although it should be noted that this distinction should not be taken too literally, particularly in geographical terms. Moving beyond 'English' pidgins and creoles, moreover, it is important to recognise that the 'French' creoles of the Indian Ocean region often appear more like their Atlantic equivalents, both because, perhaps, of the West African linguistic and ethnic backgrounds of many enslaved people forcibly brought to both areas and also because the speakers of the new varieties, and their 'lexifiers', were not native to the place of settlement. Beside the many similarities between varieties present even in this small sample lie unquestionable anomalies and dissonances. The greatest of these issues, which we will touch upon repeatedly throughout this chapter, is concerned with the question, why are some of these varieties more like their lexifiers than are others?

3.3 Where Are Pidgins and Creoles Spoken?

Where are (or have been) varieties generally termed pidgins and creoles spoken? It is not the intention of this chapter to enumerate all these varieties (an onerous task, carried out admirably elsewhere; again, Holm 1988–9 provides a particularly useful sense of the distribution of pidgins, creoles and related varieties, whose lexical origins at least derive from a range of languages, not all of which are European in origin). Nevertheless, a number of patterns can still be analysed. For instance, while pidgin and creole varieties associated with languages indigenous to a particular region, such as Chinook Jargon, spoken in British Columbia and contiguous parts of the north-west of the contiguous United States, can be found far inland, those which appear to have Western European languages as, at the very least, their primary lexical sources are normally found beside the sea or up navigable rivers. They are also quite likely to be spoken in regions which are considerably removed geographically from where the primary source for at least the vocabulary of the new variety is spoken. Thus Pijin is spoken in Solomon Islands, almost as far away from England as it is possible to be and live on dry land. The waterborne nature of these varieties is likely to have been a product of ship-based exploitation and trade (of a variety of sorts, some more benign than others). Until the twentieth century, the only means by which this kind of transmission could take place was by sea.

The exception to this waterborne spread of dominant languages external to where a particular variety is spoken can be found with the largely land-based spread of Russian and Arabic, both of which also produced pidgins and creoles of various sorts. Indeed, it is interesting to note that, while waterborne Arabic was spoken for centuries along the East African littoral (for a discussion of Arabic pidgins and creoles, see Owens 2022: 412–14), it was the indigenous kiSwahili which spread into the hinterland, developing pidgin forms as a result of this expansion (for discussion, see Mazrui 2022).

It is quickly evident that, although pidgins in particular are found across a large part of the earth's surface, there are several geographical concentrations in terms of numbers of varieties spoken. Melanesia and New Guinea (see Map 3.1) represent one of these concentrations. In fact, it could be argued that these varieties stem from one original pidgin, spoken as a trade variety across a large part of the western sectors of the southern Pacific Ocean. These various purposes included the harvesting of sea slugs, a lucrative trade with particular focus on connections to China, but also the availability of seasonal employment in the sugar plantations of northern Australia (for discussion, see Keesing 1991; Siegel 1998; Koch 2011).

The other concentration of pidginisation and creolisation is associated with the islands in, and the territories surrounding, the Caribbean Sea. It is associated with the slave trade of the sixteenth to nineteenth centuries. This concentration is at least in part connected to the presence of varieties spoken on the coast of West Africa and islands off its coast during the period of European expansion in that region. Many of the descendants of these varieties continue to be spoken and have often spread into the hinterland of the original contact; some, such as Nigerian Pidgin, are spoken by many millions of people. Another smaller-scale concentration, also founded upon slavery and later based upon peonage, lies in the present or formerly French territories situated in the central Indian Ocean.

It is unsurprising, of course, that a great many of these varieties came into being primarily as a result of the European imperialist expansion from the sixteenth century on. It could be argued that, although formal European imperialism ended in the aftermath of the Second World War, the linguistic tendencies set in motion during this period have continued. In part, at least, this is due to the largely 'soft' power wielded by the United States, hegemonic globally since at least the middle of the twentieth century (and in some regions, such as the Caribbean, from much earlier). Are there differences in the presiding social, political and economic forces which produced the pidgins and creole varieties in these places, therefore?

In the Caribbean region, unsurprisingly, it was the forced importation of considerable numbers of enslaved people, largely from Africa, from the sixteenth to nineteenth centuries which encouraged the development of these varieties. The Melanesian (taken in their broadest sense) varieties, on the other hand, came into being somewhat later. While apparently set in motion by European-led, often exploitative and not entirely voluntary enterprises, the linguistic diversity of the region had long demanded the use of lingua francas of local origin. This importation of European – particularly, perhaps, English-based – dialects was a natural source for those varieties, often termed pidgins and creoles, although some specialists would prefer *expanded pidgins* for the latter, as European power grew and spread in the region. (For a discussion of this process, see Siegel 2008a: 84; see also McWhorter 2018: 47–8, who interprets these varieties as representing the development of pidgins into creoles, rather than expanded pidgins – indeed, he would not truly accept such a distinction.)

3.4 Suggestions for the Origins and Development of Pidgins

When I was a student, I was taught that creoles inevitably and solely derive from earlier pidgins, with which they share many features. The primary distinction between the two states was that the former had native speakers, while the latter did not. It was always underlined, however, that pidgins were essentially connected to a context and to specific cultural and economic developments and that the genesis of a creole from that source was only occasional and not necessarily predictable (indeed, the process was rather rare). As first language varieties, moreover, creoles could be employed by native speakers to represent any and all of the ideas which any other native variety can, something pidgins generally cannot do. Mühlhäusler (1986: 5) provides an illustration of how such a development might take place, bearing in mind that the progression from one stage to another is not guaranteed (Figure 3.1). Any of the levels proposed may represent the final developmental stage of a particular variety.

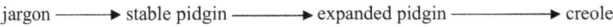

Figure 3.1 Mühlhäusler's typology of creole development.

Mühlhäusler (1986: 5) gives examples of alternative terms for each of the proposed stages: a jargon could be described as a *pre-pidgin, multilingual idiolect* or *secondary hybrid*; a stable pidgin could be termed a *pidgin, basilectal pidgin* or *tertiary hybrid*; quite regularly, an expanded pidgin is described as an *extended pidgin*.

What is presented here is a very useful schematisation. States (or levels) are achieved; sometimes (but not always), sociolinguistic factors lead to changes in the use of the variety and how speakers relate to it, thus implying movement towards a new stage. It also demonstrates how fractured the terminology used in the field was (and is).

But while these portrayals can be helpful for initial comprehension of difference and development, the reality of the classification of varieties of these types, at least according to the discussions and analyses which follow, is rather more messy (although many scholars choose to make their own interpretations seem highly straightforward, indeed, obvious). We need to consider each of the states employed in this chapter (and the following) in some depth, paying particular attention to how these states are perceived as coming into being. We will begin with pidgins.

3.4.1 A Sociolinguistic Discussion of the Development of Pidgins

Decamp (1971: 18–20) suggests that there are a number of ways in which a pidgin can develop. Unsurprisingly, one of the primary catalysts for this is trade, whether voluntary or not. A use variety practically *must* come into being as a result of longer-term or regular trade. Mute trade, aided often by signs (traditional or improvised), is only of so much use; the possibility of misunderstanding is considerable and sometimes dangerous. The use of interpreters, if such are available, is also often of limited value. Omai, the Tahitian interpreter employed by the 1768–71 Royal Navy expedition under Captain James Cook to communicate with indigenous people on their journey, was able to be understood sufficiently among Māori speakers in New Zealand for relatively easy communication. He could not understand, never mind translate, anything said to the explorers by native people on the arrival of the expedition to Australia (for a discussion, see McCormick 2013). Even if the interpreter can speak the local language, moreover, considerable misunderstanding is possible, often due to cultural practices and relationships. The practice also always left the traders at the mercy of the honesty of the interpreter.

Which (perhaps better, *whose*) language is employed as the primary source for the use variety can tell us something about the social relationships between the groups involved in trade. This desire to find common ground through language almost inevitably becomes complex when other social pressures are brought to bear. Both input varieties can contribute essentially the same amount of material to the new variety, as with Russenorsk, used for communication between Norwegian fishermen and Russian merchants in the nineteenth and early twentieth centuries; the name of the variety – 'Russian-Norwegian' – implies equality (or near equality) in the relationship between the groups. That these 'mixed' varieties are rare is a striking indication of the inequality in the social relationships which underlies the development of most mainstream pidgins (and, indeed, creoles).

Too much can be made of the idea that pidgins are primarily aids to clearer communication. There is evidence that, on several occasions in North America and elsewhere, a somewhat simplified form of a local language was developed (whether consciously or not) by native speakers. This variety was intended to stop their neighbours learning their 'true' language, possibly because they wanted to maintain a degree of secrecy in their dealings with outsiders, but also because they felt that these outsiders were not worthy to use their language in its full form. A striking example of this tendency, but one where the outsiders' language was given lexical primacy, can be found in the development of China Coast Pidgin in the late eighteenth and early nineteenth centuries. Both parties to the trading exchanges appear in the main to have considered themselves to be the other party's cultural superior. Not only did Chinese speakers not want the English-speaking traders to 'debase' their language by using it; traders appear also to have been forbidden by local and national authorities to teach the foreigners Chinese. Both sides also wished to retain a native code which users of the pidgin would not have been able to follow readily (for a discussion, see, e.g., Parkvall and Bakker 2013: 48).

Perpetual bondage slavery (with, unlike other forms of slavery, a highly circumscribed possibility of manumission) came into being in the expanding Western European world from the sixteenth century on. It was intrinsically linked to the exportation by force of enslaved people to new territories which were being exploited by the imperialist powers. It was replaced in the same and similar territories in the course of the nineteenth century by peonage (where individuals were technically free but were tied to the land either by statute or poverty). These processes and their outcomes inevitably led to the creation of classes of people who were born with severe social and economic disadvantages in relation to the other inhabitants of the territory in which they were now placed; these disadvantages were enforced by the interpretation of physical appearance. These brakes on development and equal treatment to all inhabitants were deemed by many of the dominant parts of the population to be both necessary and reflective of first 'religious' and then 'scientific' orthodoxies. Learning the dominant language (or at least a form of it, comprehensible to their 'masters' and peers) became a necessity of life for them.

The ancestors of the large South Asian population resident in Fiji (see Map 3.3), brought as labourers to the sugar plantations and elsewhere in the late nineteenth and early twentieth centuries, were in many ways forced by circumstance and their plantation environment to develop a range of use varieties. Their need to develop a group identity was also focussed by the considerable hostility felt by many of the native Fijians towards the newcomers. We will discuss Fiji Hindi in more depth in Chapter 6, but it should be noted that a pidgin form of Fijian also developed during this period and in the early period of contact with Europeans which preceded it (Parkvall and Bakker 2013: 52). The primary distinction here is that, with the first instance, it was the South Asians' native varieties which formed the basis of this new variety, while, in the contexts discussed in this chapter, the varieties began as those spoken by non-native speakers who might then become native speakers. As we have already seen, however, even this causal connection is contentious.

We could therefore claim that the development of a pidgin begins as a means of communication between populations which are diverse linguistically. That these varieties often develop in situations of dominance by one group over other groups, on many occasions brutal, cannot be ignored. But while a sociolinguistic understanding of the reasons for pidgin development has been presented, it is necessary to understand the linguistic forces at work in their creation and evolution. This will be attempted in Section 3.4.2.1.

3.4.2 Linguistic Origin of Pidgins

In many ways, the linguistic, rather than sociolinguistic, processes by which pidgin varieties come (and came) into being are straightforward to describe: speakers of two or more languages, without any language in common, are obliged to find a common variety, the lexis deriving largely from the language whose speakers possess the greatest amount of economic and social capital. The actual process of pidginisation has prompted much discussion, as we will see, primarily because, with the partial exception of Hawai'ian Pidgin English, we have very limited contemporary evidence for what happened and happens in the first stages of the process. Mechanical recording was unknown until the late nineteenth century. Those who did comment on language change in use in these types of varieties were largely not trained in the practice of accurate recording. Many (possibly most) observers, recorders and analysts, as has already been suggested, carried with them preconceptions and prejudices about the varieties and their speakers. In addition, the pidgin speakers were at best disenfranchised and, at the very worst (and all too commonly), enslaved, were rarely literate and, in any event, often did not have the leisure to discuss or analyse their own speech forms.

Some historical explanations made under these circumstances can appear simplistic. For instance, Hall's view that a pidgin is essentially a product of the contact between, as he (Hall 1966: 61) would frame it, the 'European language' and the 'Non-European Language', with the pidgin being formed from the 'Common Elements', could be taken as suggesting that there was a strongly ad hoc aspect to the processes of creation, construction and stabilisation of a pidgin. I am sure this is not really what Hall intended to convey, but the way he describes the process proposes a degree of apparently random variation in terms of linguistic choice. The idea of pidgin creation through the employment of common elements is also questionable, even if, as will be suggested in Section 3.5.2.2, many of the varieties discussed here do provide some evidence for both superstratal and substratal influence. It could be argued that the processes put forward on this occasion are actually better suited to a discussion of koine formation (as covered in Chapter 6).

Despite many of these issues, however, scholars have proposed a variety of ways in which pidgin genesis (or incremental development) could have taken place.

3.4.2.1 Monogenesis versus Polygenesis

The question of pidgin and creole origin (the two, as we have touched upon, were largely seen as intrinsically linked until the 1990s by most scholars) was dominated until the 1970s by a debate on how to analyse the ultimate origins of pidgins. The discussion revolved around the question of whether there was one pidgin underlying the origins of all (or, at least, most) pidgins (the monogenetic theory) or whether there were many occasions where pidgins came into being independently, primarily based on the varieties to hand (the polygenetic theory). Despite the disparate origins of pidgins posited by the latter, the varieties produced are typologically similar. Decamp (1971) gives a detailed and even-handed treatment of both views.

The monogenetic theory carries with it an important demonstration of awareness: most European language–based pidgins (and creoles, argued by some to be of pidgin origin) contain some Portuguese lexis, such as *savvy* 'know' or *pickaniny* (now a largely racist term for children of colour but originally used to refer to anything small, including younger children, by people from all ethnic backgrounds within a particular space). Followers of the monogenetic theory have produced the argument that pidgin Portuguese was the original European pidgin which spread, along with Portuguese armed and trading power, across the world when Portugal was the primary European power in, for instance, West Africa, India and the East Indies. Some scholars have suggested that this Portuguese pidgin is a Lusitanised version of Sabir (otherwise Lingua Franca 'language of the Franks/ Europeans'), the pidgin, based largely on Romance lexis, used until the nineteenth century around the Mediterranean (Naro 1978 presents a critical – but not necessarily negative – analysis of the Sabir origin theory). All other pidgins are, according to this analysis, relexified forms of this pidgin (we will return to this and other analyses of **relexification** in Section 3.5.2.2).

This view is attractive in a number of ways, not least in its connection to a particular point in European (and world) history, the Portuguese expansion from the fourteenth century on, which has had a greater effect on global trade patterns and social and ethnic relationships than many other changes have had. It is also worth noting that there appears to be evidence for the descent of some pidgins from earlier varieties, for some of which we actually have witness (with a few, but sufficient, examples to analyse). A number of Melanesian and New Guinea English-lexified creoles, including Bislama (spoken in Vanuatu), Pijin (spoken in Solomon Islands) and Tok Pisin (spoken in Papua New Guinea), are so similar to each other that a close relationship would have to be assumed; the same can be said for at least some of the creoles spoken in Suriname (see Case Study 3). Would the Portuguese elements in many pidgins support the idea of a much more macro relationship across a considerable period? Is it possible that Portuguese acted as the metaphorical 'glue' for the products of profound language contact around the world?

There are nevertheless very good reasons to suspect that the monogenetic theory does not work as well as it first appears to. In the first instance, it is Eurocentric. There are several pidgin varieties which involve contact between a range of indigenous languages, such as Delaware Jargon in the eastern United States or Sango in central Africa, where most or all of the original inputs were non-European. Inevitably, Portuguese influence on these varieties is, at best, dubious (nor would it suit the historical narrative). But in structural terms, these varieties have many similarities with other varieties where a European connection is viable. This might be taken to mean that there are shared linguistic components present in all pidginisation events, a point to which we will return on a number of occasions.

The primary virtue of the polygenetic theory is that it provides and presents a contrastive interrogation of the issues produced by any analysis of the monogenetic theory. Its central point is that the act of pidginisation is unique on all occasions. A more nuanced view would be that, while descent from variety to variety is always possible in all linguistic situations, the original 'genesis' of this particular pidgin 'tradition' is unique. While this seems a more realistic interpretation of the evidence than the monogenetic theory proposes, it still does not explain the structural similarities between varieties which, logically viewed, would be most unlikely to have affected each other, such as Chinook Jargon and Icelandic Pidgin Basque. But too much can probably be made of these apparent similarities, even when the lexifier is essentially the same language.

When the evidence is sifted finely, therefore, it seems likely that both the monogenetic and the polygenetic theories of origin act more as means of viewing the issue, rather than as full explanations for the problem. Both theories also appear relatively uninterested in the developmental patterns put in place by native speakers as they begin to speak the new variety.

3.4.2.2 A Systematic Analysis of the Process of Pidgin Development

No matter the nature of pidgin genesis, however, several scholars have suggested that a pidgin does not (at least always) spring fully formed into the repertoire of speakers (this is in line with Mühlhäusler's typology, described earlier). Instead, there is a tendency in some contexts for a variety initially to begin as a form of language much less capable of carrying out many of the tasks of 'normal' varieties; over time, some varieties will be used in more domains and for more purposes.

Foreigner Talk I started studying French at the age of fourteen, eventually receiving an O-grade at sixteen (I already had some knowledge of German and Latin, both of which I continued studying for considerably longer than I did French). Learning French was made considerably easier by my knowledge of Latin, along with the level of French borrowings present in English. I can read a French newspaper (albeit with difficulty: I would not be able to read a novel). I can certainly read scholarly articles in that language, although only really if they are concerned with my specialisms. These abilities are all passive in nature, however. My spoken French is execrable.

My own impression, as well as that of others, is that I at least appear to be plucking words – mainly nouns and adjectives – out of the air with a limited relationship to either inflectional morphology or syntax. It must be excruciating to listen to this ad hoc explosion of (I hope) meaningful syllables. What I am describing here is something which non-linguists often describe as 'pidgin'. Such an identification would be inaccurate, however. In fact, what is being represented in my 'French' is a state which should really be termed something like foreigner talk, largely the product of a highly fragmented acquisition of a language, in particular when a person learns a language in their teens or later.

Some scholars, such as Hall (1962), have referred to this as baby talk. This implies a pre-existing linguistic model designed by adults for communication with young children. The condescension inherent in this type of analogy would have been particularly marked where native speakers are much higher in the social hierarchy than the learners. It is likely that the two processes represent very similar developments (particularly since what we have as a result of the second process is initially the variety produced by the native speaker, rather than the learner).

Despite their somewhat unwieldy natures, linguistic phenomena of this sort have their uses. It is possible to employ them to buy and sell, up to a point, although always with the worry that what you think you are saying may be rather different from its interpretation by the listener. There is also a strong possibility that you will not be able to understand responses given to you. It would be fair to say, I think, that this type of communication would not even be seen as second best.

Jargons There are occasions, however, when the originally ad hoc nature of a foreigner talk variety (if it can be termed such) has faded somewhat: a degree of regularity at all levels of its structure has come into being. Having said that, the variety cannot be seen as a bona fide *language*. Let us imagine a multilingual, non-literate region, probably at some time in the past. While the different ethnolinguistic communities generally kept themselves separate at a social level, trade before all other social functions was conducted across the region. Relationships between the peoples of the region were quite stable. It is likely that many people would have had command of more than one language; this would have been unlikely to be the case for *all* the local inhabitants for *all* languages. Over time, vehicles of communication developed whereby speakers could communicate with speakers of other languages, albeit within constrained contexts. A relatively small number of words, particularly when accompanied by effective gestures, can prove highly effective in trade.

As already suggested, this stage in the development of a lingua franca is, unlike foreigner talk, one in which a structured use of language, at least in terms of lexical choice, prevails. It is not ad hoc. Equally, this type of language cannot really be used for anything other than a trade transaction. It would be impossible to use it for a meaningful and open-ended conversation. The term *jargon* could be used to describe this state – a state, in fact, which can have considerable longevity. Jargons certainly developed during the period of European imperial expansion beginning in the early modern period. The early spread of Malay words and phrases across what is now Indonesia in the sixteenth and seventeenth centuries may also represent an example of this type of process, associated with both trade and Muslim missionary efforts (for discussion, see, e.g., Collins 2022, as well as, with a more general focus, Ostler 2022). For some varieties at least, the step towards broader understanding and wider communication is achieved.

(Stable) Pidgin Of all the terms used in this chapter (possibly in this book), *pidgin* is probably the best known by non-specialist readers. Practically everyone is likely to have a sense of what the word means. Yet this very knowledge can actually obscure the ways in which students of linguistic contact analyse a state which is not always straightforward to define. Mühlhäusler (1986: 5) remarks that

> pidgins are examples of partially targeted or non-targeted second language systems as communication requirements become demanding. Pidgin languages by definition have no native speakers, they are social rather than individual solutions, and hence are characterized by norms of acceptability.

Parkvall and Bakker (2013: 2) attempt their own definition, suggesting that a pidgin

1. is a language that is conventionalised (and not spontaneous);
2. is used as a lingua franca in a contact situation;
3. is native to no one;
4. fulfils only restricted communicative functions;
5. draws to some extent on one or more of the languages spoken or known by the groups in contact as sources;
6. has some norms of forms and usage and hence some stability;
7. is highly reduced lexically and grammatically compared to its input languages.

They note that 'most of these are social criteria and that only the last one relates to structure' (22). In the rest of this section and in Section 3.5, we will recognise this diversity (but also similarity) in definition and interpretation, while providing some background to the development of pidgins and related phenomena.

Whether derived from earlier jargons or brought into being in some other way (essentially always through necessity), pidgins remain limited in their communicative utility, particularly where they are formed and employed in a trade or work context (as they often are), in situations where people from different linguistic backgrounds have no pre-existing lingua franca. Nevertheless, pidgins are structured in similar (if not identical) ways to 'real' languages. Unlike for a jargon, it is possible to hold an in-depth conversation in a pidgin, even if the topics available for discussion might be limited (with a definite preponderance of words for trade and other relationships). Many analysts see pidgins (and their proposed forerunners) as being structurally 'simplified'. It is certainly true that at some levels, this might be the case: it may be more straightforward to learn a pidgin than would be true for a 'mainstream' language. As we have seen, how simplification – *rationalisation*, as was suggested earlier, might be the better term – as a process can be interpreted is problematical in a variety of ways.

Expanded Pidgins/Pidgincreoles Over time, a pidgin may begin to be employed in a far larger set of contexts, primarily because it has become the use language of a considerable range of people found in a work context, urban conglomeration or anywhere where there is a concentration of people involved in similar occupations, where previously a pidgin has served as a form of community communication. These are often termed *expanded pidgins*. They are also occasionally called *pidgin-creoles*, primarily because the varieties produced are similar in terms of population and usage to creoles. The primary distinction between creoles and expanded pidgins, according to some analysts, is that expanded pidgins do not have native speakers, while creoles do (indeed, native speakers of a creole may make up the whole or at least a significant part of an idealised population in a particular place). Bartens (2013: 69–70) claims that

> it is therefore *no longer justified to argue that a pidgin can only evolve into a creole when spoken by a population that has acquired it as its first language.* Instead, the original feature of a creole language is that it can fill all the communicative and stylistic functions that are needed in a speech community.

But too much can be made of this distinction: expanded pidgins *do* sometimes have native speakers. While most speakers of Nigerian Pidgin or Tok Pisin, for example, have a different first language, both varieties do have first language speakers, normally living side by side with second language users. Native speakers of Tok Pisin in particular have assumed considerable importance within their society (for further discussion, see Siegel 2008a: 5; Bakker 2008: 139). Many expanded pidgins have considerable longevity. In at least their most expanded forms, therefore, these types of language are capable of carrying the same amount of information as any other variety can.

3.5   Creole Genesis and Development

What are creoles, linguistically and sociolinguistically, therefore? This apparently straightforward question continues to cause significant issues for scholars. A large part of the rest of this chapter will be concerned with potential answers to this question.

Since they share so many linguistic and sociolinguistic features, it is natural that many scholars have assumed that a creole is the product of the nativisation of an (expanded) pidgin variety. This interpretation has increasingly been rejected, often vociferously, by some scholars. Much of the rest of this chapter will be concerned with these disputes and their historical background.

3.5.1 Creole Origin in Pidgins?

The transit from pidgin to creole appears straightforward: a language variety without native speakers develops into the native language for some speakers at least, largely through social developments. Decamp (1971: 16–17) recounts the scholarly history of how the connection (perhaps less obvious than most of us would assume) between pidgins and creoles was established. While a number of inter-war scholars discussed the idea, it was, Decamp suggests, Hall (1962) who followed the idea to its logical conclusion, seeing the origin of a creole in a prior pidgin as a recognisable process (although one which few pidgins have followed). But there are strong objections within the scholarly community to a straightforward perception of the genesis of creoles being rooted solely in the nativisation of pidgins. Let us consider the issue from (essentially) first principles.

To what extent are creoles the natural outcome of the nativisation of pidgins? In some ways, analysing this question bears a considerable resemblance to wilfully disappearing down a rabbit hole. Despite protestations from some adherents to the uniformitarian viewpoint (as discussed earlier and in particular in Section 3.5.3), there can be little doubt that at least *some* creoles are very similar to *some* pidgins in their linguistic natures. This does not mean that these states are necessarily interconnected by a causal relationship based on descent: likeness does not immediately and intrinsically imply common parentage. We must be very careful not to fall into a 'but they must be' type of argument. Nevertheless, we have to take seriously the reality of the similarity between the two states as a first principle in any argument, particularly when their speakers inhabit the same environment or ones similar to each other. McWhorter (2018: 8) – arguably, as we will see, the most prominent creole exceptionalist – speaks forcefully for the reality of this connection. There seems to be little opportunity for common ground between uniformitarian and exceptionalist views on creole origin (although, as we will see, there may be some commonalities between the two schools, even if these are not recognised by their protagonists). What can be said is that, even *if* the developmental connection between pidgins and creoles is relatively straightforward, most pidgins never develop into creoles (Parkvall and Bakker 2013: 25). Their existence as a non-native variety is maintained only for as long as they are useful.

The apparent connection between pidgins and creoles *may* be a true one, on at least some occasions. Terms like *expanded pidgin* and *pidgincreole may* work better in these circumstances than the blanket use of the term *creole*. It would be wrong to argue, however, that these terms (and the states they represent) do not at the very least resemble each other (sometimes, in fact, linguistics, like most scholarly disciplines, seems to employ more terms than the states it is attempting to describe actually *need*). A number of scholars have made much of the possibility that substratal influences affected the development and nature of pidgins and creoles. Many other specialists have downplayed (or even dismissed) the importance of this phenomenon.

A further issue which needs to be recognised is that a distinction in nature is likely to exist between indigenous creoles, where either the dominant or the dominated languages (or, indeed, both) are autochthonous to the region where the creole is spoken (as with, perhaps, Tok Pisin or Nigerian Pidgin), and exogenous creoles, where none of the contributory varieties is native to the regions in which it is spoken, such as Haitian Creole (Bartens 2013: 66, following Chaudenson 1974). To what extent does this distinction affect the development of the varieties involved?

3.5.2 The Quarrel at the Heart of the Matter

At the heart of contemporary analyses of creole origin and development is a fundamental disagreement over what a 'creole' is. To some scholars, the 'straightforward' analysis given earlier remains the default position for the analysis of creole genesis. They consider the **basilect**, the variety least like 'mainstream' varieties of the lexifier language (of which more shortly), spoken in a context where oral ability (and often literacy) in the dominant language is growing, to be most representative of the original creole. These scholars adhere to the creole exceptionalist view that pidgins are the ultimate source of creoles. This discussion of what the basilect actually represents is central to this debate.

Decamp (1971: 28–30) provides a particularly clear description of what is generally described as the post-creole continuum, as taken from the creole exceptionalist viewpoint. The linguistic strata which underline this continuum can be laid out as in Figure 3.2, with the variety with greatest social prestige placed highest.

The basilect, according to many creolists, is the variety closest to the original creole, while the **acrolect** is closest to the standard variety of the lexifier language. The **mesolect** is a 'halfway house' between the two absolute states. The sociolinguistic point, however, is that individual speakers can move (perhaps *commute*) along the continuum, depending on the context in which they find themselves. This is the case in many postcolonial contexts (in Jamaica, for instance, politicians can shift along the continuum from a somewhat locally accented Standard English when outside the country to something like basilect when 'on the stump' in certain places). While practically everyone in all societies 'commutes' in this way quite regularly, it is the distance possible in the post-creole environment which marks off this continuum from most other everyday personal and customary linguistic journeys.

Mühlhäusler (1986: 11) provides a more complex analysis of the processes involved: he puts forward a double set of analyses, the first of which – developmental dimension – is primarily linguistic, and the second being restructuring, which has

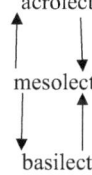

Figure 3.2 Strata of the post-creole continuum.

stronger sociolinguistic features, although these inevitably have linguistic repercussions.

As mentioned earlier, the development dimension as Mühlhäusler presents it can be represented as shown in Figure 3.1. In addition to this analysis, restructuring adds more information, which is inherently dynamic. Thus, over time, an expanded pidgin will, under the influence of the lexifier language, become part of a post-pidgin continuum, until finally it essentially becomes a variant of the language.

Mühlhäusler suggests a similar structural journey for creoles along the post-creole continuum (as he and many other analysts perceive it). Although he does not explicitly state that a movement towards merger with the *lexifier language* is an inevitable result of the post-creole continuum, it can, I believe, be claimed that the former normally comes after the latter.

If we follow this portrayal of the post-creole period in which a more egalitarian (or at least less oppressive) societal structure develops, more people will inevitably have access to mainstream education in what was often the colonial language, particularly perhaps among the socially aspirant middle classes (regularly termed, confusingly from our point of view, the creole class), in a postcolonial situation. Inevitably, this means that, according to this analysis, the basilect of twenty years from now is likely to be more like the mesolect, rather than the basilect, of today, while the mesolect of the future will be more like the acrolect of now, and so on. This type of development is likely to be indistinguishable from the ways in which convergence takes place between traditional dialects and the written standard in a literate culture (see, e.g., Millar, Barras and Bonnici 2014). Having said this, however, the forces of covert prestige will inevitably establish that at least some aspects of earlier basilects in particular will be retained by some people in some contexts. These conflicting tendencies lead to an increasingly broad control of different linguistic variants by many speakers.

For uniformitarians, however, creoles, if we can even term them such, are at least primarily and originally varieties of the dominant language of a particular territory – often of a territory which has been, or is in the process of being, colonised by settlers from elsewhere. The primary difference between creoles and other varieties, according to this analytical position, is not necessarily linguistic. Creoles were perceived by earlier scholars as being of a fundamentally different nature to the 'true' dialects of a particular language because of where they were spoken and by whom, rather than through any linguistic distinctiveness. This dichotomy, essentially false, following their analysis, has remained unchallenged to the present day in creole exceptionalist analyses. In contrast, from the uniformitarian point of view, the new variety began life, instead, as a rather 'mainstream' (but not normally the standard) variety of the dominant language, but gradually became significantly less so because of the linguistic input from an influx of adult learners, mostly recently enslaved and carried involuntarily from a range of places, who had far less access to the original dominant varieties because of the development of plantation systems (rather than the earlier homestead system, of which more in Section 3.5.3.2). Rigid segregation between populations, based on race and servile status, created an echo chamber effect inclined

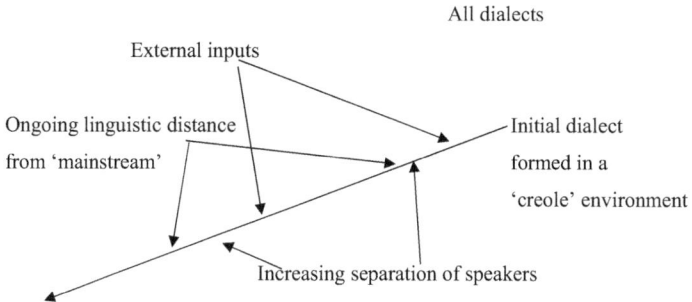

Figure 3.3 The uniformitarian creole continuum.

towards innovation (since contact with 'mainstream' varieties had lessened considerably).

Despite the demographic preponderance of later speakers, supporters of uniformitarianism would claim that, due to the founder effect, the effect which an early powerful population can have over the development of language use in a particular territory even if that population proves not to be the majority, the early nature of the dialect would affect its later development rather more than the later mass influences, in particular in terms of maintaining ties to the vernaculars which preceded and coexisted with them. Nevertheless, these later, 'plantation' inputs would create a basilect, very different in origin from that proposed earlier from a creole exceptionalist viewpoint (see Figure 3.3). The basilect would instead be perceived as the most recently produced variety of the creole, particularly distant from the 'mainstream' varieties from which its ancestor sprang. From this viewpoint, present acrolectal and mesolectal varieties would have had earlier predecessors than the basilectal. In theory, the last would diverge increasingly, but sociolinguistic forces, not least, as already suggested, mass education employing the prestige variety, would encourage most speakers to move closer in a convergent process. It is quite possible that this would bring the basilect closer to the mesolect, if the prestige variety were a major presence in the territory and literacy acquisition were possible. In other territories where the lexifier variety was seldom heard, the postulated process, if it happened at all, was of a rather less straightforward nature. The situation among speakers of varieties of Melanesian creole would fit this latter situation particularly well.

Before we go any further, it should be noted that neither of these means of illustrating creole development can explain why some pidgins and creoles are closer to their lexifiers on all occasions than are others. The creoles spoken in Jamaica or Réunion are considerably more 'mainstream' than Saramaccan in Suriname or Tok Pisin in Papua New Guinea.

That such stark and often visceral disagreement should be present in what was once a field where debate was regularly of a small-scale nature and focussed on detail is striking. What created this level of dissent? While a number of routes can be plotted towards this outcome, we will here consider breakthroughs in views on first and second language acquisition beginning in the 1970s and how these affected the views of some creolists.

3.5.2.1 The Language Bioprogram Hypothesis

Bickerton's concept of a **language bioprogram hypothesis** underlying the creation of creole varieties is grounded in the theoretical understanding of the process of first language learning by children in particular. As Mufwene points out regularly in his work, it was these interests, connected to the evolving ideas of Chomsky and his disciples, as well as to psycholinguistic theory, which led to the mainstreaming, in the 1980s, of the study of creoles in linguistics. Bickerton's model for creole genesis had interesting parallels in the study of child language acquisition.

Many of the existing students of creolisation were willing at the time to be at least open to the ideas underlying the bioprogram hypothesis, since a large part of the immediate analytical apparatus suggested by Bickerton appeared to echo the previously accepted primary tenets on creole genesis and their connection to the pidginisation process. From an early period, however, doubts began to arise for many scholars about how well the hypothesis actually mapped on to the field experience or study of earlier examples of particular creoles, which many creolists had gained. Much of what follows in this chapter is concerned with the discussion which proceeded from the promulgation of this hypothesis, as well as the highly contentious nature of much of this debate. This is very much a live issue.

Firstly, we will consider the main arguments underlying the language bioprogram hypothesis. Although I am personally convinced that later scholarship has demonstrated that the hypothesis, at best, cannot be anything more than a partial contribution to the scholarly study of creole genesis, I believe that Bickerton's suggestion is brilliant.

The hypothesis represents a complex, but also attractive, set of concepts, which can be stated in a straightforward (albeit reductive) way. When no lingua franca is readily available in a multiple-language-contact context, all humans possess an innate capacity to produce a 'simplified' form of language, based (largely) upon the variety dominant in that territory, although created according to the precepts of Universal Grammar (particularly popular at the time within the evolving generative paradigm). This variety will rapidly become the first language of the first native generation.

Bickerton's work on these matters can most readily (and succinctly) be found in Bickerton ((1981) 2016; 1984). From the late 1980s until his death in 2018, his focus moved away from pidgins and creoles themselves to one more centred on language genesis as a whole (Siegel 2008b: 192 presents a discussion of Bickerton's later work in relation to its reception). This may have been due to the eventual reception of his suggestions and analyses by most creolists, but, in typically forthright – even pugnacious – style, Bickerton ((1981) 2016: vii, emphasis original) comments that

> despite repeated attempts to refute them [his views expressed in that book] (and, of course, unfounded claims that this work or that *has* successfully refuted them) there is no need to change the central contentions of the original book, e.g. that creole languages arise in a single generation, and are created from an original, virtually structureless, pidgin by children who have an access to universal grammar unavailable to their parents.

3.5 Creole Genesis and Development

While it might be claimed that he protests too much (his analysis of what a pidgin is is, at least at times, unusual), this short passage is an excellent summary of the central features of his views. Let us lay these out in more detail:

1. Creole languages 'arise in a single generation'. This is generally the first generation born in a particular place to parents who had come from somewhere else, whether voluntarily or involuntarily (often through the exertion of considerable force), speaking different first languages, who have developed something like a pidgin.
2. The creole variety is based on this 'original, virtually structureless, pidgin' employed in the children's community, primarily, we can assume, within the home, since the proposed creole must have begun to come into being at an early stage in the children's development.
3. The new variety is not based wholly on the parental or community pidgin. Universal Grammar is employed to create a structured language.
4. This is the case because, as Bickerton would claim, Universal Grammar has essentially the same 'roots' present in the ways any child learns their first language. The process is always based on patterns and structures which are innate to them. Because creole varieties have no true first language input, Universal Grammar input is probably central. This explains why creoles are very similar to each other structurally, no matter the lexifier language.

In addition, although not mentioned in this passage, Bickerton regularly expressed his distrust of the suggestion by a range of experts that many of the shared structures, as well as many of the features which mark off differences between creoles, are due to influence from linguistic substrata (this is with the exception of lexical influence, which, given the evidence, would be impossible to deny). He felt particular contempt for these views. He refers to their supporters as *substratomaniacs*, who are purveyors of the cafeteria problem (picking any and only evidence that suits your argument), throughout. Going beyond the rhetoric, however, his view that scholars from this school are guilty of overstatement and cherry-picking does hit home at times (although see Section 3.5.2.2; see also Bickerton (1984) 2016: 29 and, for a particularly strong refutation of this type of view, Veenstra 2008: 219 and 223).

But in his critical analysis of Bickerton's ideas on this matter, Siegel (2008a: 104) points out that a belief that transfer of features from substratal languages to the creole (or, indeed, any language) must result in exactly the same features recurring in exactly the same way in exactly the same position is simplistic. Siegel (2001: 78) quotes Mufwene:

> There is no empirical evidence that a language is transmitted wholesale from one group to another. ... It would be wrong to suppose that particular features ... cannot have been selected from different sources initially for the purposes of establishing successful communication with the unplanned result of producing a new language variety.

In other words, the view among scholars more sociolinguistically minded than Bickerton is that it is individuals in communication who affect language, not the clash between abstract systems (see also Siegel 2008a: 107, 110, 114–15, 148, 168, 170–71). Siegel (2008a: 181) also points out that transfer of features from the lexifier in a way other than the natural development proposed in the uniformitarian programme (see Section 3.5.3.2) is also symptomatic of this type of contact. Siegel (2008a: 278) brings together a number of issues with Bickerton's choice of substratal language to analyse as potential sources for Hawai'ian Pidgin structures. Bickerton chose not Chinese dialects (or, indeed, Hawai'ian) for this analysis but rather Japanese and various Filipino languages, even though speakers of the latter languages were comparatively late arrivals to the islands.

From the beginning of his argument, Bickerton ((1981) 2016: 5–6) is obliged to demand certain curtailments to what he means by *creole*. Essentially, he is discussing only plantation creole: creoles developed in 'fort' or 'enclave' contexts, or where the creole has developed without permanent mass migration, are not included in his analysis. Thus varieties such as China Coast Pidgin and the Melanesian creoles (as well as, perhaps, Nigerian Pidgin) are essentially ignored.

He also notes a second issue (Bickerton 1984: 177), related to the level to which a creole shares structural features with its lexifier. He perceives this as a continuum (similar, but not conceptually the same as, the creole exceptionalist post-creole continuum mentioned earlier). Essentially, he suggests, those varieties least like the lexifier are those which have had the least interference from the superstratal variety. Thus varieties like Saramaccan (a Suriname creole, discussed in Sections 3.2.3.1 and Case Study 3) were created in a state of maroonage, where enslaved people escaped or otherwise left the colony to which they had been brought, not long after the plantation process began. Their secession from the life their enslavers had decreed for them meant that full-scale contact with the lexifier was removed early on in their variety's development. Following the creole exceptionalist post-creole continuum hypothesis, a variety of this sort has never developed beyond what we from the outside might term the basilect stage. It is therefore straightforward to perceive Saramaccan as a discrete language, with some limited connection to English.

At the other end of Bickerton's continuum are the creole varieties spoken on Réunion in the Indian Ocean (for an analysis rooted in a uniformitarian interpretation, see Chaudenson (1992) 2012, 2001). French has been a dominant – even hegemonic – presence on the island for an overwhelming period. This has led to the original creole gradually becoming merged with colloquial varieties of French (this explains, Bickerton claims, the difference between the status of Réunion Creole and that of Haiti, where French has not been omnipresent in the country, except among the richest members of that society, for more than two centuries. Somewhere in between the two extremes is Mauritian Creole, mentioned earlier, a French creole spoken in a society dominated by English from the Revolutionary and Napoleonic Wars on).

3.5.2.2 Analysis and Discussion

Bickerton's proposals need to be taken seriously. Nevertheless, it might be suggested that, having stated them so forcefully, he left himself open to criticism of cherry-picking (in fact, the very cafeteria problem he criticises so vociferously) to suit his arguments. Essentially, the following questions need to be asked:

1. Are all creoles actually as similar to each other as Bickerton suggested?
2. Are any creoles produced solely by the first native generation?
3. Are substratal influences genuinely insubstantial?
4. Does the basilect always predate the mesolect and acrolect?

Much of what follows in this chapter is based upon attempts to address these challenges. It could, in fact, be argued that the fissures already extant within creole studies began to become acute in the 1980s when Derek Bickerton put forward the bioprogram hypothesis: it suddenly became necessary to nail your colours to the mast. It should nevertheless be noted that many of the issues involved have been present since the topic of creole genesis first began to be considered. To come fully prepared to these theoretical positions, however, we will consider two issues which are central to Bickerton's viewpoint: the generation in which creoles come into being and the nature of substratal influence.

In Which Generation Are Creoles Formed? A central feature of Bickerton's stance on the genesis of creoles is that these varieties were formed in a relatively brief (and no doubt deeply stressful) period by adult second language learners and, in particular, their offspring, who made up the first-generation residents in the new territories. This, proponents of the bioprogram hypothesis would claim, explains the 'simplified' nature of the structure of creoles, along with the apparent structural similarities found between those varieties and pidgins (particularly, but not exclusively, those associated with the European slave trade in the seventeenth, eighteenth and early nineteenth centuries). These 'creators' were forced to go through this process because they had little or no opportunity for choosing a lingua franca from one of the languages coming into contact. The universals associated by some theoretical models with adult language learning would support this, since they are founded on the belief that adults can produce only a simplified version of a newly learned language, while children, particularly younger children, if anything, make the learned language more complicated.

Therefore the first native generation learned only this new variety; it is likely that, since variation was commonplace across the community, further simplification would follow from this (although the model would suggest that elaboration might also be inherent in such developments; similar changes will be discussed in Chapter 6).

But there is a problem with this attractive argument. Considerable evidence exists, across a wide range of contexts, that the first languages of the initial migrants (whether involuntary or not) were learned by the first native generation (we might also bring in our understanding of the effects of language shift upon the target language, as discussed in Chapter 2). At the earliest, it is the *second* native generation who have limited, if any, ability in their grandparents' languages. Bickerton based many of his findings upon his observation and analysis of the history of Hawai'ian Creole.

This variety's time depth is considerably shallower than is the case for most of the Caribbean and Atlantic varieties, largely being formed in the early twentieth century (although with some early attestations in the late nineteenth), thus making it attractive to analysts. Records of various sorts exist for the backgrounds of the migrants, along with their language use, in ways that earlier creole speakers, seen as property rather than employees, had little or none. The Hawai'ian evidence informs us that many children born in the islands with non-Anglophone migrant parents could speak their parents' language; after all, there is considerable evidence for ethnic residential enclaves during the early days of new settlement. A Portuguese speaker, for instance, was likely to live near to other speakers of that language. Moreover, mass education (with a strongly anti-creole – and possibly anti-ancestral language – bias) was freely available to all of the first native generation. Common cause meant that people from different backgrounds used the creole as a dominant personal variety, which was handed on to their children.

Based upon these and related points, Siegel (2008a: 63; see also 277–8), a major figure in the study of Hawai'ian Creole himself, states that 'it seems clear that with regard to features of the VP [verb phrase], Hawai'i Creole does not conform to the bioprogram prototype now and most likely never did'. This point is underlined in relation to the analyses of a range of varieties discussed in Veenstra (2008: 234); Becker and Veenstra (2003) present a schematisation of how complex transfers of different varieties across a range of contexts can be. These are all important points which essentially dismantle the central props of Bickerton's argument (even if, as Veenstra 2008: 234 suggests, a case could be made for a 'weak' version of the hypothesis).

Substratal Influence in Creole Formation To what extent do the languages spoken as first language (or, perhaps, as heritage language) by people who also use pidgins and creoles affect these pidgins and creoles? This seems an easy question to answer, but there are issues with it at a number of linguistic levels. As has already been pointed out, moreover, a number of scholars – most notably Bickerton – are agnostic about, if not actually antagonistic towards, the importance of these types of transfers.

It is fairly easy to find substratal evidence in creoles in relation to lexis. Let us take African American Vernacular English (admittedly a variety whose status in relation to creolisation is complex, as we will see in Chapter 4). This variety (or hub of varieties) has gifted other forms of North American English a small number of words, such as *juke* (as in *jukebox* and the clandestine *juke-joint*), probably originally referring to illicit sex, and *goobers* 'peanuts'. All of these, and a relatively small number of others, are fairly likely to have originated in African languages. If we pass to varieties which could be classified without much dissent as pidgins and creoles, substratal vocabulary is significantly more visible (although still not dominant), as can be seen in the transfers from the Congolese language Ntandu to the Saramaccan creole of Suriname, laid out by Smith (2015).

The problem is, however, that lexical borrowing is straightforward in process and analysis. In the previous sentence I have used four loanwords: *problem* was borrowed by speakers of English either directly from Latin or via French; the same is true for *process*; the third, *lexical*, is based around a Greek word, with Latin derivational morphology, while *analysis* retains a Greek plural (*analyses*). I do have some Latin and French (but very limited Greek); nevertheless, to me, as with most native speakers, these are English terms (which, of course, they are – although my impression is that *problem* and *process* (and probably *analysis*) are much more commonly known and used in everyday language than *lexical*). Many Japanese words – for instance, *karaoke* and *sushi* – were borrowed into English (and many other languages) in the 1980s and 1990s, when Japanese (popular) culture (or at least an external perception and representation of it) was particularly fashionable. Hardly anyone in the English-speaking world, beyond a small number of scholars and some people involved in business of whatever sort with Japan, could and can speak Japanese. The words involved were therefore spread through a small number of people we would now term *influencers*.

Lexis as a whole, as well as in relation to individual words and phrases, is not part of a system which stands by itself. Instead, words and phrases are 'lost' from everyday use, or become current, for whatever reason. The language carries on, and often, speakers barely notice the change. Just because you use a borrowed word does not mean that you have a cultural connection with the speakers of the languages from which it has been borrowed. Normally, you have knowledge of a word having been borrowed only when it happens during your time. Otherwise, how would you know?

When we look at substratal lexical influence upon a creole, therefore, the numerical level of borrowings may tell us something about the dominance of a particular language (or, rather, its speakers) in the demographic mix, but it is difficult to take any analysis much further. Mufwene (2001: 23), not himself a believer in substratal influence as a major factor in the creation of creoles, suggests that this type of influence is more often the background rather than the foreground of change in these contexts. He also observes, however, that substratal influences may be stronger where the plantation stage (of which more shortly), when enslaved people had limited access to native speakers of the dominant language, began earlier in the creolisation process, when the influence of the former languages of enslaved people would be particularly strong (Mufwene 2001: 43; see also 67).

The borrowing of substratal morphosyntax and phonology is much more difficult to locate and analyse successfully in pidgins and creoles (or, indeed, most languages). That is not to say that there is no such influence, but it is regularly difficult to trace (although we will be considering an example of just such a transfer later).

Many languages are spoken along the coast of West Africa and in its hinterland (indeed, Nigeria is among the most linguistically diverse states in the world). Given that most people who were enslaved in the Caribbean and its surrounding territories came from that region, we can only assume that many languages were spoken in the same concentrations of population. The former creolist view that this multilingual reality was preferred and perpetuated within the enslaved population by their 'owners' as a means of lessening the risk of rebellion cannot now stand (it is likely that any 'advantage' of this type would have lasted only for a generation – if that – in any event), but the multilingualism was real enough.

It is highly probable, therefore, that some features found in Caribbean creoles with an English lexifier which are not found in more 'mainstream' varieties of English can also be found in some West African languages (or even one). It is possible, of course, that these similarities might represent evidence of substratal influence. Critics of this type of effect, including those coming from both uniformitarian and creole exceptionalist positions (which will be discussed in a few pages; they are also to be found, as we have seen, in the somewhat earlier views of Bickerton), point out that, at least at a macro level, explanations of this sort can appear to be cherry-picking – finding evidence in various, often contradictory places to suit the argument (rather than employing the analysis of data to form the argument; indeed, this type of evidence could become pseudo-science in a similar way to 'creation science'). Nevertheless, there does appear to be some evidence for substratal influence on the phonologies and structures of creoles. Perhaps the most striking feature of the former is the survival from a range of West African languages in some Caribbean creoles of lexical tone (for a discussion, see Castillo and Faraclas 2006).

Two structural features which can only readily be explained as substratal in nature are found with the Melanesian varieties (which, as has already been pointed out, are largely used alongside the languages which many users speak natively). These include, as already touched upon in Section 3.2.2, verb transitivity marking and dual (and sometimes trial) pronouns. Neither of these features is found in mainstream forms of English (there *were* dual pronouns in early forms of that language, but they had ceased to be used by the thirteenth century at the latest). Marking of transitivity on the verb is also found in some Asian and Oceanic forms of English.

What is striking about these features is that they appear to echo similar structural phenomena in many of the native languages spoken in Melanesia and New Guinea; indeed, where these features are used less in local languages, they are found less in the expanded pidgin/creole, despite the great similarities in other terms in that variety across the region (Siegel 2008a: esp. 87–9; see also 91, 170). What is also striking, however, is that the categories represented are formed from the raw materials of English, not a local variety (the transitive marker *-em*, for instance, is most likely to be descended from English *him* or the widespread colloquial form *em* 'them'). It is the concept which is passed across. Moreover, the structural marking in apparently borrowed structure of this type in the new variety is less nuanced (or complex, depending on your viewpoint) than is the case with the surrounding varieties (for further discussion, see Siegel 2008a: 87–91, 186; Meyerhoff 2008).

Having said all this, however, the papers in Lefebvre (2011) demonstrate how much information on structural substratal influence can be gained through knowledge of a range of languages and concentration on patterns rather than unique examples.

It can therefore be said that, while it is not negligible, there is at best limited evidence that the linguistic nature of substratal languages influenced the development of pidgins and creoles in a profound and direct way. Much more was abandoned from the first languages of those who produced the new varieties than was carried over. This suggests that, with the possible exception of the Melanesian varieties, while there were many inputs involved in the creation of pidgins and creoles, only one variety, the lexifier, was entitled and central, whether for social and economic reasons or merely because of its ubiquity. This situation is in many ways like the koines we will discuss further in Chapter 6, but with considerably more marked societal inequalities and a far higher level of group and individual trauma present during the formation of the new linguistic variety.

Inherent to this discussion is a question which has dominated the debate on creole origins for the last fifty years: when did populations abandon their native languages entirely in favour of the new and fully functioning creole? This issue is central to some of the major disagreements in post-Bickerton creole studies. Alongside this question is a concern over the extent to which creoles can genuinely be considered separate entities if creolisation cannot be framed as the spontaneous and genetically programmed process Bickerton envisaged.

3.5.3 Post-Bickerton Interpretations

As a result of the various interlocking debates about Bickerton's views, two main schools of thought on creole origin now exist, albeit with considerable variation within them. Creole exceptionalism and uniformitarianism, which have been introduced and discussed in brief on a number of occasions in this chapter, employ the primary evidence discussed here in strikingly different (indeed, often adversarial) terms. We will now consider these competing proposals in depth.

3.5.3.1 Creole Exceptionalism

Probably the most widely recognised present proponent of creole exceptionalism is John H. McWhorter. In a sense – but only a sense – his work represents a continuation of Bickerton's, but with the distinction that McWhorter does not fully connect creole genesis with the language bioprogram hypothesis (itself perceived, in its fullest form, with rather less enthusiasm by the general linguistics community than was the case in the 1980s; McWhorter 2018: 2 emphasises this distinction). Nor does McWhorter subscribe to the idea that first native generation adults (or, indeed, the immigrant generation) brought a variety into being without input from the second native generation. He also appears willing, perhaps overwilling at times, to consider substrate varieties as being influential on an incipient creole's nature.

At the heart of the creole exceptionalist view, however, is the idea that elements at least of what causes the development of varieties of this sort are unique to the creolisation process: they are not the same as the processes of change found in other types of language development. This implies that a creole is a specific type of language affected by contact and change in ways which other forms of language are not, not only in their evolution but in fact in their very nature.

McWhorter has a wider analytical focus than Bickerton. Both analysed Caribbean varieties, for instance, but Bickerton focussed primarily on the context of Hawai'i in some ways abnormal in relation to its beginnings and the level of information we possess on what happened to the variety. Because of this broader analysis, McWhorter's work appears empirically strong. Indeed, his regular retorts to his often highly vocal opponents in the uniformitarian camp (to be discussed shortly) are that they prefer argumentation to exemplification, comparing the wealth of exemplification in his work with the lack of such in that of his opponents (McWhorter 2018: 4). This proposed discrepancy is, in fact, something of a caricature, but that does not mean that it is not a useful rhetorical weapon. In his work he proposes that categories exist which mark off a creole as a creole (although he also says that it is not necessarily the case that all creole varieties possess all of these, even if they may, implicitly, have possessed them in the past, before lexifier varieties became much more available – and authoritative – as mass literacy spread). He refers to these as the Creole Prototype. He does offer the following warning, however:

> In terms of what those three features are, the nature of memory naturally reduces the proposal to 'creoles have no inflection, no tone, and no lexicalization'. However, taken literally, that formulation is hopelessly inadequate. Creoles tend to have an inflection or three; many creoles make ample use of tone in various functions; and it would be impossible for a human language to utterly lack lexicalization of some degree.
> (McWhorter 2018: 21)

Despite this caveat, an important issue remains: a number of these 'unique' creole features appear to be found in a range of other languages where a creole interpretation of their history would be at the very least unlikely. At the same time, many creoles do not possess all of these features, nor do some seem to have done so in the past. To be fair, McWhorter recognises this (immediately after the passage given, he notes that 'a Prototype prediction that actually accounts for the data must be more precise'), but the argument he makes sometimes comes close to special pleading. Cherry-picking, as we have seen, a criticism so commonly employed towards opposing viewpoints in this field, might also be suspected here.

This observation does not mean that everything McWhorter suggests is anywhere near worthless: far from it. Mufwene (2008: 40) comments, however, that 'there is nothing in the structure of creoles that supports the "discontinuity" hypothesis'; he also sees McWhorter's views as being one of 'pulverization' of the linguistic material which forms a creole (see Mufwene 2001). In fact, both McWhorter's and Mufwene's points might be seen as overstatements – albeit carrying some truth – in relation to creole development as a whole. The truth is that, as with the ideas of so many scholars in this field, a quest for a *universal* definition of 'creole' leaves McWhorter open to the use of quite legitimate counter-examples. Having said this, he is not scared of moving his analysis beyond his default plantation-based focus, since he occasionally discusses the Melanesian varieties, for instance, even if this is only fitfully carried out convincingly. In being courageous enough to extend his analysis beyond his comfort zone, he differs from some of his most vocal opponents. His own views are put succinctly thus (McWhorter 2018: 29–30):

> The Creole Prototype is most purely exemplified by those creoles that have lived separately from their lexifiers, such as Saramaccan in the Surinamese rainforest. However, social history has hardly afforded all creoles this kind of 'splendid isolation'. … Creoles conform to the Prototype in degrees and claims that this renders the CE [creole exceptionalist] unfalsifiable are themselves unscientific. … Elsewhere in linguistics, clinality is readily accepted.

3.5.3.2 Uniformitarianism

The opposing viewpoint, here termed **uniformitarianism**, springs from a reasonable assumption: creole varieties which have a particular language as their lexifier (a term avoided or often placed in quotation marks by proponents of the viewpoint) are not independent languages but rather varieties of that language. Mufwene (2008: 36) suggests forcefully that

> this 'discontinuity hypothesis' does not explain why creoles retain such large proportions of their vocabularies from their lexifiers (up to 95% in Gullah … over 85% in Saramaccan, one of the most 'radical' creoles), nor why we can link so many of their structural features to their European ancestors [see, e.g., for French creoles, Chaudenson (1992) 2012, 2001, 2003; Corne 1999; see also, for English creoles, Mufwene 2001].

The use of referencing of this type shows both the strength of the research undercurrent in uniformitarianism and its prizing of prior scholarship as evidence for correctness (although some scholars from this school, such as Klein and Adams 2017, do stress the African origin of the lexis of some varieties more strongly). Part of the reason why creole varieties have not regularly been analysed as dialects of the language with which they share a large part of their lexis is because, uniformitarians claim, comparisons are normally made to the standard variety of the language, rather than the nonstandard (and often considerably more diverse) 'native' varieties. Such an omission is particularly unfortunate when, in the seventeenth and eighteenth centuries, most speakers of any language had at best limited access to literacy. These non-literate varieties were precisely those spoken by the indentured servants and others with whom enslaved people and other lower-status migrants most came into contact.

An addition to this argument made by some adherents to this school is that some other scholars fail (and have failed) to perceive this connection because they consider languages associated with black people (and other minority communities) as being somehow separate from (and implicitly lesser than) the language of white people who live in the same place. There can be little doubt that this is an example of racist thinking. Most modern creole exceptionalists do not appear to hold such views, but it is certainly the case that analyses of this type did have racist – or at least imperialist – ideas underlying them originally. De Graff (2005: 576) observes that the exceptionalist viewpoint has been produced by 'a set of sociohistorically rooted dogmas, with foundations in (neo)colonial power relations' (see also Aboh and Ansaldo 2007). McWhorter (2018: 89) touches upon this point, responding that scholars in his exceptionalist camp in fact 'marvel at the [creole] creators' restoration of cognitive normality' in what must have been an exceptional situation linguistically, as well as socially. This type of view might itself be analysed as demonstrating *othering* (see Section 3.1.2), however, particularly if you are opposed to the underlying argument.

Moving away from this charged debate, Mufwene (2001: 103) makes a number of astute points about the social rather than linguistic nature of creolisation. Mufwene (2008) represents a particularly thorough statement of this school's thought; while small-scale elements of his argument can certainly be questioned, as a whole, it holds together well.

Many of the views held by uniformitarians are based more on the historical record than on linguistic evidence in relation to earlier states of a creole's development. Unsurprisingly perhaps, the latter type of evidence is not entirely trustworthy – in many ways it is archetypal 'dirty data' (if there is any evidence at all, although see the discussion of the creole varieties of Suriname in Case Study 3). Uniformitarians point out that, in the early stages of an exploitation colony's development, the enslaved population is generally much outweighed by the free population, especially when combined in many early modern colonies with the indentured servants, who agreed to work off their transportation across to their new homes by labouring for a certain number of years for those who paid their passage (in some colonies, convict labour was exploited as well). In reductive terms, white people outnumbered black people. The large-scale plantations which developed as the enslaved population began to outweigh the white population did not exist at the time of settlement, when most enslaved people were housed with, or near to, their 'masters', who generally lived in relatively simple homesteads at the time. Contact with their varieties, and those of the indentured servants, was intense and intimate. Following this argument, the first generations of speakers of the creole would have realised something relatively close to the nonstandard varieties spoken around them, albeit with some influence both from native languages and the fact that most had learned what to them was a new language as adults.

The argument (indeed, ideological position) derived by the uniformitarians from these facts is that these creoles developed in a similar way to all other varieties of a language where the standard variety does not exist or is not available to a large part of the community because of a lack of literacy. Mufwene (2008: 42) observes, following Chaudenson's argumentation, that 'the so-called "creolization" process is largely an extension of restructuring processes that had already started in the relevant "lexifiers"', referring to historical changes in both the Romance and Germanic languages in relation to their ancestors. What he suggests is, of course, correct; it could be argued that it does not represent the whole story, however.

The **divergence** between varieties of the same language would be exacerbated, the uniformitarians would hold, by the reality of slavery. Unlike the cross-generational transfer of features found with most language varieties, the bringing in of new human 'cargo' for at least a large part of the eighteenth century outweighed the transfer of enslaved status by birth through what was in many ways equivalent to the traditional family group. The changes involved in the learning of the creole by adults would therefore be duplicated and amplified, probably repeatedly.

In traditional creole exceptionalist analyses, the basilect found in post-creole contexts (as discussed in Section 3.5) is claimed to represent the most 'genuine' form of the original creole – the one least affected by contact with the lexifier language. The uniformitarians, as we have seen, turn this argument on its head, however: the basilect represents the most recent form of the creole, the one most distant from the original contact variety – in many ways a mainstream dialect, equivalent and similar to other dialects of the same language. Mufwene (2008: 192; see also 199) states that

> as the proportion of nonnative speakers grew, sometimes to the majority within the non-European population, there was room for more and more xenolectal [external/foreign variety] influence on the structure of the evolving vernacular and for divergence from the European varieties. It is thus that the relevant creole vernaculars developed, by gradual restructuring, away from the original colonial European koines, without any evidence of break in the "transmission" of the European languages, contrary to the myth fostered in much of the relevant literature.

No one, it is argued, would claim that these European languages should be seen as abnormal in their development, as is argued for these 'black' varieties (this is not an accurate portrayal, in fact: some linguistic 'radicals' have claimed pidgin or creole status for English at least; see Chapter 6). In a sense, the argument runs, there is no such thing as a creole (although Siegel 2008: 53–4 points out that the process of basilectalisation suggested by this school is very close to what other creolists would consider pidginisation).

There are, of course, many attractive features to this set of arguments. It does seem to fit the historical evidence (at least in the Atlantic-Caribbean and Indian Ocean contexts) somewhat better than other models for creole genesis and development do. On the other hand, the second language transmission explanation in the model is not as different as might be argued from other mainstream models of creole genesis, albeit in relation to the most developed form of the variety, the one least like the metropolitan varieties of the languages, being the latest, rather than the earliest, to develop. Moreover, as we have already touched upon, many creoles were (and are) not found in these social circumstances. It would be easy to see these as expanded pidgins, because most speakers do not have them as a first language. Some do, however. Furthermore, many speakers of these varieties do not have close everyday ties to the lexifier variety and its speakers; indeed, their varieties are spread with little or no reference to them. This may always have been the case.

Siegel (2008a: 171) expresses a number of telling criticisms of the uniformitarian school's views:

> First of all, Melanesian Pidgin, Hawai'i Creole, and Roper Kriol [spoken in northern Australia] each did have a restricted pidgin predecessor. Second, it is clear that transfer of features from substrate languages occurred, not just reinforcement of existing features of the lexifier by the substrate languages. Third, the existence of some morphology from the lexifier – e.g. in Hawai'i Creole – does not necessarily mean continuous transmission, as the lexifier could have been one of the sources of features in the morphological expansion of the preceding pidgin. Fourth, the comparative formal simplicity and kinds of grammaticalization found in Hawai'i Creole and Roper Kriol emerged in one or two generations – much more comprehensively and rapidly than in conventional change.

Siegel adds elsewhere (Siegel 2008a: 272) that 'it is difficult, then, to understand how the passing on of these approximations of approximations can be considered normal language transmission'.

It may be significant that the varieties which Siegel (2008a) concentrates on barely overlap geographically with those studied by Bickerton and hardly at all in relation to the uniformitarians. He does, however, suggest (Siegel 2008b: 210) that 'other sources of simplified features may have included various unstable L2 varieties, as well as foreigner talk'.

3.6 Discussion

When we begin to analyse what creoles actually are, basing our analysis upon as wide a range as possible of varieties identified as being a member of that state or class, it quickly becomes apparent that taking either the creole exceptionalist or the uniformitarian viewpoint as the final (indeed, only) word on the subject, while considering opposing views as illusory, perhaps even wilfully delusional, is dangerous. Why should this be the case?

In the first instance, creoles have nearly always been spoken by people with at least some regular contact with speakers of more 'mainstream' varieties of the lexifier, without question inherently connected to all 'mainstream' dialects through absolute genetic descent. Where the lexifier was not regularly spoken in the creole environment, such as with the Melanesian pidgins, lack of immediate similarity to the lexifier is unquestionable, primarily, it could be argued, because comprehensibility between the two varieties is at best curtailed.

Secondly, many of the claimed universals are actually generally more true for some places and language varieties than others. The uniformitarian position, as espoused by Mufwene and others, is best suited to the linguistic histories and ecologies of the creoles found in most of the Caribbean and in the (former and present) French territories in the Indian Ocean. They are far less workable in relation to other language varieties, such as those spoken on island territories in the Pacific Ocean, where speakers are generally indigenous to where they are settled. The more thoughtful holders of this view – and, indeed, of the opposing viewpoint – demonstrate an awareness of this issue, although many, often of the second generation of followers of a particular standpoint, take a far more rigid view of the opposing ideas. The insights gained from uniformitarian analyses can be applied only in certain contexts at certain times; the same can normally be said for some scholars' espousal of creole exceptionalist ideas.

By the same token, the belief that creolisation involves an absolute and abrupt rupture from the lexifier stands in contrast to the reality that this does not appear to be the case with some varieties, not least African American Vernacular English, although, as we will see in Chapter 4, this variety could be seen as an outlier from the point of view of either prevailing school. This is an issue even if we accept, as we saw in our discussion of the post-creole continuum, that later sociolinguistic patterns evinced in the patterns of history of the territories involved partly 'healed' the rift. Nevertheless, Tok Pisin is a separate language (at least according to linguistic analysis), except, perhaps, in relation to the other Melanesian varieties.

The question, then, is, are all of the creoles focussed on in the literature absolutely analogical in their natures and historical development? If they are not, could creoles be seen as a constellation of discrete but related states whose origins may fall more readily into the creole exceptionalist or, for that matter, the uniformitarian camp, while other discrete states fall rather less near to either theoretical and analytical pole? How these varieties develop depends to a large extent upon the sociolinguistic forces at work during their genesis and in the evolving contexts in which they develop. These forces differ in strength from place to place (and from socio-historical context to socio-historical context), but they are likely to have been present in all contexts (McWhorter 2018: 29 suggests as much, albeit from his own school's point of view). A break in effective continuity does not rule out influences caused by close engagement with the lexifier (or whatever term is preferred by particular scholars). First language influence does not countermand second language influence. There is a possibility for irony in the fact that a debate which is centred so strongly on the nature of the (post-creole) continuum can actually be claimed to be itself a product of a continuum of different origin explanations proposed by the different schools within the field.

Siegel (2008b: 209) observes that,

> of course, both [the creole exceptionalist and uniformitarian] views could be true. Alleyne surmises that for English-lexified creoles, maximal restructuring occurred at the beginning of historical development, whereas for French-lexified creoles, it occurred at the end through cumulative divergent changes.

While this is likely to be too strong a wording in terms of the dichotomy proposed between developments, based on lexifier language, it would hardly be surprising if different varieties developed in several different ways within similar constraints.

It could be claimed, therefore, that we leave our discussion of the creole origin debate with little or no more certainty than we entered it. In many ways, this is a correct assumption. What might have been achieved, however, is a deeper and broader sense of the effects which language contact has had on the varieties developed by an often disenfranchised population when faced with both linguistic and sociolinguistic forces which are beyond their control. This remains the case even if, as seems likely, Mufwene (2008: 17, basing this on the views of Weinreich 1953; see also Mufwene 2008: 71; he is probably overstressing the argument in 2008: 199, however) is correct in underlining the importance of individual speakers during creolisation. But such a view could be accused of not recognising the importance of the *invisible hand* (Keller 1994), working within speech communities to facilitate a common set of developments, whether these be economic or linguistic. Linguistic drift (as discussed in the Glossary) assumes such a general tendency and direction within the apparent individual behaviour across a group. In the same work, Mufwene (2008: 43) suggests that 'this complex web of colonial migration defies a unilinear account of the evolution of creoles'. Singler (2008: 333) states that

> creoles are not a tightly defined group. Efforts by McWhorter to provide a linguistic definition of creoles notwithstanding, the languages of the world do not divide into creoles and non-creoles by any set of rigorously defined criteria.

This statement may be intended to provide support for a (moderate) uniformitarian viewpoint. But it also appears to support the idea that an at least perceived continuum exists between 'creole' states. The multiple-source and multiple-development explanation suggested here may well be the reality underlying this perception.

Case Study 3   The Suriname Creoles

Suriname lies on the northern coast of South America (of which it is the smallest sovereign state) and is bounded by Guyana (formerly British Guiana), Brazil, the French *département* of Guiane and the Atlantic Ocean (see Map 3.3). The country has somewhat over 600,000 inhabitants. Its coastal lands can be said to be subtropical in climate and environment with, historically at least, traditional production and trade practices being concerned with raw materials, such as sugar. The country also has considerable mineral deposits, exploited in a systematic manner from the early twentieth century on. Without travelling far up one of the country's many rivers, however, quite dense rainforest ecology becomes the norm, although the banks of the rivers and their hinterland are generally cultivated commercially. Suriname's capital, Paramaribo, presently has a population of somewhat under 250,000.

The largest ethnic and cultural groups in contemporary Suriname are made up of people whose ancestors migrated there from what are now Indonesia and South

Asia. Historically, however, the territories involved were inhabited by speakers of Arawak and Carib languages. Some speakers of these languages remain; many inhabitants of Suriname, whatever their surface cultural and ethnic associations, have First Nation ancestors. From the seventeenth until the nineteenth century at least, however, the largest single ethnic group was made up of the descendants of people of African origin (most notably, but not necessarily only, from the coastal territories of West Africa and around the mouth and to the south of the Congo River). As a demographic profile of this sort, particularly when based in the Americas, suggests, Suriname's modern history is grounded in slavery. Its complex linguistic history also came into being through this type of exploitation, as discussed in Migge (2003) and Arends (2017).

The ongoing development of Suriname, through which we perceive the country's present **linguistic ecology**, is essentially a result of Dutch imperialism from the seventeenth century on, as the contemporary ethnic composition suggests. The country became an autonomous territory under the Dutch Crown in 1954, before achieving full independence in 1975. This apparent stable continuity of governance is somewhat at variance with the earliest history of European involvement in the region, however. Evidence for this complexity can be seen in the fact that an English-lexified creole, Sranan /sra'naŋ/, is the lingua franca of the country, no matter the speaker's background. Other English-based creoles, most notably Saramaccan, discussed briefly in Section 3.2.3.1, are spoken by a considerable number of people. Following is a brief example of the first variety, where boldface represents Dutch words and phrases.

M   e   fter u   wan ptjin tori f ä   ten   di   m b   ê
I   PROG tell you a   little story of the time when I   ANT HAB
g â skoro. Te   di   m bîn g a skoro, m bj a   ait   jari.
go to school time when I begin go to school I ANT have eight years
M ben kmop a   pranasi, te zeggen   ben ... mi mâ mek   mi
I   ANT come from   plantation that is to say ANT   my ma made me
a pranasi, da m   k â foto. Dan di   m bî, m g a josjosj klas
on plantation then I came to town then when I begin I go to nursery class
Fa   m tan tu dee   nom a josjosj, dan den poj mi a ... a eerste klas.
When I am two days only at nursery then they put me   in first form
PROG = progressive; ANT = anterior; HAB = habitual
(Holm 1988-9: II, 438, from Voorhoeve 1962: 57)

This passage is essentially opaque, without special knowledge, to most speakers of English. Partly this is because of the way the passage is laid out, with particles supplying grammatical information being represented as separate units, rather than as clitics: the latter might be more representative of the flow of speech (it is worth noting that Holm's source is a work concerned with Sranan syntax). This foregrounding of these features, and the grammatical information which underlies them, emphasises in many ways the distance Sranan represents from the 'mainstream', particularly since the anterior aspect tense is not normally expressed in all but a few varieties of English.

Beyond this, a number of morphosyntactic features which distinguish this variety from many varieties of English are present. Perhaps most striking is the use of present tense forms for actions in the past, such as *mi mâ mek mi*. This usage could stem from the habit of using this tense in past narrative, found in many languages. Nevertheless, the fact that such usage is found alongside the lexical expressions of aspect should be borne in mind.

In terms of vocabulary, there is less to say. Alongside the almost ubiquitous Portuguese borrowing *ptjin* 'small', there are a few words where their origin is obscured by pronunciation, such as *foto* 'town; originally, fort'. The use of Dutch words and phrases in reference to official contexts is also noteworthy (many years ago, a student of English origin remarked to me that these were the easiest parts of the passage to follow).

It is the phonology apparently represented in the passage which is particularly striking, however. There is apparent confusion of /l/ and /r/ in words like *skoro* and *pranasi*, as well as non-rhoticity in *foto*. This same word, along with others, has an epenthetic final vowel which is common among the Suriname creoles. The confusion between consonants in the former may well represent a substratal influence from a West African language (or languages). They may all be taken as evidence for the lengthy separation of the language from its lexifier: there was little or no 'mainstream' English present throughout the period Sranan was developing to 'correct' these phenomena.

A Brief Sociolinguistic History of Suriname

This is not the place to recount the full history of seventeenth-century Suriname. Nevertheless, it needs to be noted that the middle decades of that century were taken up by transfers of power in the territory between the two main Protestant maritime powers in Europe, England and what was then the United Provinces of the Netherlands. The two countries had almost identical exploitation strategies for the region, based heavily upon the importation of enslaved Africans to work on plantations. Suriname does not appear to have gone through a full homestead stage, as suggested for other territories; the same is true, of course, for Hawai'i (Siegel 2008a: 50–51). In fact, McWhorter (2018: 6) takes considerable pleasure in pointing out how this reality flies in the face of a strong trend, often invoked, of the uniformitarian position. Permanent Dutch rule was only established in 1667, as part of a general post-war settlement between the two countries.

Over the years, creolists and others have suggested that direct English language input into the development of the colony ceased with this final handover of power, thus making its breach with the lexifier language much earlier than is normally the case with creoles from this background (Mühlhäusler 1986: 11 provides a nuanced discussion of these points). The reality is rather more complex, however. There is evidence for plantations continuing to be owned by people with English names until the end of the eighteenth century at least, although this does not counter the reality that, in official domains, English would have lost status rapidly after the handover. While the Dutch were (and are) generally pragmatic about language use in their territories (in comparison with the French, for instance), in particular perhaps in relation to their holdings in the Caribbean region, their language nevertheless became the sole language of law, administration and, eventually, education.

Religion, in its organised Christian guise, which in any event was long denied to enslaved people, should also have been Dutch dominant. But the territory's ethnolinguistic complexity (and the effort of establishing the Dutch Reformed Church in the colony's often challenging terrain) rendered this less absolute than might have been expected. This was particularly the case the farther away from the main centres of Dutch control, and sometimes the larger plantations, missions were. The Moravian Brethren, active in the region from the eighteenth century on, were particularly keen to have creole varieties used in proselytisation and worship.

In addition, a considerable number of Sephardic Jews, many of them speakers of Portuguese and Spanish, moved to the territory during this period from areas of north-eastern Brazil which had briefly been controlled by the Dutch, who were generally considered less anti-Semitic than many other European powers at the time. There is a long-standing debate among scholars about whether these immigrants brought enslaved people with them (for further discussion, see Arends 2017). Furthermore, during the late seventeenth and early eighteenth centuries, a considerable number of French-speaking Protestants entered the territory to escape persecution in France. Even in the white community, therefore, Dutch, while ostensibly hegemonic, was never omnipresent at a personal level. The development of the creoles of Suriname demonstrates this point strongly.

By the same token, the period since the end of the Second World War has witnessed a considerable migration of people from Suriname, of various cultural backgrounds, to the Netherlands. Sranan in particular is now a minority language of some importance and considerable speaker numbers in that country.

The Descent of the Suriname Creoles

As has already been stated in Section 3.2.3.1, Suriname is home to several English-lexified creole varieties. According to Arends (2017), these have developed primarily from one source (although the detail of such an observation inevitably needs to be qualified in a variety of ways). Arends (2017: 8) lays out these relationships in such a way that Sranan appears to have had a discrete ancestry from the beginnings of the then English colony. The primary distinctions which underlie this singling out of Sranan are related both to its number of speakers and to the fact that it is spoken in the most populous and 'settled' areas, both (in the past) by enslaved people and also by many people of European and other origins. A number of the other Surinamese creoles, Saramaccan having by far the largest number of speakers, are spoken by people whose linguistic ancestors had escaped slavery – the maroons. From a purely pragmatic viewpoint, it is much more straightforward to reconstruct a plausible history for Sranan, which was regularly commented upon during its development, than for the other varieties. Moreover, the different social origins of these varieties appear to be perpetuated in lexical choice in particular.

Nevertheless, for historical linguists, a striking element in any discussion of the 'family tree' of the English-lexified creoles of Suriname is the speed by which they have diverged from each other. Three hundred fifty years may seem a considerable period. But in terms of language change, this may not be the case: it is important that we consider the extent to which diversification within the Suriname varieties compares with that of other 'new' varieties of English formed in the modern period.

Varieties such as Australian and New Zealand English have a shallower time depth than Sranan and Saramaccan, by at least a hundred years. They began to crystallise as independent varieties in the late eighteenth century at the very earliest. At least until very recently, no geographical variation has been discernible with these varieties. This suggests that two hundred years must be too brief a period to develop the type of geographical dialect continuum present in territories where English has had a presence of a thousand years and more, as with England and south-east Scotland.

On the other hand, North American English, which began to develop in the course of the seventeenth century, exhibits considerable geographical variation. On this occasion there is considerable geographical variation along the eastern coast and, perhaps to a lesser extent, east of the Mississippi River. With the exception of Texas, the farther west you travel, the less these distinctions are apparent. A strong argument could be made that this is due to there having been a period in the colonisation process when the varieties of a language carried into the new settlement by colonists koineised into one largely homogenous unit; after a considerable period, distinctions began to appear, largely because of geography. We will discuss these issues further in Chapter 6.

The Suriname 'English' varieties, therefore, fall somewhere between North American and Southern Hemisphere varieties of English in terms of time depth of initial formation. We might expect, therefore, that different places in Suriname would have notably different dialects but that the distinctions present would be unlikely to impede comprehension across considerable distances. This is not the reality of the situation, however, probably because the varieties involved are not part of a mainstream dialect divergence process. Creoles may already be discrete in terms of developmental patterns *before* they diverge geographically. Native speakers of one Suriname creole have at the very least great difficulty in understanding speakers of the others, even when they are aware that these are cut from the same, essentially English, cloth. This state of affairs seems to bear rather more similarity to the apprehension of relationship felt by speakers of English towards Dutch (and vice versa): frustratingly close, but not close enough to achieve mutual intelligibility. It is worth noting that these two languages have been linguistically distinct for far longer than have the creoles of Suriname. How can we explain this difference between 'mainstream' and creole varieties?

In the first instance, we are likely to have to accept that limited (and sometimes deeply prejudiced) discussion and analysis of the Suriname varieties in the eighteenth and nineteenth centuries in particular mean that we cannot always (or often) see what is developing on the ground, except in the most general terms.

Perhaps the most obvious explanation might be the lack of input from other, more 'mainstream' varieties of English, due to the Dutch takeover. This argument can only go so far, however. As we have already seen, evidence suggests that prestige English speakers continued to live in Suriname after 1667. Many of those who remained were associated with the development and exploitation of the plantations and their inhabitants. Nevertheless, the dual influence of Dutch and English, with Portuguese as a potential junior partner, would have probably acted as a disruptor of 'mainstream' English transfer. The influence of Dutch (and, to a lesser extent, Portuguese) is present in all Suriname varieties, particularly in lexis but also structurally. Perhaps because Dutch and English are closely related, interference between competing structures is likely to have been everywhere. The influence of Portuguese (*not* a close relative of either English or Dutch) may conversely have interfered with the original structures because of issues in second language acquisition in both directions. With all this in mind, it is necessary to recognise that the maroon varieties experienced a different set of influences (or the same influences, but in strikingly different proportions) than did the varieties which formed Sranan.

The influence of African languages on the developing creoles must also be recognised, particularly since some of these languages continued to be spoken into the nineteenth century in Suriname. In contradiction to some scholars' viewpoints, Suriname was not a linguistic tabula rasa. Many enslaved people would have brought cultural and linguistic 'baggage' with them, even if this was largely of an intangible sort. While, as with Dutch and Portuguese, the influence of African languages is easiest to trace in lexis, several scholars (most notably McWhorter 2018) have demonstrated structural influence from African languages in particular in these contexts. So long as speakers of these languages were present in Suriname, their learning of the local creoles would be affected by their own language use. This same second language influence would also have affected the ways in which the creole developed, a process we discussed in relation to language shift in Chapter 2. These influences may have acted more strongly on the maroon varieties than on Sranan. It is also eminently possible that the linguistic mix of ancestral languages was different for the first generations of speakers of the different creoles.

Finally, the situation in which the native speakers of the Suriname creoles found themselves was very different from what was the case for most other new varieties. Suriname is a large territory which is difficult to transit (even in comparison to mountainous territories like Jamaica). Moreover, speakers of the Suriname creoles lived, at least originally, largely in a state of oppression and subjection. Although enslaved people were often in the majority in the Suriname colony in the eighteenth century, their agency in controlling their lives and how they were perceived was highly curtailed. Finally, and perhaps most strikingly in relation to North American English, the effects of literacy in English on the local vernacular were – to a large extent, are – absent for most of the people living in Suriname, except as a school subject in the last century or so. The new creole varieties were not constrained by anything comparable to the literate centre and its centripetal strength, as found in most colonisation circumstances. This is an important point, because, at least with this variety, the basilectal form of the various creoles appears to be original, rather than representing varieties which are closer to the 'mainstream' of English. Indeed, McWhorter (2018: 7) argued for Sranan coming about as the result of 'a stark abbreviation of language and built outwards', in other words, a creole following his exceptionalist interpretation, adding that 'we must recall that the English component of Sranan was recruited not just as "features", but in the form of constructions and contrasts simplified – i.e. pidginized'.

3.7 Conclusion

As we have seen, while most scholars agree on what a pidgin is (and often how it came into being), theoretical analyses of the origins and development of creoles exhibit considerable dissent, sometimes expressed in a forceful way.

Particular focus has been given to the creole exceptionalist and uniformitarian schools of interpretation, themselves the products of the intellectual foment caused by Bickerton's espousal of the linguistic bioprogram hypothesis. At first glance, these analyses seem utterly incapable of synthesis: idealising somewhat, the creole exceptionalist viewpoint sees the form of the creole least like the lexifier as being its oldest (and also most 'authentic'); the uniformitarian school would see this same variety as, all things being equal, the most innovative.

As we have also seen, however, both models can only have a chance of holding if only certain types of creoles are analysed. The Melanesian varieties in particular do not fit comfortably within either theoretical position. As was suggested in Section 3.6, we may have to accept that, rather than there being one type of creole formed in one way, there is instead a range of ways in which this might happen, depending on both linguistic and, perhaps particularly, sociolinguistic contexts.

Exercises

1. Choose a 'radical' creole, such as Saramaccan or Tok Pisin. Taking both sociolinguistic and linguistic analyses into consideration, are these varieties *languages* or *dialects*? (You might like to look at Millar 2005 for a discussion of the sociolinguistic debate on the meanings of these terms.)
2. This chapter concentrated almost entirely on English-based creoles. Choose a pidgin or creole which does not have a European language as its lexifier (such as Lingua Geral or Delaware Jargon). To what extent (and at what levels) are these similar in development and nature to the varieties discussed here?
3. You have almost inexhaustible research funds (and a rather loose relationship with ethical standards). You recruit fifty people who are monolingual in

a language not shared with anyone else in the group. You then leave the volunteers on a remote island. They are not allowed to leave the island and return; no contact with the outside world is permitted (except weekly deliveries of food and other necessities, brought by people who do not speak any of the subjects' languages). What do you think will happen linguistically by the end of one year? What about by the end of five years?

Suggested Reading

As this chapter demonstrates, discussions of the origins and natures of pidgins and creoles are highly contentious. I defined two central positions as the creole exceptionalist model and the uniformitarian position.

The former position is particularly well represented by the work of John H. McWhorter. His book of 2018 is perhaps his most developed statement on the matter, although the caveats mentioned about this model should be borne in mind. In my view the classic work on the uniformitarian position is Mufwene (2001). Chaudenson (2001) and De Graff (2005) are also very much worth reading. The latter is a particularly striking example of the polemical nature of the ongoing debate. Ansaldo (2009) is an even-handed discussion of other analyses from this starting point.

4 Semi-creoles
Varieties with Creole-like Features Which Are Not Creoles

Introduction

There appears to be a grey area between the perceived linguistic nature of creoles (and pidgins) and 'mainstream' dialects of a language. Towards the end of Chapter 3 we discussed circumstances in which varieties described as creoles appeared to be structurally more like their presumed lexifier source than is the case with other apparently creolised varieties.

Because of the difficulties in categorisation mentioned earlier, therefore, the best means of description appears to be through exemplification and discussion. In this chapter we will be considering the histories and natures of Pitcairn Island (and Norfolk Island) Vernacular English (the varieties are often known as *Pitkern* and *Norf'k* by speakers), St Helena Vernacular English, Afrikaans and African American Vernacular English (AAVE). All of these varieties, to a lesser or greater extent, have creole-like features but are not creoles. The chapter as a whole will end with a discussion not only of what has been considered but also with some thoughts on how the development of creoles and similar varieties can be best analysed and categorised.

4.1 Definition of *Semi-creole*

Pitkern and Norf'k, St Helena Vernacular English, Afrikaans and AAVE are 'halfway house' varieties that appear to have gone through something like the fundamental restructuring many associate with creolisation, but this has only been partly achieved. Scholars have termed such varieties, among other things, *creoloids* and *partly restructured vernaculars*. Displaying a degree of impatience, Mufwene (2008: 41) refers to 'so-called "semi-creoles"'. Despite this in many ways understandable frustration, however, I will use **semi-creole** here as the default term, primarily because, although no one descriptive term can truly be said to represent all the facets and analytical difficulties of these particular varieties, *semi-creole* appears to me to be the most lacking in a direct connection to any one of the competing models of creole origin discussed in Chapter 3 (for a well-argued case for this view, see Holm 2004: 22).

4.2 Pitkern (and Norf'k)

Of all territories where English speakers live in any numbers, the history of Pitcairn Island (see Map 3.1); actually an archipelago, but only one island is inhabited) is, at least when considered from a distance, the most romantic. The people who settled the island – among the most isolated on earth – in 1789 have been portrayed, often with considerable poetic licence, in several novels and at least two films. This prominence is primarily due to today's islanders being descended largely from the mutineers on HMS *Bounty* and their Tahitian wives, along with several of their male companions, brought for their (presumed) 'local knowledge'. They hid from the Royal Navy, away from the main trade routes. Unfortunately, we have limited knowledge of what happened during the lifetime in which, we assume, the local variety of English began to develop (although all evidence suggests that the period was at times violent and bloody). By the time full contact was resumed with the Royal Navy in the second decade of the nineteenth century, only one of the mutineers had survived, along with a number of Tahitian women and their children. From what we can reconstruct, most of the Englishmen (within whose numbers there was, in fact, someone from the West Indies, who is likely to have been at least partly African in origin) had died, whether peacefully or through violent confrontation, considerably before.

4.2.1 The Linguistic Variety Which Developed

We would expect that a 'simple' use language, a pidgin, probably with English as its lexifier, would have developed within a population dominated demographically by speakers of Tahitian. Indeed, varieties of this sort were found across the South Pacific in the eighteenth century, in some ways precursors to the European-based varieties which proliferated over the next hundred years (Drechsel 2014). Neither of these outcomes was achieved. Why is this?

While it is difficult to be certain about events reconstructed from the small amount of information available, it is apparent that Pitcairn was, from an early period, far from egalitarian in its social relationships. English speakers were dominant and able to impose their language on the others. There is evidence that some knowledge of Tahitian was maintained in the community until at least the second generation. Indeed, several words from that language are retained in the islands' lexis (Mühlhäusler 2020: chap. 6); most of these relate to flora and fauna. That language's position appears always to have been subsidiary and subaltern, however.

Nevertheless, the fact that some of those transmitting English to the next generation were not native speakers of that language should have led to more restructuring – perhaps even creolisation – than actually took place. It can be assumed that literacy was not evenly distributed among the *Bounty* mutineers. Officers like Fletcher Christian are likely to have been fully literate, but many of the sailors would have had, at most, limited reading skills. It is also quite likely that the first native generation, with primary input from non-literate mothers with second language ability in English, would have had lower reading and writing skills than their fathers. Yet the written word (in particular, the Bible), and therefore Standard English, was revered by the community. In the course of the 1820s, literacy spread along with evangelical forms of Christianity; again, the Bible was at its heart. Thus, from at least the second native generation on, the availability and importance of Standard English lay at the heart of the community. It is likely that this presence altered the trajectory of the development of the local variety (for further discussion of the cultural history of Pitcairn Island, see Amoamo 2013; for a nuanced discussion, see also Mühlhäusler 2007 and, in particular, Mühlhäusler 2020: chap. 8).

In 1856, overcrowding on Pitcairn Island led the British colonial authorities to evacuate the territory, moving the inhabitants to the rather larger and less isolated Norfolk Island – until not long before their migration the primary punishment colony for those sent to Australia for penal servitude. That this relocation was not entirely popular with those who migrated can be demonstrated by the fact that, within a few years, a minority returned to Pitcairn Island. While those Pitcairners who remained in Norfolk Island were never the sole inhabitants, it was only after the Second World War that immigration from other sources became considerable. Norfolk Island is presently administratively part of New South Wales, while Pitcairn Island is administered as a British Overseas Territory, albeit one with considerable everyday autonomy.

4.2.2 Examples of Pitkern

With these points in mind, let us consider two (written) examples of Pitcairn dialect. The first (as reproduced in Mühlhäusler 2020: 32) was recorded from a local 'boy' by Raine (1824: 461) based on his interactions with speakers while visiting the island in 1821:

> Suppose one man strike me, I no strike again, for the Book says, suppose one strike you on one side, turn the other to him; suppose he bad man strike me, I no strike him, because no good that; suppose he kill me, he can't kill the soul – He no can grasp that, that go to God, much better place than here.

Compare this to a much later example, reproduced by Mühlhäusler (2020: 53) from a collection of stories collected by Pitcairn children, edited by the Pitcairner Meralda Warren. The book was intended for use in schools, primarily to encourage use and literacy in the variety by its younger native speakers, and presented in Warren's (2008) own orthography:

> Du Tedside es good un. Mrs T lev do dere. She come ya from Galapagos.
>   Mussa when he ell, Sambo go down fer feed her Mullon. Sometime wi si da Got. We luv a go down fer swim un Fishen fer Nanwhere un a White Fish.

Mühlhäusler provides a translation (to which I have added my own translation, here represented in square brackets, for a clause which appears to have been omitted by accident):

> Tedside is special because Mrs T lives down there. She is a Galapagos tortoise. [When she is ill], Sambo mostly goes down to feed her watermelon. We see goats there sometimes too. We swim down there and go fishing for namwe [otherwise *namwee*; a local fish species] and white fish.

The two texts are strikingly different linguistically from each other, particularly in terms of their relationship to Standard English. It might be expected that the earlier recording would realise a much more divergent language, particularly because Pitcairn Island had so recently emerged into the world again and literacy was low, while literacy in Standard English is now high on the island and communication with the outside world is essentially ubiquitous.

A number of reasons could be given for this discrepancy. Firstly, there is the very real possibility that Pitcairn dialect *is* actually diverging from other varieties of English, even if literacy in Standard English is now the norm. Indeed, this reality might actually encourage writers of Pitkern to emphasise difference, although not necessarily entirely successfully, as the variation between <wi> and <We> in such a small passage is likely to demonstrate. Secondly, the first passage is written by, and from the point of view of, a complete outsider. Raine is likely to have moulded the language presented to him into something closer to Standard English, even if the passage nonetheless contains features, such as deletion of copula or a strikingly different means of marking negation, which are unquestionably not standard (or even 'mainstream'). In fact, this may be why Raine employed nonstandard usage of this type: they give a sense of difference without compromising comprehension. Warren, on the other hand, is an insider with an interest in the variety who is likely to wish to emphasise the difference between Pitkern and Standard English. It might also be possible that the biblical reference in the first passage brought the boy's language closer to that of the island's primary authority; at best, this can only be seen as being a secondary catalyst for particular usage, however.

4.2.3 Discussion

As the work of scholars such as Laycock (1989) demonstrate, there has long been dissent over what type of variety the dialects of Pitcairn and Norfolk Islands are. There are certainly features which are similar to those of creoles, but not of the same level of effect and occurrence: Pitkern is much more readily comprehensible to other speakers of English than most creole varieties are. Most of the time, the variety seems rather like a highly divergent dialect, not dissimilar to the ways in which the dialects of Scots are perceived from the perspective of speakers of the south-east England dialects (or, indeed, those of the American Midwest). Given the lack of information about the first generation of English speakers born on Pitcairn, it is difficult to draw absolute conclusions about the origins of the variety. It is quite probable, however, that a pidgin was spoken on the island, possibly brought into being by the need for communication between English and Tahitian speakers. Although this variety did not prevail, aspects of its structure were carried across into the more 'mainstream' variety employed by the descendants of the dominant English-speaking males. Pitkern can therefore be seen as a divergent nonstandard variety which has inherited some pidginised or creolised features. This survival was made more straightforward because of the small number of 'mainstream' inputs available in the first generations of the community's and variety's development.

4.3 The English of St Helena

St Helena is primarily known outside the island itself as Napoleon Bonaparte's final place of (enforced) exile, from 1815 to 1821. In fact, its choice as an 'open prison' for someone considered by many to be the most dangerous man in Europe could be taken as evidence that the island was perceived by the British authorities, who acted as his gaoler, as something of a backwater. To some extent, this is the case: St Helena has never been a major trading centre and lies off the main trade routes of the South Atlantic. Until 2015 it could be reached only by sea. This relatively isolated environment inevitably led to the language use of the territory being something of a unique test bed for linguistic variation and change (this and the following paragraphs are primarily based on the work published in Schreier's 2008 monograph).

St Helena is unique in another way: it is the only former British colony in the Southern Hemisphere where slavery was introduced and practiced (the presence of slavery in South Africa into the nineteenth century is a product of the Dutch imperial presence at the Cape of Good Hope until the Revolutionary and Napoleonic Wars). The reason for this anomaly is that its colonisation began at an early date: the late 1650s (while all other Southern Hemisphere varieties date from, at the earliest, the later eighteenth century). Until the time of Bonaparte's exile, it was a possession of the (English, later British) East India Company, rather than being ruled directly by the Westminster government. Given the relative closeness of St Helena to West Africa, along with the ingrained European traditions of slaving in that region, it is quite striking that, although there were West African people among those enslaved for labour on St Helena, most were from Madagascar. We can therefore assume that Malagasy was spoken by a considerable part of the inhabitants of the island in the eighteenth century (although, perhaps surprisingly, there is very limited evidence for influence from that language upon even the lexis, normally the level of language most readily affected by contact, of the local varieties of English).

Another striking (and unexpected) feature of St Helenian (the locally preferred adjective) culture and history is that, unlike most places where slavery has been a major part of the economy, racism is now practically unknown. Moreover, most inhabitants are of mixed race. It may be that isolation and the sometimes pressing need to achieve something beyond mere survival encouraged the avoidance of prejudice.

4.3.1 St Helenian Vernacular English: A Brief Description

What is St Helenian Vernacular English like, therefore, bearing in mind that both possession of education and social status will affect some inhabitants more than others, as is the case practically everywhere? Phonologically, the dialect is in many ways a mainstream Southern Hemisphere variety of English, with, naturally, its own particularities. A number of features do stand out, however: /w/ and /v/ have merged, often at [β], in vernacular speech, while /f/ and /v/ are employed in place of /θ/ and /ð/ in TH contexts. These changes are not unknown in a range of southeast England varieties, past and present, but they are also sporadically found in English-lexified pidgins and creoles around the world (particularly, perhaps, in the Atlantic-Caribbean region, as evinced in our discussion of Gullah in Chapter 3; AAVE speakers also regularly employ 'TH-fronting').

There is more to say about morphosyntax, perhaps. Many features of this type (here all derived from Schreier's fieldwork), such as the 'double comparative', *people were more genuiner than what they are today*, are widespread in nonstandard varieties; others, such as *she had to get operation*, are rather more unusual in the speech of native speakers of English. Subject and object distinctions are often non-existent, as with *us come up Peak Hill way see* (this structure is found in Yorkshire English, for instance, but is also common in many pidgins and creoles). The use of possessive *they* (*that's they occupation*) is also commonplace in St Helenian Vernacular English, another feature found in a range of other varieties sometimes classified as creoles, along with AAVE.

The norms of Standard English verb–subject concord are not always represented in St Helenian speech (as with *I's quite happy*; *I think they's divorce*). Features of this type do occur in many English dialects; they are certainly more common in some contact-influenced varieties. What is particularly striking, however, is, when compared to the 'mainstream' equivalents, the presence of means to express aspectual distinctions in verbs, such as habitual *be* (*it don't be pain like fore days it don't be real pain*), habitual *do* (*that's what all of us do query*) and the completive *done* construction: *I done beat him now*. Again, many of these constructions are analogous to features found in Atlantic-Caribbean English-based varieties and AAVE. This does not necessarily mean that there was direct influence between one region and the other, but it does suggest that these were common features in the contact variety 'pool', which 'bubbled up' regularly.

Finally, and perhaps most surprising, is the 'past infinitive' structure, as with *my daddy used to got the flax* 'my daddy used to get [i.e. collect, harvest] the flax' and *I didn't went out nowhere* 'I didn't go out anywhere'. With one exception (which we will deal with shortly), this construction, by no means unknown in other languages, is peculiar to St Helena within English. It is not a prototypical creole form, but it is certainly unexpected and may well tell us something about the historical development of the variety.

As with the other varieties discussed in this chapter, there can be little doubt that St Helenian Vernacular English has creole-like features, as well as some features which, while not necessarily creole, are certainly unusual within an English framework. In other ways, however, the dialect demonstrates closeness to nonstandard varieties in (southern) England, bearing in mind the community's greater developmental time depth in comparison with, for instance, Australia and New Zealand. Given the size of both the island and the number of its inhabitants, it is difficult to imagine the extent to which a specifically creole-using and -developing community could come into being. But, before the stabilisation of the present vernacular, it is quite possible that something like a post-creole continuum existed, with a basilect which possessed features which were at least highly divergent from the acrolectal norm. A small piece of evidence for this might be found in the form of English used on another South Atlantic island (although, as ever, we need to be careful that we do not make too much of a small piece of evidence).

4.3.2 Comparative Evidence from Tristan da Cunha English

Tristan da Cunha English is spoken in the most isolated place on earth, by around 250 people (see Map 4.1). This variety, described and analysed by Schreier (2003), is in most ways a mainstream Southern Hemisphere dialect (comparable, therefore, to the English of New Zealand, for instance), dating back to the middle of the nineteenth century, descended primarily from a nonstandard southern English dialect or set of dialects, no matter the rather diverse origins and experiences of the early settlers. One feature stands out, however: the use of a past infinitive (as with *all we*

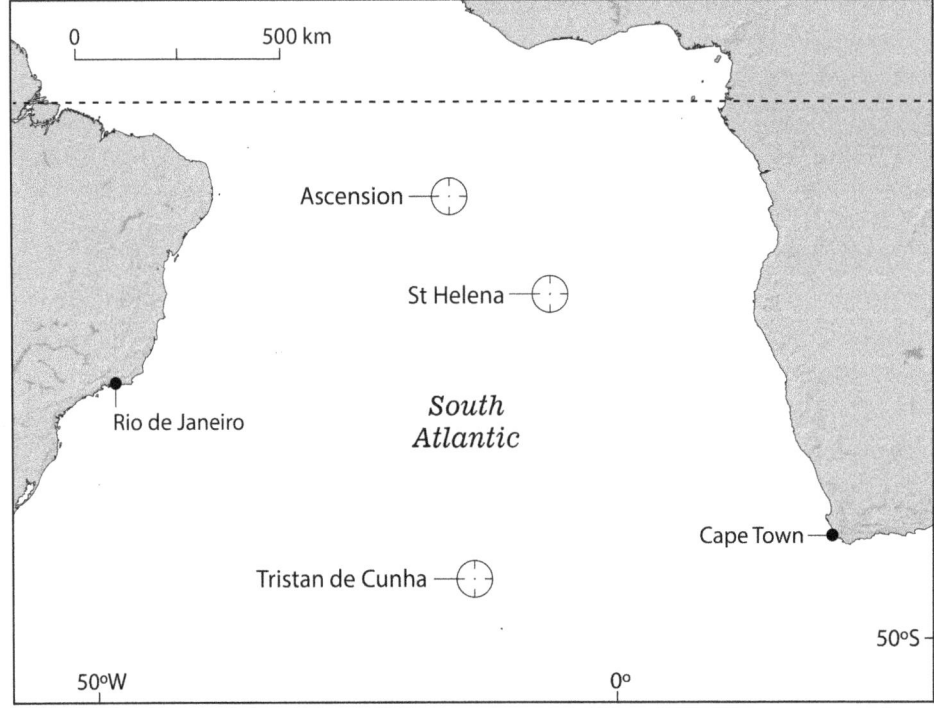

Map 4.1 St Helena and Tristan da Cunha in their geographical settings.

usta done 'all we used to do', from Schreier's material). Strikingly, this is similar to (although more restricted in use than) some St Helenian Vernacular English structures.

Of course, just because two varieties share a structural feature does not necessarily mean that there is a common source. Although now administered within the same unit, along with Ascension Island, St Helena and Tristan da Cunha are nowhere near each other and are strikingly different from each other ecologically and historically; their inhabitants rarely had much contact until Tristanian children started to go to St Helena for their secondary education in the relatively recent past.

But if we reach back to the earliest history of the present Tristan da Cunha settlement, we find an event which might explain this apparent transfer. In an attempt to stabilise what was an extremely violent environment among the all-male population of the island (the survivors of shipwrecks, as well as men who had been stranded), a mid nineteenth-century Anglican missionary offered passage and inducements for St Helenian women to come to the southern settlement as wives for the men on Tristan. They are the foremothers of the present settlement. While we do not know much about the social origins of the women, it does not seem likely that they would have come from the wealthier parts of the St Helenian community. The idea of marrying half-crazed men in a new and unknown place can only have been attractive to people who had practically nothing. Before the stabilisation of St Helena English, these poor – historically enslaved – women may well have spoken something like a basilect of a creole-like language variety. Some of this at least was passed on to their offspring (and probably to some of the non-native speakers who lived on the island for considerable periods). In a sense, Tristan da Cunha English provides brief and partial glimpses of what St Helena English was like 150 years ago.

Although evidence is limited, therefore, it would not be unreasonable to assume that small-scale contact events at the very least similar in outputs to that found in creolisation contexts were present in St Helena. This is not the immediate ancestor of the present vernacular, however, which is a compromise koine (see Chapter 6) of a range of different varieties of English, including second language forms of a number of types.

4.4 Afrikaans

Afrikaans represents something of a linguistic conundrum (this argument derives much from Holm 2004, while not necessarily reaching the same conclusions; for sociolinguistic detail on the language use of literate users of 'Dutch', of various forms, in southern Africa in the nineteenth century, see also Deumert 2001, 2004). In some ways, it is a colonial variety of Dutch, derived from the dialects of the Hollands in particular. Following this argument, it could be compared to the development of varieties such as New Zealand English (see Chapter 6) or, indeed, South African English (see, e.g., Lass 1987, 1990, 1995), albeit with a considerably greater time depth than these two Englishes possess in relation to the 'home' variety. There are other features of Afrikaans, however, which would not be normal for any variety of Dutch. Most strikingly for our purposes, many features found in Afrikaans are similar to features found regularly in creole varieties. In other words, there are features found in any form of Afrikaans which mark it off as different from any European variety of Dutch:

- loss of all traces of ablaut (as in the distinction in English between *sing*, *sang* and *sung*) and the distinction between strong and weak verbs
- loss of all regular verb endings of person, number and tense
- replacement of the past tense by perfect aspect, marked by prefixed *ge-*
- overt marking of direct object position
- loss of gender in the article system (Mesthrie 2004: 531)
- multiple negative concord (Holm 2004; Combrink 1978)

To the penultimate of these points might be added the complete loss of morphological marking for grammatical case on nouns and adjectives, still at least partly active in Dutch when the two varieties separated at the beginning of the eighteenth century (and still present in place names and family names in the Netherlands and Belgium). Some of these features (such as the preference for perfective over simple past marking) are in line with, as we will see in Case Study 5, nonstandard usage across a large part of central Europe. Many are essentially peculiar to Afrikaans and have no Dutch analogues, however. Some features can be attributed to contact with other languages; some appear largely to be evidence for the breakdown which happens in situations in which people are using a language other than their own as a means of communication.

4.4.1 What Linguistic State Does Afrikaans Inhabit?

But Afrikaans is not a creole, a reality emphasised by the fact that there is a degree of mutual intelligibility possible between speakers of mainstream varieties of Afrikaans and speakers of Dutch when speaking their native varieties, without great efforts in accommodation on either part. Much of this conundrum derives from the past of southern Africa since the first exertion of Dutch power in the region in the early seventeenth century.

Further contact-induced developments which do not involve direct transfer can also be mentioned for Afrikaans. Looking at this language from an external perspective, it is understandable that we should consider written Afrikaans as representative of the language as a whole. In a sense, of course, this is correct. It is in this variety that Afrikaans speakers who are fully literate in that language express themselves in writing. Yet it is also quite conservative in relation to other Afrikaans native speaker varieties, such as that of poor rural whites or members of the community of 'Cape Coloureds', as well as the Orange River varieties, spoken today in the far north of South Africa and southern Namibia, used primarily by persons of colour who moved there in the nineteenth century. This is without taking into consideration non-native speaker varieties, such as Fly-Taal, developed as a means of communication by economic migrants under apartheid, from all over Africa to the south of the great lakes, to the mines and other large endeavours of South Africa. Standard Afrikaans is closer to the Dutch of the Netherlands than all but the most 'careful' varieties spoken in South Africa. Until the twentieth century, Standard Dutch was the language of law in the country; it was also the language of holy writ in the Reformed Church, an organisation of central importance to Afrikaner society.

4.4.2 Contrastive Examples

Something of the nature and diversity of the Netherlandic varieties used in South Africa and elsewhere can be seen in the following brief excerpts (derived from Holm 1988–9: II, 352) from the Parable of the Prodigal Son (Luke 15:11–12): 'A man had two sons. The younger of them said to his father, "Father, give me the share of the estate that will belong to me."'

The first example represents what we can assume to be fairly conservative Standard Dutch of the (late) nineteenth century:

Een	*zeker*	*mensch*	*had*	*twee*	*zonen.*	*En*	*de*	*jongste*	*van*	*hen*	*zeide*
a	certain	man	had	two	sons	and	the	youngest	of	them	said

tot	*den*	*vader:*	*vader*	*geef*	*miij*	*het deel*	*des goeds,*	*dat*	*mijtoekomt.*
to	the	father	father	give	me	the part	of-the property	that	mebelongs

(Valkhoff 1966; nineteenth-century Bible translation)

The language employed maintains grammatical gender distinctions, so that *het deel* 'the part' expresses its membership of the neuter gender class through the demonstrative pronoun/definite article used, while *de jongste* 'the youngest' expresses common gender (in most Dutch dialects, as in many Germanic varieties, the original masculine and feminine gender classes have fallen together). Grammatical case is largely moribund, but the remnant of the genitive case, *des goeds*, is still present, even if it is highly likely that many varieties of Dutch had already replaced this synthetic means of demonstrating possession by various forms of periphrasis (see Chapter 5 for further discussion). *Tot den vader* may also represent the survival of an accusative/dative form of the definite article/simple demonstrative pronoun. This feature was already highly archaic at the time of the translation.

Here is the equivalent text in Standard Afrikaans:

'n	*Man*	*het*	*twee*	*seuns*	*gehad.*	*En*	*die*	*jongste*	*van*	*hulle*	*het*	*vir*	*sy*	*vader*
a	man	has	two	sons	had	and	the	youngest	of	them	has	to	his	father

gesê:	*Vader,*	*gee*	*my*	*die*	*deel*	*van*	*die*	*eiendom*	*wat*	*my*	*toekom.*
said	father	give	me	the	part	of	the	property	that	me	belongs

(Valkhoff 1966)

Before we begin this analysis, we should note that this written version will, like the Dutch equivalent, be likely to be rather conservative in its usage, compared even to the upper-middle-class norms of the time, given the passage's status as holy writ. Moreover, this text would undoubtedly have been influenced by the Dutch text, which was the norm in most Reformed Churches into the twentieth century (and would, again, have had particular status in these contexts).

That being said, the text does demonstrate marked structural differences in relation to the Standard Dutch (most of the differences in lexis are more likely to represent differences of personal and group choice in these circumstances, rather than major distinctions between varieties). Grammatical gender, for instance, appears no longer to be inherent in the system (rather than Dutch *het deel*, *die deel* is realised, for instance, sharing the same determiner as *die jongste*). A number of the other differences found, such as the periphrastic expression of possession (*van die eiendom*) or the use of the *have*-perfect where Standard Dutch employs the historically 'correct' simple past (as with *het twee seuns gehad* as against *had twee zonen*), are, as already suggested, found in colloquial Dutch and its relatives in the Netherlands, Belgium and beyond. It would be difficult to claim that these were 'creole' features. Strikingly, the rules of element order of Continental West Germanic (such as verb in final position in subordinate clauses – *wat my toekom*) are adhered to. The use of *wat* (equivalent to English *what*) as a relative pronoun is highly marked in the Dutch context, but the feature does appear in some dialects of English (including many creoles), is found in some southern German dialects and is the norm in most Romance varieties.

When all of this is borne in mind, it is striking that the 'Cape Coloured' Afrikaans text Holm provides is structurally close to the Standard Afrikaans. The primary textual differences appear, in fact, to be matters of levels of formality:

'n Man het twee seuns gehet. En die kleinste van hulle het vir sy pa
a man has two sons had and the youngest of them has to his father

gesê: Pa, ge vir my die deel van die erf wat myne is.
said father give to me the part of the property that mine is
(D. Makhudu, personal communication to Holm)

It is necessary to recognise, however, that these similarities are likely to be rather less prevalent in the spoken form, particularly in highly colloquial contexts. Moreover, as is the case with most short excerpts of this type, we cannot be certain what has not been inadvertently left out (for instance, Afrikaans, unlike other Germanic languages, marks direct object by a preceding particle, as is the case in many creoles and other languages).

4.4.3 Socio-historical Background

Why (and how), then, did this divergence take place? Why is Afrikaans not to Netherlands Dutch what American English is to British English?

Before servants of the Dutch East India Company established a small way station at what is now Cape Town for ships travelling to South Asia, present-day Indonesia and beyond, the primary inhabitants of the region were speakers of various Khoikhoi languages. Most were herders of cattle. When the Dutch arrived, the local native groups assumed different postures in relation to the new arrivals. There was considerable peaceful coexistence, but also occasional, sometimes extreme, violence, from which, despite their comparatively advanced weapons technology, the Europeans did not always emerge victorious. As the colony around Cape Town expanded, many Khoikhoi people became integral parts of the colony, whether as free (although not necessarily equal) citizens or held in some form of bondage. They performed a range of tasks within the colony, from being farm labourers to children's nurses (for which role they were particularly prized). There was much intermarriage (whether of an official or 'country' sort). The products of these unions were the first 'Cape Coloureds'. From an early period, Dutch spread into these communities, initially as a second and, eventually, in a distinctive first language form.

To begin with at least, the Dutch territories at the Cape of Good Hope were a small cog in a large wheel; over time, however, the importance of Cape Town, both as a trading and victualling centre and as a settlement hub in a territory with a Mediterranean climate, became increasingly clear. The Dutch mercantile empire began, in the seventeenth century, to become a major territorial power through the extension of their control from their forts to their hinterlands, while also exploiting connections which the Portuguese had established, as the latter empire contracted. Dutch trade was not focussed on slavery in the way that seventeenth- and eighteenth-century English (later British) trade was, but Dutch soldiers, administrators and merchants had no compunction about exploiting people in this way to strengthen and develop their power bases. Thus enslaved people from East Africa and, in particular, Madagascar were brought to the Cape, as were many people from what is now Indonesia (in particular, Java). Many of this latter group were brought in a state of indentured servitude rather than slavery, although the line between these two types of lack of liberty was inevitably blurred. Primarily because of religious differences, the Indonesian element of the population of Cape Town remained largely discrete (indeed, their cultural presence is still highly visible in parts of the city today). The populations of East African and Malagasy origin, however, quickly became subsumed into the multiracial reality of the region. In both cases, nevertheless, local varieties of colloquial Dutch quickly became central to their linguistic reality (even if, as in the Muslim communities, knowledge of Arabic and other languages survived). As with the Khoikhoi speakers, however, second language influence on first language acquisition was inevitable.

It should be noted, moreover, that European migrants to the Cape were not all native speakers of Dutch. Many German speakers were among the settlers (in fact, a few of them held rank within the colony). In the late seventeenth and early eighteenth centuries, a considerable number of French Protestants, fleeing persecution at home, settled at the Cape. As is always the case with large-scale ports, moreover, a considerable number of individuals, speaking several different languages, were resident in the colony, either permanently or for considerable periods. Finally, as British power grew in India and elsewhere around the Indian Ocean, Cape Town was regularly visited by English speakers, some of whom are likely, for whatever reason, to have remained there. Even before the British takeover of the colony during the Revolutionary and Napoleonic Wars, therefore, English would regularly have been heard. It is very unlikely that at least long-term residents from an English language background would not have had some command of the local varieties of Dutch, however, even after the transfer of power.

Despite this linguistic takeover, as already stated, some people from mixed-race backgrounds are themselves native speakers of Afrikaans (although members of many of the communities who make up this rather amorphous group have begun to switch to English over the last half century). Many of these native speakers live in Cape Town and its vicinity. This ethnic mix among Afrikaans speakers was often ignored (or even submerged) under the apartheid regime, where (white) Afrikaner purity in blood and ideology was foregrounded. This idealised connection, even communion, was associated with the *voortreks* of the nineteenth century, when Afrikaner farmers and their families left the Cape Colony, associated increasingly with British rule and the English language, for the High Veldt and beyond, intending to set up self-governing and godly territories. They were normally in direct confrontation and conflict with the Bantu-speaking nations which were already settled in the same territories. The majority of Afrikaans speakers remained in the Cape Province, however. But, while not invisible, these mixed-race inhabitants were *not* Afrikaners. Their contribution to the development of that language was often downplayed, if not ignored, particularly because this shared development was seen as a 'dirty secret' by some ideologues (for further discussion of the past and present linguistic ecology of South Africa, see Mesthrie 2004).

4.4.4 Afrikaans Is Not a Creole

Afrikaans is not a creole, at least as most creolists would define this state. It does have creole-like features, however, even if there is no evidence that people during the foundation of the Dutch colony at the Cape believed that an entirely new variety was coming into being. That does not mean that no forms of pidgin Dutch were spoken in those early days by anyone, particularly given the multilingual environment Cape Town was becoming. There are reports from the period of 'broken Dutch' being spoken by enslaved people and servants in the new city and its hinterland. Everyday contact with more prestigious and mainstream varieties of Dutch may well have hindered the spread of any creole which might have developed from this, particularly in such a socially stratified context. At the same time, however, elements of the 'broken Dutch' would have found a place even in the most elevated households through the presence of servants and, in particular, the use of nurses who did not speak Dutch as a first language but regularly had greater (or at least more intimate) contact with young children than had their parents. Almost inevitably, many features of the 'broken' variety would have been internalised by young learners. Since only the most privileged members of Cape society were likely to be in the position to travel regularly to the Netherlands (and most Dutch seamen and business travellers would have spoken their own dialect Dutch rather than the standard in any event), the new African dialect could develop and follow its own way without much interference. This might well have been encouraged by there being a sizeable white (and therefore privileged) population who did not speak any variety of Dutch as a first language. Elements of their own 'broken' varieties of the hegemonic language may well have influenced the local dialect's development as well, given their social standing.

Support for the proposed 'injection' of creole-like linguistic material through a range of pidginisations, which took place at the same time as the more Dutch-focussed variety which became Afrikaans, can be found by an analysis of the Orange River variety of the language, separated geographically from most other speakers through the migration of people of mixed race (Holm 2004: 137).

Case Study 4 African American Vernacular English

An early memory: watching a Saturday evening variety show on the television sometime in the early 1970s (I was probably six or seven), I saw a song-and-dance number based on Irving Berlin's 'Alexander's Ragtime Band' (despite its name, actually a very early example of jazz-tinged pop, from 1911). It is an attractive song and one of the earliest examples of musical syncopation to be used in the popular music mainstream. One line jumped out at me, however:

That's just the bestest band what am, Honey Lamb.

I found the use of *am* (rather than *is*) fascinating (I recognised the use of *what* and *bestest* as nonstandard, although they are not turns of phrase that speakers of my own dialect would use). I asked my mother why *am* was being used in this context; she prevaricated but eventually suggested that it might represent the way American black people spoke in the past. This is not actually true, but I can see why she said it. The varieties which many African American or Afro-Caribbean people speak have never included features of this sort. But there is a genre, minstrelsy, a representation of black life and culture at its 'safest' (as perceived by white people), broadly associated with the second half of the nineteenth century, in which white people often impersonated black people and employed 'incorrect' language of this sort. Irving Berlin is tapping into this tradition; he even namechecks 'Swanee River' in the song, arguably the archetypal minstrel show piece. (It is worth noting that Berlin himself was not a native speaker of English; the same 'invented' grammatical feature can be found in another minstrel ballad, 'The Old Folks at Home': *all de world am sad and dreary*. This song was written by Stephen Foster, a white northerner, who died during the American Civil War.)

Of course, dialects are often parodied by outsiders. No Scots speaker, for instance, has ever said 'it's a braw, bricht, moonlicht nicht the nicht', partly because it is ungrammatical: '(h)it's a braw, bricht, munelichtit nicht the nicht' would be closer to reality. But although Scottish people may sometimes suffer from ethnocultural discrimination in England and elsewhere, the legacy of slavery does not hang over them. Scots speakers may be considered odd because of the way they speak, their political allegiances and so on, but this is not generally explained as being due to lack of intelligence. Most Scots also pass for any other person of North-West European origin.

But most speakers of creoles or similar varieties are different ethnically from those who possess or possessed greater economic and political power in the territories in which they are settled. The prejudice which hangs over the language(s) of the enslaved and their descendants is still very much alive and can warp our analyses, even (perhaps particularly) when elements of the subaltern language are at best commodified for the dominant population. In present-day popular culture, AAVE is both omnipresent and historically misunderstood.

Socio-historical Background

The reasons for there being people of African descent in what is now the United States are, of course, both well known and perennially contentious in relation to their effects and results up to the present day. In brief, large numbers of people, primarily from West Africa and the Congo to Angola region (although other parts of Africa were also represented), were brought across the Atlantic involuntarily and sold into chattel slavery (which meant that enslaved people were rarely able to achieve freedom, in marked distinction to what was possible with many other forms of slavery in the past or current at the time). While the 'peculiar institution' was, by the nineteenth century, confined to the southern states (in particular the southern parts of this region), it is worth noting that, until the Revolutionary War at least, slavery was also commonplace across the North, with concentrations in parts of New York State and New Jersey, and elsewhere. It has been described as America's original sin (Wallis 2016; along with racism, if the two can truly be distinguished in this context – I write this as someone from a country, Scotland, whose collective hands are not clean in this matter).

North American slavery is often associated with the large-scale plantation economic model, where considerable numbers of enslaved people were forced to labour in the production of often extremely lucrative cash crops, including tobacco, indigo, rice and, before everything else, cotton, the last of which becoming highly profitable with the introduction of the cotton gin in the mid 1790s. This invention industrialised a previously time-consuming process, as well as being a vital underlying reason for the continuation of slavery into the second half of the nineteenth century in the United States. As the urban areas of the South industrialised in that century, unfree people of African origin also worked in industries of various sizes; many were forced to assume the role of household servants, in considerable numbers in the richest homes (Morgan 1998 is a particularly comprehensive discussion of how slavery developed and spread in the Lowcountry of South Carolina and the Chesapeake region of Virginia, demonstrating connections and disconnects between the enslaved population and the white inhabitants).

But the plantations were not present in all places during the period when the first enslaved people were brought to the colonies. In the seventeenth and early eighteenth centuries, a considerable number of enslaved people, as we saw in relation to other contexts in Chapter 3, lived in homesteads, in close proximity to their owners and other servants who were not considered chattels but were bound to work for a given time for the same people. It was in the eighteenth century that the great plantation system became the norm (it is likely that it became dominant considerably earlier in South Carolina and the colonies which sprang from it, such as Georgia, than in Virginia and its hinterland). While the new economic realities of the eighteenth century demanded the importation of many enslaved Africans, the generations of black people in the English (and then British) colonies which preceded them had often had different social and sociolinguistic relationships with speakers of English. Elements of their experience are likely to have been passed on into the new mass environment (Winford 2015 and Schneider 2015 provide lucid and non-partisan descriptions and analyses of the sociohistorical forces and events underlying the development of the variety).

Even after emancipation in 1863, the situation for most African Americans did not improve materially. Slavery was replaced by the state of sharecropper, a form of peonage where former masters assumed a monopoly or near monopoly on the production and sale of cotton from the allotments provided for that purpose. After a brief political effervescence in the aftermath of the Civil War, black people were excluded, often violently, from the decision-making process at local, state and union levels by an increasing number of Jim Crow laws and the near-institutionalised unofficial implementation of terror. Despite being in the majority in a number of states in the Deep South, African Americans were marginalised (for a nuanced discussion of these matters, see Ayers 2007: esp. chap. 6). It is unsurprising, therefore, that, when the opportunity to move north to better paying jobs and a freer environment arrived, to begin with in the economic boom caused by the First World War, many did so. By the middle of the twentieth century, the West had become as attractive. Legal segregation had never existed in these places, but something similar came into being unofficially, with the poorest parts of cities becoming associated with 'race'. As the events of 2020 demonstrated, white attitudes towards African Americans have, perhaps, ameliorated (in particular, towards the black middle classes), but oppression and repression still lurk just beneath the surface in certain contexts (for a discussion of the nature of the 'Great Migration', see Wilkerson 2020; Gregory 2005).

We would expect, therefore, that long-term circumstances of disenfranchisement and marginalisation, founded on slavery, would have created a fully fledged creole in the United States. But, with the exception of Gullah, spoken now in the Sea Islands off South Carolina and Georgia (for a recent discussion, see Weldon and Moody 2015; see also Section 3.2.3.2), this does not appear to be the case. AAVE is much closer to mainstream varieties of English than is the case with, for instance, Tok Pisin or even Jamaican dialect. Why is this the case?

Examples and Analysis

A starting point for our discussion of the development of this variety is that it should not be assumed that AAVE has no creole-like features, such as those we analysed with other varieties in Chapter 3. This needs to be emphasised. Nevertheless, a large part of the make-up of the dialect is not at all distant from mainstream 'white' nonstandard varieties of North American English.

Here are two examples. The first was recorded in the third decade of the twentieth century, but the speaker was enslaved until his early teens:

> Billy McRae, Jasper, Texas, born 1852, recorded in the 1930s
> That crew of Yankees would go **tru**. Next time you see, there come a whole troop of Yankees, all ridin' **horseses**, big guns a-hangin' on in there, all like that you know. Yeah. We all would stan' lookin' at um, all going home.
> An I said, I ask um, I said, **I duh ask um**, I she, 'Mámá, whàh dé, whàh dé go: n?' Said, 'Dey all going home now.' (Sutcliffe 2001: 137, emphasis and orthography as in original)

(Sutcliffe makes much throughout his paper of a difference between what he terms *Plantation Mesolect*, here in bold, and AAVE; this absolute distinction will not be followed up here.)

With this brief excerpt, there is little or nothing to say about lexis in comparison with other varieties of English. Phonologically, the use of /t/ and /d/ for /θ/ and /ð/ is highly marked in these contexts. Some structural features, such as *a-hangin'*, are hangovers found in both Black and White Southern Vernaculars of a construction often perceived as archaic, if not actually opaque, by other users of English.

The second example is a rightly famous one, dating from the late 1960s. JL is the fieldworker; Larry is a fifteen-year-old African American male, living in the largely African American neighbourhood of Harlem in New York City. He is a gang member and perceived as a 'problem student' at school. He is also a highly thoughtful person and a gifted speaker:

JL: What happens to you after you die? Do you know?
LARRY: Yeah, I know.
JL: What?
LARRY: After they put you in the ground, your body turns into-ah-bones, an' shit.
JL: What happens to your spirit?
LARRY: Your spirit – soon as you die, your spirit leaves you.
JL: Where does the spirit go?
LARRY: Well, it all depends ...
JL: On what?
LARRY: You know, like some people say if you're good an' shit, your spirit goin' t'heaven ... 'n' if you bad, your spirit goin' to hell. Well, bullshit! Your spirit goin' to hell anyway, good or bad.
JL: Why?
LARRY: Why? I'll tell you why. 'Cause you see, doesn' nobody really know that it's a God, y'know, 'cause I mean I have seen black gods, pink gods, white gods,

all colour gods, and don't nobody know it's really a God. An' when they be sayin' if you good, you goin' t'heaven, tha's bullshit, 'cause you ain't goin' to no heaven, 'cause it ain't no heaven for you to go to. (Labov (1969) 1972: 193–4)

Of course much of what Larry says is mainstream colloquial English. Without access to a recording of the piece, it would be impossible to say for a large part of the excerpt what geographical and ethnic background the speaker had. Features in Larry's speech, however, such as the occasional omission of copulas (for instance, *if you good*) and the use of *be* as an habitual marker (as in *when they be sayin'*), are archetypically AAVE in nature and have analogues in varieties which are classified as creoles.

AAVE: A *Decreolised* Creole?

When faced with this type of evidence, it is reasonable to assume that what we have now is evidence for the decreolised end of a post-creole continuum (as interpreted by creole exceptionalists; see Section 3.5.2), where even the densest forms of the dialect are at most mesolectal in relation to earlier varieties. The basilect, we assume, was far more creole-like but is no longer present in the contemporary form of the variety. This was indeed the primary argument of many scholars in the 1970s and 1980s. There are considerable issues about accepting such a view, however, at least in its entirety (for recent discussion – indeed, often heated debate – see Rickford 2015; Van Herk 2015; Mufwene 2014a, 2015; the first stirrings of much of this debate can be found in Poplack 2000).

In the first instance, why would decreolisation take place in the United States, where slavery remained ubiquitous well into the mid nineteenth century in certain parts of the country? The same process of decreolisation (if it is interpreted as such) is rather less advanced in Jamaica, where slavery was abolished a generation earlier (although, of course, the economic and social relationships between those formerly enslaved and their 'masters' altered far less and not quickly). This could be taken to imply that something exceptional happened to the speech of people of African origin in the United States. To what extent is this a fair assumption?

Given the extent to which, from the eighteenth century on, enslaved people and their descendants were segregated from the white community in those regions, why would a more mainstream dialect have developed there? Are the histories and sociolinguistic development of enslaved people of African origin in the United States different from analogous populations elsewhere?

More importantly, indeed crucially, there is little or no evidence for earlier versions of AAVE being more creole-like than is the case with the present varieties (indeed, some scholars would see modern AAVE as having diverged from an earlier variety much closer to the southern 'norm'; see, e.g., Bailey 2001). Nineteenth-century written versions of African American folk tales and anecdotes exist (not, admittedly, particularly trustworthy, given that they were intended for a largely white audience). There is also evidence from African American 'colonies' founded in the nineteenth century, in Nova Scotia (in Canada), the Dominican Republic, Liberia and elsewhere, where connections with the Deep South have been largely severed for at least 150 years. Recordings (written or mechanically stored), made in the 1930s, of the recollections of elderly people who had been enslaved in their childhoods and youth are also available. The language evidenced on all of these occasions is also not particularly creole-like.

It may be that the black people associated with these external regions were not representative of African Americans as a whole: the Samaná colony in the Dominican Republic had a considerable number of free, northern, educated pioneers, for instance. It is also the case that the people recorded in the 1930s had often been employed (involuntarily, naturally) in the houses of their owners. While the potential for abuse – in particular, sexual abuse – was considerable in such close proximity to entitled white people, and while the hours were long, the work was not back-breaking in the way that was true for field hands. This might explain why this particular segment of the enslaved population lived longest and why their language was most affected by that of middle-class whites.

This set of arguments does not work as well for the colony in Nova Scotia, since it was founded by enslaved people who had escaped from bondage via the Underground Railroad and have remained a distinct and economically deprived minority in their new home. These final pioneers are probably as representative of the black population of the southern states in the nineteenth century as can be found anywhere. The language of their descendants appears no more creole in its features than do the languages of all of the linguistic colonies represented here (discussion of the issues flowing from this evidence can be found in Schneider 2015; Kautsch 2002; Miethaner 2014; Sutcliffe 2001; Van Herk 2015; Poplack and Tagliamonte 2001; Poplack and Sankoff 1987).

Why does this discrepancy exist? There are, of course, no direct answers to this question. As already said, however, during the homestead phase with which a number of creole formations are associated, people of African descent were much more closely connected to their 'owners' than was the case in most of the later plantation environments. Holm (2004) sees this process as an example of partial restructuring: as the result of competing forces of creolisation and 'normalisation'. There is, in fact, limited evidence for this contest, although, instinctively, something like this would be very likely to have happened; indeed, it connects well with some of the discussion given in Chapter 6 in particular. It is likely, therefore, that contact with a number of different kinds of native speaker varieties (and, indeed, non-native speaker varieties) would have produced speakers of an English which, while having some non-native speaker traits, including substratal influence, would have been strikingly similar to, although not the same as, that used by many poorer white people. This situation is analogous to what is found in the American South today (although there is some debate, as presented in Bailey 1997, over how old present-day White Southern Vernacular English actually is; see, e.g., Wolfram 1974; discussion of the connections between AAVE and the white vernacular Englishes of the American South can be found in Bailey 2001; Feagin 1979).

When large-scale plantations became more commonplace in the course of the eighteenth century, it was, this theoretical model suggests, the homestead language variety speakers who became the 'trainers' of those newly brought from Africa and elsewhere. Part of this training consisted in the passing on of the language of their owners and other whites with whom they all had contact, whether voluntarily or not. New varieties would have come into being because of the proportion of non-native speakers learning at this time, thereby encouraging the new vernaculars to diverge from their white equivalents. It is certainly possible that creole-like varieties developed in some places, but these did not take over the whole, instead only influencing parts of the new dialect(s). Given that, in the early years of the nineteenth century in particular, the development of new staples, as well as the long-term depletion of minerals in soils, caused by the cultivation of crops like tobacco, along with the spread of disease in some crops, led to mass migration of owners and enslaved populations towards the west, different (often, we can assume, differing) varieties must inevitably have been mixed in everyday communication. This in itself led to dialect levelling (see Chapter 6) and the spread of presumed creole-like features into virgin territory. By 1860 at least, a recognisably black form of English had developed which, while possessing some creole features, was essentially a mainstream dialect of English.

This is a believable narrative; it is very likely to be a fair representation of what actually happened during this period. Some nagging issues remain, however, not least in relation to the reason why this particular region's language form, born out of slavery, should be so un-creole in many ways. Given that many parts of the Deep South had (indeed, some still have) a majority African American population, why is the variety so unlike those produced in similar situations in, for example, the Caribbean? Mufwene's (2001) foregrounding of the founder principle as central to the survival of the earlier homestead varieties appears convincing. But many scholars connected to the uniformitarian school (as discussed in Chapter 3) would emphasise the similar forces at work in other slavery-induced varieties in which the modern realisation is much more 'creole' in nature. The distance between the 'more creole' and 'less creole' outcomes, discussed here and in Chapter 3, still needs to be recognised. The reasons for this gap have not yet been fully appreciated, never mind analysed.

4.5 Conclusion

Each of the situations discussed in this chapter is in many ways unique: in terms of location, speaker numbers, social environment and so on. They also have much in common, however. Each possesses features which resemble those found in the creoles discussed in Chapter 3. Other features, however, appear closer in nature to the mainstream dialects of that particular language. What has brought about this discrepancy?

It we follow the uniformitarian position analysed in Chapter 3, vernaculars of this kind represent language types which have not gone so far in developing a creole-like basilect, instead remaining close enough to the 'mainstream' for that language to be treated under most circumstances as a somewhat eccentric member of the 'inner circle'. They therefore represent the 'missing link' in the uniformitarian model. This view is attractive when we consider that the linguistic distinctions between the Pitkern and Norf'k vernaculars and, for example, Jamaican dialect or the creole French of Réunion are not at all great (some scholars would claim that these differences are not truly meaningful).

But there are issues with a complete acceptance of this viewpoint as the only possible explanation for these varieties' development. Could it be argued, for instance, that individual or group decisions among speakers of these creole-like varieties really did forge closer links to the mainstream of a particular language than was the case where undoubted creoles developed? This can be readily seen in the development of the Englishes of Pitcairn Island and St Helena. In the former, Standard English, while the native code of few of the original settlers, was revered, in particular because of its connection to scripture; with St Helena, the connections forged across the community in the hard times through which the island passed regularly, particularly fruitful after the emancipation of enslaved people across the British Empire in 1833, encouraged the development of something like a koine, as discussed further in Chapter 6. As we will see, it is much more difficult to make an argument of this type for AAVE. Unlike the other varieties discussed in this chapter, AAVE is (and was) spoken by a large population whose experience, while similar in some ways to speakers of both semi-creoles and creoles, was highly discrete in relation to work, geographical location and a range of other features. Koineisation events are nevertheless likely to have been commonplace in situations in which large-scale population movements and mixing were a regular part of life.

Would it be possible to see the origins and development of the varieties discussed in this chapter as representing a discrete type? Could something like a small-scale creolisation have taken place within a community? For whatever reason, including perhaps those mentioned earlier, these micro-creolisation events did not produce a variety which survived long as a separate unit. Some of its features bled into the less radical local varieties which were also coming into being at the same time, however. Considering the evidence discussed, this type of event – or series of events – would have been more likely to have happened with St Helenian Vernacular English, Afrikaans or AAVE than with Pitkern, where something like an unstable pidgin at the heart of the community in the first generation of settlement may have provided the unexpected, creole-like features in the later, stable local vernacular.

Exercises

1. Does what we know about semi-creoles affect the way we approach the origins and development of creoles proper?

2. Research what we know about other semi-creoles not mentioned in this chapter. You might want to look at Singlish (the local vernacular form of English spoken in Singapore and surrounding areas), Brazilian Vernacular Portuguese or the varieties of vernacular Spanish spoken in the Caribbean area.

- How different are any of these from varieties normally designated as creole, such as those spoken on Réunion (discussed in Chapter 3)?
- How different are the semi-creoles you have researched from 'mainstream' dialects of their lexifier languages?

Suggested Reading

Holm (2004) is a highly effective treatment of semi-creoles. Many of the works recommended at the end of Chapter 3 would also be useful, in particular, perhaps, those that favour the uniformitarian view.

5 Macro-convergence

Introduction

In this chapter we will take a focussed look at the results of contact between languages which are at most distantly related, and often completely unrelated. We will consider these contacts at a relatively intimate level, before looking at **language areas**, large-scale regions where different languages become more like each other over long periods. Finally, we will look at a number of issues connected to a 'genetic' view of language relationships, paying particular attention to the 'Altaic' languages.

5.1 The Convergence of Distantly Related or Unrelated Languages

Linguistic variation and linguistic change are universal and perpetual. But not all change involves divergence from other varieties, even though this has been the primary concern of most historical linguists since the inception of that discipline. Sometimes languages converge. On occasion this can happen between near relatives, as occurred in the development of Fiji Hindi, which we will consider in Chapter 6. But on other occasions, languages which are not close to each other can also converge in usage. The language use patterns observed in Kupwar, a village in south-central India, offer a striking example (the classic description is Gumperz and Wilson 1971; Hock 1991: 502–4 presents a particularly clear discussion of the evidence).

Kupwar lies on the boundary in South Asia between areas where the Dravidian languages (such as Tamil and Malayalam) are spoken by most people and those where the Indo-European Indic languages (such as Hindi and Gujarati) are spoken by the majority (see Map 5.1). This borderline reality is reflected in the presence of speakers of Marathi (an Indo-European language) and Kannada and Telugu (both Dravidian languages) within the village. Strikingly, speakers of the different languages come from different caste and religious backgrounds. Marathi is spoken by landless labourers and 'untouchables', Telugu by low-status Hindu ropemakers, Kannada by Jain landholders and fairly high-status Hindu artisans, but they interact on a daily basis. Speakers of Urdu, also an Indo-European variety, but associated with the Delhi area and the greater Gangetic plain of northern India, is also spoken by a considerable number of Muslim metal workers, whose ancestors had come to the village several centuries before the research was carried out.

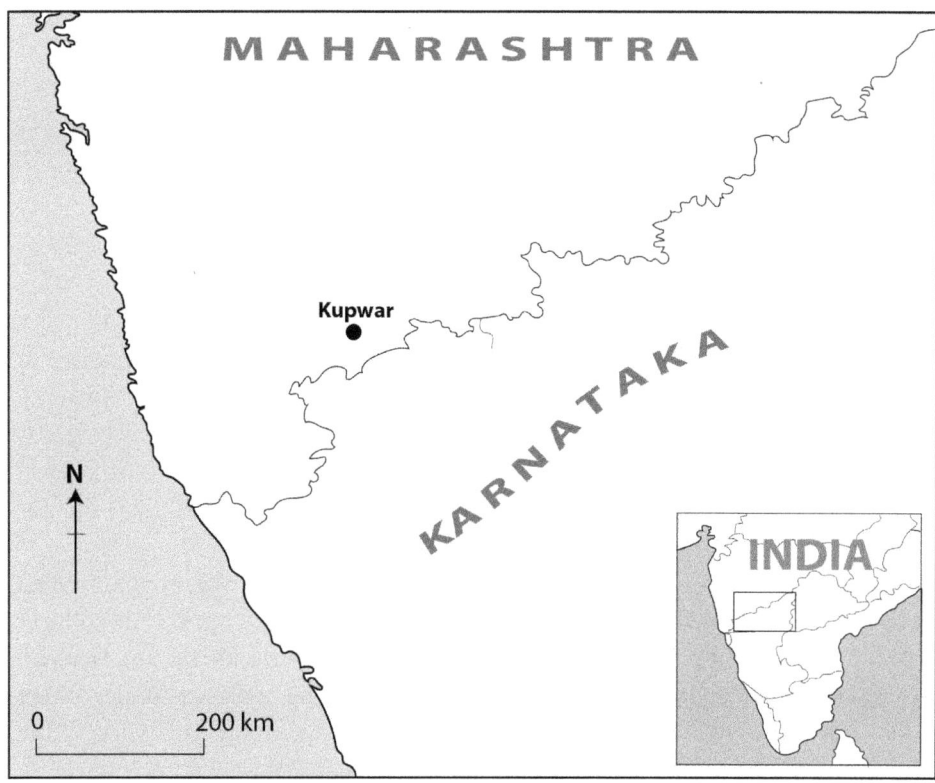

Map 5.1 Kupwar, a village in south-central India, and its environs.

Table 5.1 Morphosyntactic similarities in Kupwar Urdu, Marathi and Kannada

URDU	pala	jəra	kat	ke	le	ke	a	–	yə
MARATHI	pala	jəra	kap	un	ghe	un	a	l	o
KANNADA	tapala	jəra	khod	i	təgond	i	bə	–	yn
	greens	some	cut	Abs.	take	Abs.	come	TA	

'Having cut some greens, having taken (them), I came'
= 'I cut some greens and brought them'[a]–

[a] For a recent treatment, see Hock and Joseph (2019: 347–8).

Although related, Marathi and Urdu are not mutually comprehensible, beyond an awareness of shared roots; inevitably, no mutual comprehension is possible between either of those languages and Kannada (or, indeed, Telugu, which does not feature in this particular discussion). In Kupwar, an unexpected linguistic phenomenon regularly occurs, however. Similar morphosyntactic structures can be found in the three local languages, as illustrated in Table 5.1.

This convergence is confined, as far as we can tell, to the village; in other places in the same territories the three languages have entirely discrete ways of producing the meaning underlying the structure. It should be noted that the

Table 5.2 Inflectional morphemes in Greek, Fertek Greek and Turkish

	GREEK	FERTEK GREEK	TURKISH
'wife'	yinék-a	nék-a	kadın
'wives'	yinék-es	nék-es	kadın-lar
'of the wife'	yinék-as	nék-a-yu	kadın-ın
'of the wives'	yinék-on	nék-es-yu	kadın-lar-ın

linguistic convergence in Kupwar does not generally involve the borrowing of words; instead, it is a common concept and order of elements which appear to have developed between the languages. Considerable multilingualism must exist, but social barriers of various sorts prohibit the movement of lexical items from language to language – particularly, perhaps, when they do not serve a grammatical function.

At a more focussed level, these phenomena can be seen in the ways in which Turkish affected Fertek Greek, formerly spoken in Cappadocia in central Anatolia, in Table 5.2 illustrated by Dawkins (1916), as reported by Matras (2013: 76). Here we have evidence for an originally fusional typology being replaced, under direct Turkish influence, by an agglutinative one (although, as with the discussion of the Turkic influence on Armenian described in Chapter 1, it is the conceptual framework which is borrowed, not the actual morphology). Long-term contact at the very least encourages linguistic convergence.

5.2 Divergence and the Linguistic Family Tree Model

Historical linguistics, the study of language change, derives from the late eighteenth-century intellectual ferment related to the pursuit of sources (and of 'genuineness'), originally grounded in central and northern Europe. English speakers often highlight the fact that the scientific 'discovery' of what we now know as the Indo-European languages derives from observations by a (senior) servant of the East India Company; this may be an overstatement, however. The German-speaking lands (and before them, arguably, the territories of the Danish Crown) were at the heart of moving from the piecemeal observation of similarities between disparate languages, modern and ancient, to a full understanding of the *mechanisms* of change. Evolutionary biology (and, later, genetics), along with textual criticism of ancient – to begin with, biblical – texts, was at the heart of these intellectual developments. There was considerable cross-pollination between these fields and ours, with scholars like Jacob Grimm (1785–1863) being both a philologist (in relation, but not confined, to the folk tale collection and analysis he and his brother carried out) and an historical linguist. The systematic analysis these fields provided to each other is undoubtedly the primary strength of each.

As Darwinian evolutionary theory became the bedrock for many branches of science (as well as, with sometimes less positive results, politics, sociology and economics), the dominant model of evolution through descent began to preside over the thinking behind the study of historical language change as well. Historical linguists, such as the *Junggrammatiker* 'Neogrammarians' of the middle and later nineteenth century, saw change as being essentially a steady (some might say mechanical, even mechanistic) development away from a single parent, with mutual disparity of linguistic usage based upon scientific rule-driven principles eventually creating systems which were mutually unintelligible. While language contact had to be acknowledged, this was generally approached as being lexical in nature; it was even treated with contempt. Pidgins and creoles, for instance, were regularly viewed through racist attitudes, as were *Mischsprachen* 'mixed languages', such as, in their interpretation, English (*misch-* and its compounds were and are highly loaded and contentious semantically). In other words, the sub-Darwinian approach they espoused was perceived as the absolute norm; any evidence which suggested different models of interpretation was often ignored or treated as an aberration.

Of course, there is a great deal to be said for the central precepts of neogrammarian theory and practice. I use it regularly in my teaching and work. But there are also severe flaws inherent in the approach in relation to the dirty reality of language change. It is a convenient myth. An analogy to this can be found in physics. For over two centuries, Newtonian theories were preeminent in relation to our understanding of the nature of the universe. Einsteinian physics proved that a range of Newton's ideas are faulty. Nevertheless, the latter are still regularly used, particularly in more general and less advanced discussion, such as in school classrooms, because they describe our terrestrial reality well and are straightforward to interpret.

Unlike the natural evolution of at least the 'higher' species (as it turns out, most), languages do not have the two sources of DNA necessary for fully fledged variation of characteristics present in their offspring (extreme cases such as Michif, discussed in Chapter 1, being very rare indeed), instead relying on a single source. Moreover, dialect continua bring into doubt the idea of the neat separation of offspring characteristics proposed by the Darwinian model.

One of the greatest of these issues relates to the often profound effects linguistic contact has had and has on language development. It might be argued, in fact, that linguistic change, if it *is* of an evolutionary nature, is actually closer to Lamarckian theories of evolution (for a critique, see Goldman 2021: chap. 3), where experience within their lifetime by parents can affect their offspring, rather than Darwinian, where change is essentially random and unconscious. Thus, as well as a particular language demonstrating descent from its ancestors, it also carries with it the material it has derived through contact both in the present and in the past (often the distant past).

The Germanic subfamily can be analysed as an example of both the great insights and the drawbacks produced by an adherence to this inherently genetic view of linguistic change (see Figure 5.1). Several of these languages have had written witness for a considerable period, with some, such as Gothic, being recorded from

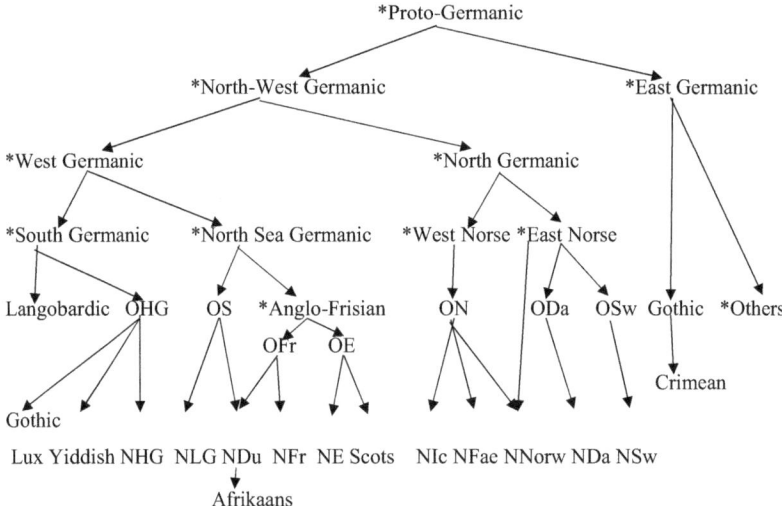

Figure 5.1 A simplified 'family tree' (*Stammbaum*) of the Germanic subfamily.

the fourth century on and German and English from the seventh (there are also runic inscriptions dating from at least the fifth century, representing something close to a variety we will discuss in greater depth shortly). By the time these records were available, a sundering between varieties had taken place, albeit with some varieties appearing closer to each other than other varieties.

Thus German and English bear considerable similarities when first recorded, while Gothic appears to have already travelled a considerable distance along its own path of development, even when it is first recorded. When we bring in the first recorded versions of other Germanic varieties (Old Saxon, the ancestor of Modern Low German, recorded from the eighth century, the ancestor of the modern North Germanic languages, from around the same time in runes and from the eleventh century in Roman script, and Dutch and Frisian in the course of the Middle Ages), we can begin to produce a description of descent – a *Stammbaum* or family tree – of the Germanic subfamily of Indo-European.

East Germanic, the only member of which for which we have a considerable corpus being Gothic, appears to have split from the other Germanic varieties at a relatively early date. This analysis is based upon the fact that it does not realise (and, indeed, could not have developed) a range of features central to the other varieties, such as *Umlaut* (otherwise known as *i-mutation*).

Most historical linguists would then posit a variety termed Proto-North-West Germanic, a form of which might be represented in some of the earliest runic inscriptions (although the ways in which the runes were produced, the materials employed and the very development of the craft of rune-making itself make a straightforward equation of spoken language and written representation problematical). Sometime in the early Christian centuries, this united language, we posit, split into two parts – West Germanic and North Germanic – through diverging phonologies and structural features. Some mutual intelligibility was likely to have continued for some time afterwards, however, in particular between the ancestors of English and Danish, which appear to have been spoken in close geographical proximity in what is now Schleswig in Germany and Jutland in Denmark, before the English infiltration of Britain began in earnest as Roman power and authority collapsed on that island.

From at least the ninth century, the North Germanic varieties divided into West Norse and East Norse varieties, with the former being somewhat more conservative than the latter at all linguistic levels. Uncontroversially, West Norse varieties include Faeroese and Icelandic; the Norse dialect of Greenland, which disappeared in the late Middle Ages, and the Norn dialects of Orkney and Shetland, whose last native speakers lived in the eighteenth century (for further discussion, see Chapter 2), were also members of this grouping. Modern East Norse varieties include Swedish and Danish; the traditional dialects of Gotland, the long island in the eastern Baltic basin, can be analysed as a separate member of this grouping (albeit now dialectalised under Standard Swedish). But the status of Norwegian within this analytical structure is problematical.

The most common genetic analysis of the West Germanic languages is that, from early on, a split developed between the North Sea Germanic languages – including English and Frisian and, at least to some extent, also Dutch and Low German – and High German varieties, which some scholars would analyse as a discrete subgrouping, often termed *South Germanic*. There are issues in the analysis of the ancestral connections of most of the Continental West Germanic languages, however.

These 'genetic' delineations are useful mnemonics with considerable grounding in the historical linguistic reality. They cannot explain everything, however. Modern Norwegian, for instance, stands as a halfway house between West Norse and East Norse (see Map 6.3). The western dialects of the language, reflected particularly in the Nynorsk standard variety of Norwegian, are phonologically West Norse (for instance, in their preservation of the diphthong in *haust* 'autumn', in comparison to the monophthong in Danish (and East Norwegian) *høst*); their morphosyntactic structures are often more conservative in their usage than those found in eastern Norwegian, Danish and Swedish. Nevertheless, they are undoubtedly structurally closer to these East Norse varieties than they are to unquestionably West Norse varieties, such as Faeroese or Icelandic. Grammatical case, for instance, so strongly preserved in the insular West Norse languages, is vestigial in all but a small and unrepresentative set of Norwegian dialects. This can be analysed in two ways (although the proposed processes are probably interconnected). Either what we see in Norwegian represents the remnants of a dialect continuum between supposedly polar West Norse and East Norse groupings (thereby questioning the earlier absolute split between them) or East Norse developments gradually infiltrating originally West Norse varieties (thereby foregrounding change in affiliation due to contact-induced spread). Both interpretations are, in fact, likely to be correct.

With the Continental West Germanic languages, dialectological analyses also undermine many of the postulated genetic splits. On the ground, at least before mass literacy in standard varieties became the norm by the end of the nineteenth century, a dialect continuum existed in all the varieties spoken between Switzerland and the lowlands of the Netherlands and northern Germany (this analysis ignores Frisian in its various forms, where a separate ancestry is indicated, although all Frisian dialects have partaken to some extent in the changes which have passed through this continuum). Indeed, those features which *do* mark off the modern Middle and Upper German dialects (most notably the Second Germanic Consonant Shift – compare the final consonant in Modern English *book* /k/, Modern Dutch *boek* /k/ and Modern High German *Buch* /x/) have a striking geographical distribution which suggests that they developed in the first instance in the southern dialects. The Swiss German varieties, for instance, appear to have taken these changes to their logical conclusion in all positions, while their use is increasingly constrained the farther north the dialects are spoken; the complexity of the 'Rhenish Fan', where Low and High German features are found in the same dialect, normally in an ordered, rather than random, manner, also has to be borne in mind. This diffusion can be analysed as a form of dialect contact leading to the production of new dialects with new alignments.

Focussing on Modern Dutch in particular, it may be possible to analyse the apparent anomalies in its phonological system in particular as being a result of linguistic contact. At heart, Dutch is a Low Frankish variety, closely related to other Frankish dialects, including Luxembourgish. Features of the language cannot be readily analysed as being of Frankish origin, however. Some appear closer to the Saxon dialects spoken across northern Germany and in the eastern Netherlands. Others appear closer to Frisian usage. It could be argued, in fact, that modern Standard Dutch (and its close relatives in the Hollands, Zeeland and Brabant) is a contact variety, possibly representing a new dialect (or dialects) created by the settlement of the new lands produced by reclamation for agriculture of the sea bottom from the early Middle Ages on.

Thus contact can sometimes confound descent.

5.3 Convergence as a Countervailing Force in Linguistic Change: The Balkan Language Area

It can therefore be claimed that linguistic contact in a variety of forms presents an alternative mode for analysing change which acts as a counterbalance to the idea of genetic development. This becomes even more pertinent when we turn to the development of Germanic languages like English, Afrikaans or Yiddish, where contact has played a particularly powerful role in their development.

From this evidence we can observe that not all features a particular language has can reasonably be analysed as descending from its 'parent'. Often the language's geographical neighbours, no matter their own parentage, seem to have more in common with each other than with their ancestors. What this actually means is a point to which we will return shortly. In the meantime, however, let us consider a relatively straightforward set of examples of this type of diffusion of common features. Campbell and Poser (2008: chap. 10) are cautious to the point of scepticism about convergence. But while the points they make against, for instance, Dixon's (1997) *punctuated equilibrium model* carry weight, the evidence presented in this chapter does suggest that contact-based convergence is a regular linguistic development. No argument is being made that *all* features within a language are affected by usage in another language; some features *are*, however.

Multiple coalescences across linguistic boundaries can be seen as *areal features*; if a sufficient number of these occur in the same essential area, we can speak about a *Sprachbund*, a 'linguistic union/area' (although, as we will see, what a bald assertion like this actually means is open to considerable discussion). We will turn now to the most famous of these phenomena.

Most early historical linguists spoke western and central European languages and considered them 'normal'. Inevitably, the first apparently 'unusual' group of these language areas to be considered in a systematic way was located nearby in southeastern Europe: the *balkanische Sprachbund* – the Balkan Language Area (see Map 5.2)

Map 5.2 The Balkan Language Area: major languages involved.

Given its mountainous nature, it is unsurprising that this region is linguistically diverse. Languages with a considerable number of speakers, such as Greek, Albanian, Bulgarian and Macedonian, Serbian, Turkish (historically spoken throughout the Balkans and still the language of a sizeable minority in Bulgaria and parts of Greece) and Romanian, predominate now as languages of state. Other varieties, such as Arumanian (sometimes termed Vlach, historically spoken in different dialects across the 'neck' of the Balkans; now spoken by lesser numbers there and in exile communities in Romania and elsewhere) and Romani, were and are spoken in patches across the region (Carmichael 2000). Jewish varieties of Spanish were also spoken in pockets in urban areas, such as what is now Thessaloniki, until the Second World War.

But this diversity is matched by the similarities found between modern versions of these languages spoken in the Balkans, even though many of them are, at most, distantly related. These similarities can be schematised in the following way (here derived primarily from Thomason 2001: 105–9, although with my own commentary; a more in-depth and critical analysis can be found in Friedman and Joseph 2017):

1. The dative and genitive cases are identical in form (Albanian, Romanian, Bulgarian/Macedonian and Greek). Slavonic languages normally distinguish these; the Balkan Romance languages are the only Romance varieties which have retained (or possibly developed) grammatical case marking at all (an in-depth discussion of the morphosyntactic features of the area can be found in Mišeska Tomić 2006).
2. Future tense employs auxiliary use of the verb 'want' (Romanian, southern Albanian, Serbian, Bulgarian/Macedonian and Greek). Future marking in neighbouring or related languages is derived from 'have' instead, or they have no explicit future marking (coincidentally, English *will* also originally expressed volition before becoming a future marker; close relatives, like German and Dutch, use the verb *werden* 'become' as an auxiliary in the same contexts).
3. There is a postposed definite particle (Romanian, Albanian and Bulgarian/Macedonian). The morphemes employed are different in all the languages; they are derived largely from the pronoun system of the individual languages). Postposed article use occurs nowhere else in Europe, except in Basque and in the Scandinavian languages. Greek also has a definer, but it is preposed in a similar way to English (it is also of considerable antiquity); Turkish expresses the category of definiteness using different 'building blocks'.
4. Infinitive structures have been lost or are only employed in particularly marked contexts. 'I want to go' is literally 'I want that I go' (Serbian, Bulgarian/Macedonian and Greek; to some extent Albanian and Romanian). This change is practically unknown elsewhere in Europe. Older Greek varieties used an infinitive in these contexts.
5. The adjectival comparative is formed analytically ('more short') rather than synthetically ('shorter') (Albanian, Romanian, Bulgarian/Macedonian, Greek and Turkish). Other Romance languages employ this type of structure (as does,

to a degree, English: the standard variety does not allow synthetic *-er* in words of more than two syllables).
6. A direct or indirect object can or must be preceded by a particle marking it as an object (Albanian, Romanian, Bulgarian/Macedonian and Greek). This is rare elsewhere in Europe (although a similar feature is found in Afrikaans, in a departure from mainstream Dutch practice).
7. A distinction is made between reporting events witnessed by the speaker and those passed on from a second hand source (Albanian, Bulgarian/Macedonian and Turkish; to some extent Romanian). This is unknown elsewhere in Europe.
8. The numerals from 11 to 19 are constructed along the lines of 'one upon ten'. This feature also occurs in some other Slavonic languages and in Hungarian.
9. A great deal of lexis is held in common. Turkish and Greek loans are numerous in the other languages; Romanian has been influenced lexically to a considerable extent by Slavonic.

When first confronted with this evidence, it is tempting to see the Balkan Language Area as constituting a single entity; the names that we often give it, *Sprachbund* or Language Union, following its early 'discoverers' and 'explorers', such as Kopitar (1829) and Trubetzkoy (1923, 1930), encourage this equation. Yet when we consider it in more detail, it becomes apparent that the 'Balkan' features observed are not universal within the area. Perhaps, rather than seeing the phenomenon as a 'union', it would be more realistic to use the term *convergence zone*. Within this part of Europe, for whatever reason, there is a general tendency for local languages to move towards each other in usage. The shared features, however, are unevenly spread among the varieties. Some analysts (such as Hock 1991: 492–8) have gone so far as to suggest that the spread of features here is similar to the spread of features across a dialect continuum and that we can draw isoglosses across the Balkans (and, indeed, beyond, historically) in a similar (although rather more complex) way to more 'normal' linguistic situations, despite the fact that we are dealing with what are ostensibly different languages. That these extensions are particularly noteworthy in the Balkans can be explained primarily by the history and geography of the area, rather than by any innate tendencies within the participating languages. Moreover, while several 'Balkan' features can be interpreted as examples of spread and borrowing, others appear to be the products of multilingual interference.

It is worth noting, in fact, that these convergence zones, while relatively common across the world, do not always appear as 'neat' as those found in the Balkans (themselves, as we have seen, not particularly seamless when analysed in depth). Underlying this view is acceptance that each of the features of the *Sprachbund* has come about because of the spread of individual (or groups of individual) features, rather than as part of an overarching process. If this is the case, however, the assumption has to be made that isoglosses can be drawn across language boundaries for which the possibility of mutual intelligibility is significantly more problematical than is the case between closely related varieties, such as Dutch and German. This is a point to which we will return on a number of occasions in the rest of this chapter.

5.4 Large-Scale Convergence: Beyond the *Sprachbund*

The Indo-European family works well as an example of how multiple languages can be demonstrated through comparison to be relatives of each other, with an orderly line of descent from the proto-language to its subfamilies and from them to individual languages (even if some lines of descent have been 'fixed' by scholars more than have others). These can be expressed, as we have seen, through the use of a *Stammbaum*, a family tree. The comparisons which underpin this type of analysis are helped in the case of Indo-European by the survival of documents written in earlier Indo-European dialects, going back on at least one occasion more than three thousand years. Through no conscious design (apart from the fact that many of the early historical linguists spoke an Indo-European language as their mother tongue), it was the history and development of this family that was first analysed in a scholarly manner. From these analyses it was assumed that all language relationships could (indeed, *should*) work in this way. While this is true for some language families (Semitic, with greater and deeper historical witness than Indo-European, springs to mind, as does Bantu, for which a comparative lack of historical witness is countered by great formal and conceptual similarity between its members), language relationships exist where the creation of a *Stammbaum* is not helpful. With some of these, it would be fair to say that what appears to be relationship is actually evidence for contact.

5.4.1 The Uralic Languages

Members of the Uralic family are spoken in north-eastern Europe and northern Siberia (as well as, with one language, in central Europe). It is a group of languages with limited historical attestation. With the exception of a few languages spoken in Europe which are considered part of this family, such as Hungarian, Finnish, Estonian and Mordva (spoken in areas near Moscow in the Russian Federation), most of the languages affiliated to this postulated family are spoken by groupings of a few thousand at most, most of whom until quite recently followed traditional ways of life involving herding, subsistence farming and gathering and hunting; most are now fluent in the official state variety, which is often Russian. Only Finnish and Hungarian have written histories reaching back more than a few hundred years (and even with these, the time depth involved is nowhere near as deep as with Indo-European). The dangers of misassignment based on limited evidence are considerable, therefore.

The traditional means of describing the descent of the Uralic languages (following Marcantonio 2002: 2 – as we will see shortly, many of Marcantonio's ideas cannot be supported; her discussions of others' views are often insightful, however) is that Uralic is made up of two major subfamilies: Samoyedic and Finno-Ugric. Within the latter grouping, the Ugric languages are distinguished from the Finnic. The Ugric subgrouping is itself split as much by geography as by anything else, since Hungarian is, of course, spoken in central Europe (and has been for more than a thousand years), while its proposed sister languages, including Khanty (otherwise, Ostyak) and Mansi (otherwise, Vogul), are spoken in the river valleys of north-central Siberia. Within the Finnic languages, most scholars would distinguish a Baltic Finnic (or Balto-Finnic) group, containing Finnish, Estonian, Karelian, Vepsian, Livonian and a range of relatively small-scale varieties spoken in the north-eastern Baltic zone (the relationship of the Sámi dialects to Baltic Finnic is contested, although most scholars believe that, at the very least, Sámi is more closely related to Baltic Finnic than to any other Finnic groupings). The Finnic languages spoken along the upper Volga and in the Permian region of the Ural Mountains are also often considered subfamilies, although the precise membership of each group differs from scholar to scholar. Similar phenomena are perceptible for the much better attested Indo-European languages.

There are, however, issues with employing the family tree model in relation to the proposed family. The connections proposed between Magyar and the other Ugric languages are not overwhelming, even if we accept the considerable time depth of the split between the Ob-Ugric languages and their western cousin (often dated by scholars, such as Abondolo 1998a: 6 and Honti 1998: 327, as approaching around three thousand years ago). Moreover, some scholars (e.g. Viitso 1997) would be happier representing something like a family where Finnic and Ugric are not truly differentiated subfamilies, with Hungarian and the Ob-Ugric languages being classified as somewhat distantly related members of a much larger family. Even within the Baltic Finnic languages, in fact, as Laakso (2001: 204–5) suggests, basing her analysis in part on that of Salminen (1998), the family tree model does not represent well the level of contact and mutual influence found between different dialects, often repeatedly, within their development.

Abondolo (1998a) and Honti (1998) suggest that Hungarian and the Ob-Ugric languages do not seem as 'Uralic' as their presumed relatives but suggest that this in fact provides evidence for their originally lying at the innovative core, a concept which itself is at the very least dubious as a theoretical position. Languages at the centre of a family *do* often innovate, but this need not be the case, as appears to be true when comparing German with English or Lithuanian with the other Baltic Indo-European languages (or, indeed, Lithuanian in relation to Indo-European as a whole). Nevertheless, to most scholars, Hungarian should be analysed as being a distant relative of Finnish (however the Finno-Ugric family is defined) which was powerfully influenced by Turkic languages (the Magyars first appear in historical documents as part of a large Turkic confederation based on the lower Volga); a far smaller number of scholars (most notably Marcantonio 2002) take the opposing view, that Hungarian is a Turkic language which was to a degree influenced by Finnic languages far back in its history. In connection to the historiography, the relations between Hungary and the Ottoman Empire in the early modern period may have affected the ways in which these connections were and are analysed, since inhabitants of the central Danube region tended to see themselves as 'defenders of western (in other words, Christian) civilisation'. Inevitably, Marcantonio's view is highly controversial and is generally considered indefensible from a linguistic viewpoint. A far less controversial discussion of strong Turkic influence over the Finnic languages spoken around the Volga Bend can be found in Bereczki (1993).

Given that its primary Finno-Ugric prop is less than solid as a binary unit (although, as we have seen, there is an overwhelming consensus that the subfamily exists), it is unsurprising that Uralic as a whole can be questioned, at least in terms of the relationships represented by the traditional *Stammbaum*. It appears, in fact, that, while the Samoyedic languages, spoken by small groups across a large part of northern Eurasia, do seem related, the changes that have influenced some varieties but not others of that subfamily appear at times to have influenced other languages spoken nearby, including a number of Altaic varieties, Yukaghir languages and members of the Ob-Ugric grouping. As with the Balkan Language Area, but over much broader geographical space and time, it may be that what we have is a convergence zone with isoglosses crossing the territories involved, no matter the apparent origin of the language.

Nevertheless, most scholars would recognise Uralic as a genuine language family, with, like Indo-European, the reconstruction of a proto-language being possible (even if, as has been suggested, some convergence zone features need to be fed into the historical mix). But this coexistence of a *Stammbaum*-type family descent and areal diffusion is much more difficult to carry out with the Altaic languages.

5.4.2 The Altaic Languages

The Turkic languages are undoubtedly related. Indeed, for a set of languages spoken across a wide swathe of Eurasia, it is remarkable how similar they are (when we compare that similarity with the level of dissimilarity between the Germanic languages, for instance, historically spoken in a much smaller region): agglutinative in typology, for instance, with most languages realising similar subtle forms of vowel harmony. Turkic languages have been recorded, off and on, for more than a thousand years, and, largely due to records kept in China, we can place the earliest territories occupied by speakers of these languages to the (north-)west and southwest of the Han Chinese territories (for a potentially contentious discussion of this settlement, see Robbeets and Savelyev 2020). Speakers of these languages became involved in Eastern Europe during and following the collapse of Roman power along the Danube. Later Turkic-using states on the Eurasian steppe, such as the Khazars, were commented upon by Muslim writers; their languages and cultures strongly influenced the development of polities in the eastern Slav lands. While some details of exact relationship can be (and are) debated, a classical *Stammbaum* is straightforward to produce.

From the nineteenth century on, scholars have attempted to connect this family with others from central Asia, a grouping perceived (and conceived of) as the Altaic languages. Most linguists would analyse this group as including the Mongol languages and the Tungusic languages of south-eastern Siberia and Manchuria (the most famous of which being the now essentially moribund Manchu language; Evenki is probably the most discussed Tungusic language surviving to the present day). Many linguists are convinced that Altaic is a language family in the way Indo-European is (see, e.g., Robbeets 2005, 2015). Equally qualified scholars contest this idea fiercely, however (see, e.g., Vovin 2005). The latter group claim that, while, with Indo-European, common function words, such as verbs like *have* or *be*, or numerals, are found in many, if not most, of the daughter languages, this is not so obvious with Altaic, where the words in common tend to be primarily lexical rather than functional in nature (although this is partly questioned by the material in Robbeets 2015).

Some linguists would include Japanese and Korean in this family, although this is hotly contested (for a recent discussion, see Vovin 2017). The naivety of many attempts at connecting Japanese to anything beyond, possibly, Korean (an early and particularly egregious example of which being Miller 1980) is exemplified and analysed throughout Vovin's analysis; other scholars take a more optimistic view, as demonstrated by Robbeets (2017). What is striking throughout many of these discussions, at least from the point of view of someone working on Indo-European languages, is how much is made of so little evidence. Many – but not all – contributors to Robbeets and Savelyev (2020) appear to take the genetic connection between Japanese, Korean and Altaic as a given, almost if it were an act of faith. It is interesting that throughout the connection, *Altaic* as a term and a construct is largely replaced by *Transeurasian*, a super-construct based upon conflicting views on the precise analysis of relationship within Altaic. The fact that the link is suggested at all might encourage us to question the stability of the Altaic construct as a whole.

A recent treatment (Ceolin 2019) tends towards the view that an overarching Altaic construct cannot be supported by the evidence. The papers contained in Robbeets and Savilyev (2020) underline this. Some, such as Robbeets (2020a, 2020b, 2020c), appear to assume that the construct is proven, while others, such as Vajda (2020) and Brown (2020), see the Transeurasian 'family' as a product of diffusion (all of these studies base their findings on radical redevelopments of lexicostatistic ideas, a reliance which does not immediately inspire confidence in their findings). Any family resemblances do appear primarily connected more with contact than with shared descent (evidence for how intimate the contact between these varieties is can be found in the discussion of morphological transfer from Mongolic into Tungusic languages in Anderson 2020: 720–21). It is certainly a definite possibility that the languages presently identified as Altaic were actually formed in a large contact and convergence zone in central Asia over centuries, if not millennia. Apparently cognate forms actually represent transfer during lengthy and intense convergence rather than genetic relationship. Thus a Lamarckian set of evolutionary relationships seems to trump a Darwinian model of language relationship and descent, at least on this occasion.

An interesting side issue follows on from this. Even with the languages in which the *Stammbaum* model works, can we rule out contact underlying some of the relationships portrayed?

Case Study 5   'Standard Average European'

Many examples of linguistic convergence have been suggested. Most of these are found in areas less well known to speakers of major European languages, areas which many 'cosmopolitan' observers might consider 'exotic'. To bring home how common they are, however, the following will focus on potential convergences which coalesce in western and central Europe.

Having an overt expression of definite and indefinite contexts in the noun phrase (compare *I drank beer*, *I drank a beer* and *I drank the beer*) is central to the semantic structures of languages originating in Western Europe, along with several languages based in northern, central and southern parts of that continent, for instance, Italian *la casa*, English *the house,* Norwegian *huset* (with postposed definite particle). Many – perhaps most – languages spoken today do not have this feature, although they can, of course, express definite and indefinite meaning. They do so in different ways, however, often connected to the use of grammatical case and other structural features, as with Finnish (Chesterman 1991) or Russian (Leinonen 1982; Friedrich 2009), or through the employment of specific element order patterns. In Europe, in simplified terms, a line can be drawn across the continent between the Germanic and Romance languages, which have definers, and the Finno-Ugric and Slavonic languages, which do not (with the exception of Bulgarian and Macedonian, part of, as we have seen, the Balkan Language Area, and Sorbian, which has been heavily influenced by German).

This appears to suggest differences passed down through the linguistic family tree. The truth is more complex than this. With almost all of these definer-realising languages, there was a time when their ancestors did not have determiners. This is most readily observable with the Romance languages: all the modern languages of that family possess overt determiner function, but their ancestor, Latin, did not.

What can we make of these patterns? The default position might be that there is nothing unusual about this geographical distribution at all. As has already been pointed out, all human languages express definiteness, but the means by which they do so differ. Inevitably, the realisation of discrete definers is one of the ways in which this category can be expressed. From this viewpoint, the fact that this structure appears to cluster geographically is interesting but cannot be explained.

This type of 'explanation' is not helpful for a number of reasons. Would it be possible to say that what the evidence for the employment of this feature actually demonstrates is that, rather than genetic descent, mutual influence has certainly taken place among closely related varieties as a form of diffusion? But the changes also occurred between languages which were often at least not close relatives, if related at all, as the result of long-term bilingualism, in particular in frontier zones. Thus the concept of determiner-based expression of definiteness must have been particularly foregrounded across previously impervious barriers, often due to the presence of bilinguals who carried some degree of societal status.

It is likely that this change took place (at least in relation to these transfers) during the late Roman era and the period following, when ethnic, cultural and linguistic identities were particularly fluid. This influence appears to have left some evidence of how article function spread, largely because German has not completely formally separated demonstrative and definer function (*der Mann* can mean both 'the man' and 'that man', while English separates these functions by using the discrete forms *the* and *that*), suggesting that the phenomenon, having developed elsewhere, had begun to lose impetus there. Where the impetus for these developments began and how the feature spread are not the concern of this discussion. Apparent diffusion of features between languages in this part of Europe is not confined to this phenomenon, however.

Merger of Present Perfect and Simple Past

In a somewhat more circumscribed part of the same region, both Romance and Germanic varieties are jettisoning (or have jettisoned) the expression through inflectional morphology of the distinction between simple (habitual) and perfect past (English *I ate* as compared to *I have eaten*), with the latter periphrastic form being favoured. The distinction between completed and habitual action is instead generally supplied by context or the use of adverbials rather than morphological realisation. In Standard French, German and Dutch, this change is obscured by prescriptive insistence on the historical norms; in written varieties with less historical 'baggage' associated with the region, such as Luxembourgish or Wallon (the Gallo-Romance vernacular traditionally spoken in large parts of what is now southern Belgium), where the written tradition is less historically based, the new spoken reality is represented in writing. Thus where Standard German would make a distinction between *ich habe gegessen* 'I have eaten' and *ich aß* 'I ate', Luxembourgish has *ech hun giess* for both. This apparent coalescence is also present in Afrikaans, whose ancestor is derived from nonstandard Dutch varieties, in particular exported from the Hollands and Zeeland, transported from the Netherlands to southern Africa, as discussed in Chapter 4. This may give a sense of the historical depth of the development; alternatively, its presence in both Africa and the Netherlands may be an example of drift.

'Death' of the Genitive Case

Most of the Germanic languages (with the exception of English, which is untypically conservative in this matter, and Icelandic) seem to be losing, or have lost, the use of the genitive case as a means of expressing possession. Those languages which have retained a functioning grammatical case system (such as German or Faeroese) have replaced the genitive case with a circumlocution based upon a dative case construction and the use of a personal pronoun (in German, most famously, *Der Dativ ist dem Genitiv sein Tod* '[literally] the dative is to the genitive its death', a popular discussion of which can be found in Sick 2016). In languages where case is no longer an integral part of the language, such as Norwegian, constructions such as *Robert sitt hus* '[literally] Robert his house' or *huset til Robert* 'the house to Robert' are prevalent, although, unlike, say, in Luxembourgish, *Roberts hus* is still possible.

Similar changes towards prepositional usage took place early on in the development of the Romance languages, moving away from their ancestor, Latin; there is some evidence suggesting that at least some speakers of Scottish Gaelic are also moving away from genitive expression of possession towards the use of the dative case in those contexts (for discussion, see Cole 2015), so that we may well be witnessing the spread of a convergence zone feature.

Discussion

Although not exactly mapped onto each other, these geographical patterns can be analysed as representing a tendency within western and central Europe towards typological change in the same or similar ways by language varieties in close proximity, no matter their ancestry. The precise reasons for the changes involved are problematical to trace, however. Some of them may be centuries old, while others appear much more recent. It is quite possible, of course, that the nucleus of a language area always forms in such an apparently haphazard way.

5.5 Conclusion

In this chapter we have considered the effects of a range of linguistic contacts where the input varieties are not closely related, if they are related at all. We saw that quite profound changes came about through this type of contact, changes which almost inevitably affect the nature of the contact varieties, often bringing morphosyntactic material into harmony across linguistic differences which are considerable for those languages outside the contact zone.

We have viewed these phenomena in relatively small-scale contacts, such as those in Kupwar, where several languages (or some of their dialects) have come into contact over a considerable period and in a number of ways began to move towards each other in a language area. We have also considered the extent to which long-term contact at a larger scale may lead to confusion between 'genetic' relationship and 'close neighbourhood' relationship.

Contact between 'distant' language varieties is an absolute reality. The change caused by this contact can alter the nature of languages and their historical trajectories. Convergences lie at the heart of many of these events. Chapter 6 will discuss similar phenomena played out through the contact between much more closely related varieties.

Exercises

1. A number of convergence zones (otherwise, language areas) have been identified. Find out what you can about one of them. (Hint: the Caucasus is probably the best covered of these, but you need not confine yourself to this.)

2. To what extent can the scepticism expressed in this chapter towards the Altaic language family being a 'family', in the sense that Indo-European is, be applied to other language families?
3. Find out what scholars have said about, for instance, the Afro-Asiatic, Khoi-San or Austronesian language families. Could – or should – this agnosticism be applied to families such as Semitic (generally perceived as a subfamily of Afro-Asiatic) or even, despite what has been said, Indo-European, for which a traditional *Stammbaum* model is assumed and preferred?

Suggested Reading

In relation to areal linguistics, I recommend strongly the contributions to Hickey (2017), in particular the essay by Friedman and Joseph.

The works referenced in this chapter which deal with more specialised discussions are often much more approachable than might be expected. Sadly, much – but not all – of the material on the Uralic family is written in languages which are less well known than they should be, however.

6 Close Variety Convergence and Change

The Koine

Introduction

Most discussions of linguistic convergence are based on the evidence of interaction between at most distantly related languages. This is in many ways a reasonable starting point. When languages are not closely related to each other, the influence they have on each other and the products of this interaction are readily visible, particularly in relation to borrowing. It is much more straightforward to see this process when the distance between the inputs is considerable. But many examples of convergence through contact are not of this type. Closely related varieties also come into contact. On these occasions, it is the linguistic proximity of the varieties in contact which produces a particular result.

In this chapter we will consider the nature of close variety convergence and change. Focussing on the koine, a 'common denominator' dialect formed by contact between closely related varieties, we will see ways in which varieties of these types interact with each other, producing what might be seen as a simpler (or more straightforward) variety. Particular attention will be given to varieties which have developed in 'colonial' or extraterritorial contexts. Can we distinguish in these contexts between varieties brought into being through compromise between dialects of the same language and between closely related (but distinct) languages?

6.1 Closely Related Varieties and Convergence

While it is not always the case, closely related linguistic varieties tend to be found geographically near to, if not actually beside, each other. This makes sense, of course. Generally (at least historically), separation between varieties happens geographically. Before the advent of (relatively) rapid transport in the nineteenth century, with the development of a workable steam engine (and, at an individual level, the bicycle), it was physically difficult for people to move from one place to another. The cultural and linguistic nature of communities was, in the end, focussed on how far you could walk, to and fro, in a day, and potentially get up the next day and do so again. Obviously major physical barriers, such as mountains or significant expanses of water, made travel even more daunting. Over time, linguistic usage would begin to differ between places. Discrete dialects and, often, languages (the distinction between the two is not always straightforward) develop. It takes a long time before the awareness of linguistic kinship disappears entirely, however.

But the opposite is also true: closely related varieties may well begin to coalesce, partly or entirely. Largely socio-historical and sociolinguistic factors underlie this (for discussion, see Millar 2005). Primary to this process is the creation of *koines*, common, often somewhat 'rationalised' varieties.

6.2 Koineisation

There are several occasions when linguistic contact produces a degree of simplification. Chapters 3 and 4 discussed pidgins, creoles and semi-creoles, demonstrating what this simplification might mean in relation to how the language variety develops after contact. No matter how specific varieties develop, a continuum exists between those varieties which would normally be defined as full creoles and those which have creole-like appearance but where no apparent 'break' between the 'pre-creole' variety, the lexifier, and the variety has occurred.

In other words, as we have seen in Chapters 3 and 4, Afrikaans, while changed by the contacts between speakers of Dutch and other languages spoken in the Cape Colony in the seventeenth and eighteenth centuries, self-evidently remains a close relative of Dutch in a way that cannot be said for Sranan in relation to English (this view does not in any way downplay the thoroughgoing nature of many of the changes involved in the first language's development, which have moved it away from the Dutch 'mainstream'). It is possible to extend this 'diminishing cline of disruption' to include what are often referred to as koines, varieties of a language which demonstrate a degree of linguistic simplification or, to put it another way, 'rationalisation', in relation to earlier varieties.

6.2.1 Koine Glossa

The original *koine glossa* 'common language' was a variety of Greek spread by the armies of the Macedonian kings (in particular, Alexander the Great) and their successors in the second half of the fourth century BCE and perpetuated by the presence of Hellenistic kingdoms from Albania to Afghanistan for centuries afterwards (for in-depth discussion, see Horrocks 1997: 32-6). Before this extension, Greek was spoken (and written) in a range of divergent dialects within a relatively circumscribed space. Probably the most often read (and to a considerable degree the most prestigious) dialect, Attic, was associated with Athens and that city's precocious development of written discourse on politics, philosophy and history. Other written varieties appear to have been considered no less 'Greek' than Attic, however, despite the reality that literate speakers of these dialects would have been used to reading in the Athens variety, primarily because of availability. Attic, however, was a close relative of the Ionic dialects, spoken by a large population living in the

Aegean Islands and along a large swathe of the coasts of what is now western Turkey, connected with the thriving trade across the Persian Empire, of which it formed the westernmost part. Their combined geographic coverage was considerable.

Koine glossa was essentially a form of Attic carried to this new Greek world – to a new speaker population, often with a different mother tongue. But Attic has a few issues – grammatical and phonological – which make it rather less straightforward to learn and to follow. The related Ionic varieties have fewer of these issues (these apparent simplifications were often shared with other Greek varieties). Ionic forms were therefore selected (normally at most semi-consciously) within an essentially Attic framework as a means of aiding greater levels of comprehension among both native and non-native speakers of Greek.

In addition, all varieties of native speaker Greek presented a range of linguistic issues for non-native speakers. All had pitch accent, essentially a form of lexical tone, as found today in many languages of East and South-East Asia. For native speakers, of course, the system was not problematical (indeed, it is likely, as is the case with its Chinese equivalent, that it was a functionally useful system internally). Most languages spoken in the eastern Mediterranean basin and in south-west Asia at this time had no such feature; speakers of these languages would have found this feature difficult to follow and to learn. Inevitably, as *koine glossa* developed (and eventually became the primary form of both spoken and written Greek), features such as this were abandoned. It could be argued that the language lost out in terms of possessing more subtle forms of expression because of these changes (certainly linguistic conservatives have made this claim regularly ever since), but the language itself gained sociolinguistically to a considerable extent from them.

As we saw in Chapter 3, the word *simplification* has to be used guardedly when talking in linguistic terms, but certainly the *koine glossa* presented a more straightforward form of Greek which was nonetheless readily perceptible as of the same type as all other forms of the language. It is the ancestor of all modern Greek dialects, save for Tsakonian, spoken in the Peloponnese, which demonstrates at least some Doric ancestry (for a recent discussion, see Liosis 2014).

6.2.2 Modern Koines

Koine glossa is not the only koine recorded, naturally (indeed, it may not even be the earliest: the diverse populations of multilingual states like Babylon must inevitably have led to a degree of linguistic 'rationalisation' for the main use languages; for preliminary discussion, see Gzella 2021: chap. 3). Claims have been made for the language varieties spoken in capital cities and in major new settlements regularly having koine-like features (see, e.g., Kerswill and Williams 2000). Similar features can often be found in areas which had not previously been heavily settled (if at all), such as 'Fenland' in eastern England (as commented on by Britain in, among other places, his papers of 1997, 2014 and 2015), the French of Quebec (see Mougeon and Beniak 1994) or the Dutch *polders*, land reclaimed from the sea (Scholtmeijer 1999). But since the idea of simplification is regularly used in relation to the changes produced by **koineisation,** it is necessary to define the differences between koineisation and creolisation, bearing in mind that both have been associated with development through ease of learning and production. Siegel (1985: 358) suggests that 'koine formation involves continuity, in that speakers do not need to abandon their own linguistic varieties', while 'this is not so for pidgin and creole development'. Closer to the central distinction between the varieties is, as he states, that 'koine formation requires intimate and prolonged social interaction between speakers. We must assume that this is not so in pidgin and creole development, where contact is restricted.' He adds that koineisation is often a lengthy process, while pidgins and creoles come into being quickly 'from an immediate need for communication'.

This sounds clear-cut. But is it? Even avoiding the discussion over whether creole genesis is (necessarily) of the 'sudden' type suggested here (see Chapter 3), the assumption of absolute distinctions in terms of development between creoles proper, semi-creoles (or semi-reconstructed vernaculars) and koines is not fully tenable. As we have already discussed, something like a continuum must exist in these contexts. It is nonetheless important to stress Siegel's central theme: the length and intimacy of the contacts involved in koine development, along with, often, much more limited social differentiation between communities in the contact zone than would be the case in a slavery or post-slavery environment, *is* a feature which the development of koines appears to share with more 'mainstream' language change and evolution.

Koines are, in fact, essentially 'normally' developing varieties in which 'regularising' tendencies are more pronounced, and changes are more systemic, than would otherwise be the case. This is, of course, an important observation which we will discuss and analyse in more depth in the following, even if we have to accept that the apparent clear water created between 'koine' and 'mainstream' may not be as wide or as straightforward to navigate as might at first appear.

6.2.2.1 Fiji Hindi

Siegel's earlier work focussed particularly on Fiji, an archipelago in the South Pacific (see Map 3.1) where, for more than a century, there has been a large South Asian ethnolinguistic minority, descended from indentured servants brought to the islands through British imperial policy at the end of the nineteenth and beginning of the twentieth centuries. For a variety of reasons, the relationships between native Fijians and people of Indian descent have seldom, at least until recently, been entirely happy. Naturally, partly this is cultural: almost all 'native' Fijians are evangelical Christians, while the majority of the 'Indians' are Hindus and a sizeable minority are Muslims. There is a very real linguistic divide between the two parts of the populations, however. Most native Fijians speak the local Austronesian varieties, although knowledge of English, primarily but not entirely as a second language, is considerable. An overwhelming part of the South Asians native to Fiji speak Indic Indo-European languages, derived largely from varieties

Map 6.1 The Gangetic dialect continuum.

spoken 'at home' from the Punjab down through the Gangetic plain to that river's mouth (see Map 6.1).

All these Indic varieties are close relatives; I suspect that any speaker of one of them would quickly recognise this about at least most of the others. That does not mean, however, that someone from Lahore in the Pakistani Punjab would be able to follow someone speaking the native dialect of Dhaka in Bangladesh. Nevertheless, there is considerable, although not necessarily unproblematical, mutual intelligibility along the dialect continuum for a considerable length of the Ganges/Ganga, generally associated with dialect groupings often termed Braj, Awadhi and Bhojpur (to the extent that the varieties of the 'centre' involved would generally be analysed as dialects of the modern standardised language Hindi).

These potentially mutually intelligible varieties lie at the heart of our understanding of what happened linguistically to the Indic varieties of Fiji. The labourers who migrated to Fiji would have come largely from agricultural backgrounds where levels of literacy were generally low. But they would have also inhabited environments where many trained themselves (indeed were probably schooled from birth) in developing an understanding of people who lived a considerable distance away from them on the dialect continuum. This would not be purely passive; it is likely that you would also have known and practiced strategies which involved identifying potential problems for others in understanding your speech and avoiding them in ways that the largest number of people would understand.

This pattern was encouraged and developed in Fiji, in situations where group understanding was needed more. Generally, there is considerable variation in lexical use and phonological patterns between these dialects at home. But it is with inflectional material that this is particularly the case (see, e.g., Siegel 1987: 115). The Fiji variety generally reorganises these distinctions into paradigms with fewer forms, which are comprehensible across a wide range of dialects. It would not be controversial to suggest that 'simplification' and 'regularisation' were central forces at work in the development of that variety, as speakers of different varieties became united in a new and external situation.

6.2.2.2 Dialect Levelling in Western Norwegian Industrial Towns

New koineised varieties need not develop in new territories which lie considerable distances away from where the source varieties were originally spoken. Let us consider two new industrial centres in western Norway, as researched by Sandve (1976) and analysed by Kerswill (2001: 674–7). The inhabitants of both settlements are concerned primarily with metal smelting, associated with inexpensive and highly productive local hydroelectric power and with rapid connections to the Atlantic through the Hardanger Fjord, of which their native fjord forms a part (see Map 6.2).

Setting up new industrial towns (albeit on far earlier foundations) in rural western Norway (instead of in urban centres such as Bergen, Trondheim or Stavanger – none of which would themselves have had large populations at the beginning of the

Map 6.2 Odda and Tyssedal.

Table 6.1 Origins of people working in Odda and Tyssedal Smelteverk in 1916–18

Western Norway	Eastern Norway	Norway (other)	Other countries
Origin of people working at Odda Smelteverk in 1916			
81%	5%	7%	7%
Origin of people working at Tyssedal Smelteverk in 1916–18			
36%	35%	16%	12%

twentieth century) inevitably meant importing trained workers from elsewhere. With the two towns we are considering here, we have records of the origins of the first generations who worked in the factories (Table 6.1).

There are two initial points to be registered here. The first of these is that, while the two towns do not lie far from each other, with essentially the same existing local population speaking similar dialects, and are also involved in similar enterprises, the origins of the first generation of workers were strikingly different. In Odda, the overwhelming majority came from western Norway, while in Tyssedal, equal numbers of incomers came from east and west. The second point is that these distributions matter.

Norway has a small population in relation to its size. In 1910, considerably fewer than 2.5 million people lived there. But that limited population was widely spread across the country, largely living in small settlements which, given the geology of the country, were often sundered even from near neighbours. Linguistic diversity was (and is) considerable. Most notably, a major bundle of isoglosses divides the country between east (and to a degree north) and west. As discussed in Chapter 5, in some senses, the boundary between West Norse languages (Icelandic and Faeroese) and East Norse languages (Danish and Swedish) does not run along Norway's border with Sweden. Instead, it runs close to the east of the great mountainous spine of the country itself (see Map 6.3). The great distinctions – in pronunciation, word choice and inflection – between the two centres which we will briefly consider here are founded upon this linguistic distinction.

Let us look at a number of different patterns found with morpholexical features in Odda and Tyssedal and in majority West and East Norwegian (throughout represented in the International Phonetic Alphabet, rather than with local orthographic practice; the [ʁ] for /r/ is a western Norwegian feature which would be realised by locals no matter the variety employed) (Table 6.2).

With these examples, we can see a natural connection between the norms in the new towns and the geographical origins of the first settlers. It is not always as straightforward as this, however. On some occasions the two town dialects are closer to the East Norwegian pattern, even though the great majority of the first settlers in Odda were from the west (Table 6.3).

6.2 Koineisation

Table 6.2 Odda has a West Norwegian, Tyssedal an East Norwegian, variant

Odda	Tyssedal	West Norwegian	East Norwegian	
kɑstɑ	kɑstə	kɑstɑ	kɑstə	'throw' (inf)
jɛntɑ	jɛntə	jɛntɑ	jɛntə	'girl'
jɛntu	jɛntɑ	jɛntu	jɛntɑ	'the girl'
e:g	jɛi	e:g	jɛi	'I'
kvi:t	vi:t	kvi:t	vi:t	'white'
hɛimɑ	jɛmə	hɛimɑ	jɛmə	'at home'

Table 6.3 Both Odda and Tyssedal levelled towards the East Norwegian variant

Odda	Tyssedal	West Norwegian	East Norwegian	
vi:	vi:	me:	vi:	'we'
ɑlə	ɑlə	ɑdlə	ɑlə	'all' (pl)
çøt, gʉt	çøt, gʉt	çø:t, gʉ:t	çøt, gʉt	'meat', 'boy'

Map 6.3 Dialects of Norwegian.

Table 6.4 Simplified and/or interdialect forms

Odda	Tyssedal	West Norwegian		East Norwegian	
kɔmə	kɔməʁ	çe:mə	kɔmər	'come'	(present)
sɔ:və	sɔ:vəʁ	sø:və	sɔ:vər	'sleep'	(present)
ɛlvəʁ/ɛlvɑʁ	ɛlvəʁ	ɛlvɑr	ɛlvər	'rivers'	

There are also occasions in which both town dialects (albeit in different ways) seem to have developed a compromise form which is likely to have been easily comprehensible to speakers on either side of the divide (Table 6.4).

It appears that, when the West Norwegian form is markedly different at a range of levels from the East Norwegian one, the East Norwegian form may still be preferred. This is particularly the case, perhaps, because the literate industrial workers of the two towns, no matter their personal origins, had knowledge of the dominant East Norwegian standard of the language, Bokmål (at the time of the foundation of the settlements, often named *Riksmål* 'language of the kingdom'). But, for the East Norwegians, no such 'interpretive device' for West Norwegian was familiar to them (their knowledge of what is now termed Nynorsk, the western variant, is likely not to have been great). It may be, of course, that they never considered doing so (for further discussion of similar contexts elsewhere in Norway, see, among others, Neteland 2019).

This sense of apparent convergence which involves the creation of new forms and usages not confined to any one (or, indeed, any) source input is also highly marked in the development of 'new' varieties created by emigration to a new settlement.

6.3 Dialect Contact and New Variety Formation: Convergence and Divergence

What causes a language to diverge from the 'homeland' varieties when it is carried to a new place? This is a complex and difficult issue but one which research over the last thirty years or so has started to explain. We will therefore start by considering contact between what are normally taken to be dialects of the same language and the creation of new varieties. Since many of these came into being in the modern age, we know a great deal about the histories of the people who first spoke the varieties. While naturally we do not know *everything* about their development, we can be more certain with this than with many other kinds of contact, where the process began in a distant past or in situations where we have no written recent documentation and history (or both).

Let us consider in the first instance the Southern Hemisphere native speaker English varieties. With the exception of St Helena (discussed in detail in Chapter 4), the settlement colonies where English was the primary mother tongue in the Southern Hemisphere were founded at the very earliest in the late eighteenth century (and most in the nineteenth). The numbers of speakers vary considerably, with Australia (presently with around 25 million residents, almost all of whom speak English, mostly as a native language) and Tristan da Cunha (with around 250 inhabitants) making up the extremes (the Pitcairn Islands have a population of only around fifty people, but, as we have seen, its vernacular has features which bring it close to being a creole in origin and nature). Because of the relatively small historical window within which the varieties have developed (and also, perhaps, the social and geographical origins of some of the settlers; this is more contentious, as we will see), however, the varieties, no matter how sundered geographically, are linguistically similar.

Australian English is the product of well over two centuries of European settlement on that continent. That does not mean that the variety came into being the minute that the first, overwhelmingly involuntary English-speaking settlers arrived in what became Sydney. What those early days did create was large-scale contact between related varieties, not unalike, although perhaps more diffuse than, and with longer-term ongoing input of novel linguistic material from, 'home', to what we saw in Fiji, given that new English-speaking immigrants arriving has been an ongoing reality for Australians since the Second Fleet.

These settlers would, to a large extent, have maintained something like their own usage for their lifetimes, bearing in mind that they would have developed a degree of convergence when speaking to their neighbours (and quite possibly before that in the lengthy voyage to their new home), who would have been far less likely to come from a similar linguistic background to the new inhabitant than would have been the case in the 'old country'. The children of these immigrants would have been different in this respect (as in many others), however. By the time that the various Australian colonies (later, states) were setting up administrations which included compulsory education and compulsory educational inspection within their remits, in the second half of the nineteenth century (Australia did not exist as a single country until 1901), school inspectors and other authority figures were already writing and speaking about the 'deficiencies' of local pronunciation, describing it in ways which closely resemble Australian English today (for discussion, see Peters 2008; Damousi 2010). The connection between vernacular Australian English pronunciation and 'Cockney', the varieties of English spoken in traditional working-class communities in London, was also often pointed out.

These similarities are real enough. The vowel in words like *rain* (a monophthong /e/ for me) is a mid to close diphthong in Received Pronunciation (RP), originally an upper-class and upper-middle-class accent of the south-east of England but later one associated with this elite group throughout that country. Its close relative, 'Cockney', has a lower, more open diphthong. The diphthong in *ride* is pronounced closer to the centre of the mouth in working-class London speech, as it is in the traditional dialects of most of rural southern England, than is the case with RP. These features are also the norm in the Southern Hemisphere varieties. All Southern Hemisphere varieties (with a few small-scale and generally explicable exceptions) are also not fully rhotic. While this is now the norm for most of England, in the nineteenth century the feature was confined largely to south-east England and Yorkshire, with the latter of which the Southern Hemisphere varieties share little linguistically (Trudgill 2004: 67–70). Are the forms of English spoken in the Southern Hemisphere merely south-east England varieties carried overseas? How does this relate to our knowledge that people speaking different varieties of English came to these territories?

The idea that most Southern Hemisphere Englishes are essentially transported south-east England varieties is more problematical than it sounds. In the first instance, the Southern Hemisphere varieties sound like Cockney *now*; it cannot be absolutely said that this is what London varieties sounded like two hundred years ago. If London speakers did sound markedly different at that time, then what we have is an example of drift (Sapir 1921; see also Malkiel 1981) rather than direct descent: similar varieties developing in similar ways despite their speakers having only limited contact with each other, in the same way as my relatives in the United States and elsewhere share many similarities in build and character with me (and vice versa), even though their branches of our family were sundered from mine more than a hundred years ago. There is the danger of 'but there *must* be a connection' being used as an argument.

More striking, however, are those occasions when Southern Hemisphere varieties do not coincide with London varieties. A central feature of 'Cockney' and other British urban varieties is the development of /θ/ to /f/ ('TH-fronting'). While evidence is sparse, it would generally be agreed that at least some Londoners have been doing this for centuries. This feature is practically unknown among native speakers of English in the Southern Hemisphere (although it is found occasionally in the English of native Australians). The loss of /h/ in all positions is commonplace across a large part (but not all) of England; this change has been spreading since the Middle Ages. From my own experience, some South African speakers of English have this feature, but it is unknown in all other varieties from that hemisphere.

Why should these varieties be different from the apparent 'mother' variety in what are central features? Contact of various types is very likely to be the primary issue underlying them. It may also explain why, despite their obvious similarities in so many ways, Australian English and New Zealand English are also different from each other when we consider other, often central features. This is particularly marked with the short vowels (compare Australian and New Zealand pronunciations of *pin* or *pen*) but is also highly marked in lexis. Sometimes this can be seen as being culture- and ecology-specific, such as *billabong* 'water hole' or *kiwi*, referring to the iconic flightless New Zealand bird (as we saw in Chapter 1, often also used as a term for an inhabitant of New Zealand), but this does not explain the presence of words of different 'old country' origin, such as the Scots word *byre* 'cow house', used in New Zealand English. Can it be possible that proportion of settler origins has affected the final 'product'? This is all interesting. But how does it fit with our theme of linguistic contact?

Given their differences in size, as well as time depth, of English-speaker settlement, we might expect that Australian English would be the most analysed and discussed in relation to its origins. But while much ink, both scholarly and general, has been spilled on the birth and development of Australian English, it is New Zealand English which has been given the most attention in the last thirty years and about whose prior development we know more, through the serendipitous presence of a corpus of English spoken by the first generation of people of European descent born in New Zealand, recorded across a large part of the country in the immediate post-war period.

Without these recordings, we might be tempted to postulate that the first native generation would have spoken a variety which, while undoubtedly deriving some features from their parents' speech, would primarily demonstrate an orderly progression towards the apparently south-east England variety which was gradually mutating (and coalescing) to become the unique but similar New Zealand variety. Nothing could be further from the truth, as Gordon et al. (2004) and Trudgill (2004) point out.

As a group, the recordings present evidence for an apparently chaotic range of usage. Individually, speakers do not sound either New Zealand or English. They often do not sound anything like *any* speaker of English for whom we have evidence. Several speakers appear to have Scottish consonants but south-east England vowels, or vice versa. One speaker does not pronounce /h/ but does have /ʍ/ (for the <wh> words), a combination which would normally be considered typologically impossible. Siblings often sound strikingly different, although they have remained in close proximity across their lives. The same is true for close friends. It might be tempting to see this confusing diversity as being representative of an essentially low-level settlement (initially of a 'free enterprise' nature, since the British government was not, at least to begin with, keen on the colonisation of the territory), where a small population was spread across a wide area. There may be something in this, but it does not explain why such closely connected individuals should sound different. We need to dig deeper to find a more adequate solution.

In work centred round his book of 2004, Trudgill has suggested that there is an *inevitability* underlying the process of new variety construction. With New Zealand English, for instance, he highlights the origins of the pioneer English-speaking immigrants to the country. From these origins he suggests we can produce reasons for why particular features from the immigrant 'mix' survive into the present variety. Thus, in New Zealand, full rhoticity was lost because the majority of immigrants came from places where this feature was already lost (or was in the process of being lost: remember the comments made earlier about historical usage patterns being derived from modern evidence), including a large part of England. The use of /h/, on the other hand, continued because those who retained it were in a (bare) majority in the new colony: Scots, Irish people, English people from north of the Tyne and from East Anglia (/h/-fulness has largely disappeared from the last region now, but this has happened well within living memory; see Trudgill 1988). Alternatively, a near majority carried the day with this feature because its loss was *marked*: people who have full use of /h/ in their variety find /h/-dropping varieties difficult to follow. The apparently 'chaotic' nature of the pronunciations found in the 1940s recordings, Trudgill suggests, actually represents a halfway house in relation to creating this new, fundamentally population proportion-based, essentially homogenous variety.

There are highly attractive points in this argument. It would seem counterintuitive that those migrants who came in the largest numbers did not affect the new variety more than those with smaller populations. But other features, such as the founder effect (discussed in Chapters 3 and 4) or swamping (Lass 1987, 1990, 1995, 2004), where the language use of a later, more populous group overlays and replaces earlier use, might also have been of some importance. Most sociolinguists would also baulk at the apparently mechanistic view of language change: there is very little room for human agency.

What can be recognised, however, is that a new koine has come into being through both a combination and sorting of the source materials and the creation of new features anchored on, but different from, the sources (see, for instance, the changes of pronunciation in the New Zealand short vowel system, a systemic change unmatched in any other variety).

Case Study 6 The Effects of Contact between Closely Related Languages and Their Outcomes on a Broader Historical Canvas

In Chapter 5 we discussed those occasions in which complete adherence to the family tree model of ongoing change through divergence was not entirely successful in explaining the change which had taken place with some of the Germanic languages, most notably with what became Modern Dutch and the present nature(s) of Norwegian. Unlike our discussion of another Germanic variety, Afrikaans, in Chapter 4, we were forced to accept that, if change was caused by contact in relation to the ancestries of Dutch and Norwegian, this was through contact between close relatives. The following case study considers two such potential contacts of this sort for which the long-term typological outcomes were considerable.

Low German and the Scandinavian Languages in the Late Middle Ages and the Early Modern Period

In the later medieval and early modern periods, both the North Sea littoral and the Baltic Sea basin (see Map 6.4) were dominated by speakers of Low German, the native language, historically, of a considerable part of the northern European plain. Most of their activity was associated with the business of the Hanseatic League, a trading federation so powerful that it acted like a state, sending out embassies to foreign courts and developing internal and external policy which had profound effects upon the politics and economies of countries (and their languages) situated around the Baltic and North Seas. In eastern Scotland, where I live, there is considerable architectural, cultural and linguistic evidence for this influence. This is nothing compared to Scandinavia, however. Many of the cities of the region – in particular, Bergen, Malmö, Stockholm and Visby (the main settlement on the

Map 6.4 Scandinavia and the Baltic basin.

Swedish island of Gotland) – were dominated by Low German speakers (or their descendants) for centuries. In these places they took on the roles of traders and sailors and, eventually, became major players in local and national government; predictably, marriage and consequent child-rearing would have taken place regularly between Low German and Scandinavian speakers. This would inevitably have had linguistic results. Although not universally popular, to put it mildly, Low German influence spread far into the hinterlands of these and other urban centres. Low German remained a living language in these 'colonies' through close ties of business (and often family) with the Hanseatic heartland. At the very least, however, long-term residence in Scandinavia would have led to a 'rough' bilingualism.

The linguistic remnants of this influence can be found today most overtly in the level of (Low) German lexis found in the Scandinavian languages, rendering them distinctive when compared with their more conservative sisters, Faeroese and Icelandic. In Modern Norwegian, for instance, even in the more purist Nynorsk standard variety, 'to speak' and 'language' are *snakke* and *språk*, both deriving from

Low German. As is the case with French in relation to English, it is at best very difficult to produce a sentence in a Scandinavian language without using a Low German word. Low German influence is all-pervasive in lexis. How might it have affected the Scandinavian languages morphosyntactically? Or is its influence, like French with English, confined primarily to lexis, as many Scandinavian scholars believe?

In both its western and eastern forms, Old Norse, recorded during the period 1050–1400, realised a rather conservative version of the inherited Germanic inflectional morphology system in both noun and verb phrases. In the verb phrase, for instance, discrete forms largely existed for each number and person in both tenses. In the noun phrase, most 'slots' associated with grammatical case and gender, in nouns, adjectives and pronouns, retained discrete forms or were at least rather more likely to be discrete than was the case with Old English or even Old High German, even though these varieties are first recorded in Roman script four hundred years before Old Norse. Highly developed noun classes, often with separate inflectional apparatus, were also the norm.

Many of these features are well preserved in Icelandic and, to a lesser extent, Faeroese. The languages of Scandinavia are markedly different, however. Case marking, apart from a few survivals in island (and geographically remote) communities in Norway, is essentially moribund, if not vanished altogether. The descendant of the genitive case is still employed in written use but has been replaced by various periphrases in speech (this is true for Faeroese, in which the dative case is used in possessive expressions; this was discussed in more depth in Case Study 5). In Danish and many Norwegian varieties, the rich noun class marking inherited from Old Norse has essentially disappeared, although in Swedish and other dialects of Norwegian, it has been retained to a greater extent.

But it is in the verb phrase that the most marked distinctions can be found. For instance, the present indicative paradigm for Old Norse *spyrja* 'to ask' is *ek spyr* 'I ask'; *þú spyrr* 'you (sg.) ask'; *hann, hon, þat spyrr* 'he, she, it asks'; *vér spyrjum* 'we ask'; *þér spyrið* 'you (pl.) ask'; *þeir, þær, þau spyrja* 'they (masculine, feminine, neuter) ask'. In all three modern Scandinavian languages, *no* distinction is made between number and person in either verb tense. An invariant form is instead used (Norwegian Bokmål: *spørre* 'to ask' is *jeg spør* 'I ask'; *du spør* 'you (sg.) ask'; *han, hun, det spør* 'he, she, it asks'; *vi spør* 'we ask'; *dere spør* 'you (pl.) ask'; *de spør* 'they ask').

It should be noted that all of these changes are perfectly natural. What marks them out as unusual is the speed by which they passed through the Scandinavian languages in the late Middle Ages and the early modern period, well beyond those contexts where bilingualism was normal (as far as we can tell, something between one hundred and two hundred years, depending on the dialect). The question, then, is, did the contact with speakers of Low German during this period encourage (or even trigger) these changes? (Further discussion of some of these features can be found in Wührer 1954; Dahlberg 1954–6; Haugen 1976: sec. 5.2; and Ureland 1986, 1989, as well as in the papers collected in Jahr 1995. A recent treatment of the issues can be found in Baxter and Trudgill 2019.)

This is a difficult question to answer, but the fact that intense contact, large-scale societal disruption and change and major, typologically altering language change took place at essentially the same time is indicative. It is likely that the changes would have happened in any event, but not probably so quickly or so radically. The resulting language varieties were not mixed in the way that, say, Michif is. They remain solidly North Germanic in their natures. But the variety produced is a koine, with many of the structural elements which might have proved confusing to, and difficult to learn for, a Low German speaker ironed out. Underlying this must be the regular presence of bilingual households where a 'lowest common denominator' variety was passed on to children. This view is supported by evidence for major and systemic change in English in the early Middle Ages, which will be discussed subsequently.

The English 'Transition Period'

There is a long-standing debate over whether linguistic contact caused (or channelled) the great changes in morphosyntax through which English passed between 900 and 1300 (and which happened in individual dialects in what appears to have been two to three generations). These modifications are particularly marked in the noun phrase system.

Old English was a 'traditional' Germanic language, where grammatical case and gender were marked on nouns, pronouns and adjectives, with the last category also realising different endings depending on the level of grammatical information carried by other elements of the phrase. After the rapid transition, dialects showed none of these features (the one very minor exception being that late fourteenth-century London English, the dialect of Chaucer, maintaining some evidence of the distinction between 'strong' and 'weak' adjectives, as Samuels 1989a points out). Even plurality, which previously was marked on nouns, pronouns and adjectives, disappeared on the adjective and was much simplified on the noun. It remained with demonstrative (and personal) pronouns in most dialects but not on the newly discrete definite article or the adjective (the last being quite unusual in European terms). In several texts from the transition period, it is possible to see how rapid these changes actually were (see Millar 2000, 2012b: 115–18; 2016: 124–6; these also depict the progress of these changes from north to south).

Let us consider a striking example of the thoroughgoing nature of the changes involved. The English monk, writer and public man Ælfric produced a homily, *De Initio Creaturae* (On the Beginning of Creation), probably at the end of the tenth century. A number of manuscript copies of this work survive. We will concentrate on two of these, however, since they are particularly contrastive. The first of these is London, British Library, Royal 7 C.xii (hereinafter Royal), which was written in the late West Saxon *Schriftsprache* (the dominant form of written English at the time) at the time of initial composition. It is certainly in the hand of someone very close to Ælfric; the scribal hand may actually be that of Ælfric himself. The second is also the latest copy, London, British Library, Cotton Vespasian A.xxii (hereinafter Vespasian). It was probably copied (and edited to some extent) somewhere in Kent (in the far south-east of England) at the beginning of the thirteenth century. While Vespasian attempts to reproduce the Old English of the original as well as possible, there is considerable evidence that the scribe does not fully understand the nuances of what he is writing.

We do not have enough space to conduct a detailed comparison (the interested reader might want to consult Millar and Nicholls 1997 for more discussion). But the following two examples are representative of the linguistic differences demonstrated. For 'without any earthly father', Royal has *buton ælcum eorðlicum fæder*. Here the dative case with a masculine noun is represented by the *-um* endings on the premodifiers. The Vespasian equivalent, however, *buton elce eorðlice federe*, has much reduced endings morphology, using *-e*, which, by this point, was employed to mark a number of different features, including adjective plurality (which it does not represent here). Ambiguity is, if not rampant, at least highly threatening to the survival of the inherited system.

One further example, on this occasion with slightly different wording in the different manuscripts, is that Royal has *seo eorðe þe is awyrige on þinum weorce* 'the earth which is accursed in your work', while Vespasian has *se eorðe his awirigd on þine weorce* 'the earth is cursed in your work'. As with the previous example, the endings system in Vespasian is curtailed in comparison with Royal. Equally striking, however, is the use of grammatical gender-specific definers. Royal has the historically 'correct' *seo eorðe* 'the earth', where *seo* is the form of the definer associated with feminine nouns (like *eorðe*) in the nominative case. Vespasian, however, has *se eorðe*, where *se* was historically only grammatical when used with a member of the masculine gender class in the nominative case.

These are only a few examples. This apparent breakdown can be plotted across England and is inexorable and fast (as can be seen in the language of the Continuations to the *Peterborough Chronicle*) (for a discussion, see Millar 2012b: 113–18).

As was demonstrated in our preceding discussion of the linguistic results of the contact between Low German and the Scandinavian varieties from circa 1400 to circa 1700, the changes involved in the transition between Old and Middle English are quite striking but do not involve anything 'unnatural' in terms of what the results of the changes were. The speed through which the changes passed within the speech communities involved *is* dramatic, however. The changes effected in the 'transition period' could readily have happened without linguistic contact.

But it could be argued that the presence of considerable numbers of Norse speakers in northern England during the period, speaking discrete but similar varieties to those spoken by the indigenous English, should at the very least be considered as a potential spur to the change, particularly since, as Samuels (1989b, 1989c) demonstrates, it is from this region, the Great Scandinavian Belt (see Map 6.5), that the changes radiated. Some scholars have taken quite extreme views on this, not least two (Emonds and Faarlund 2014; see also Emonds 2011), who have suggested that Modern English is actually a North Germanic variety, rather than a direct descendant of Old English (a suggestion which, it should be

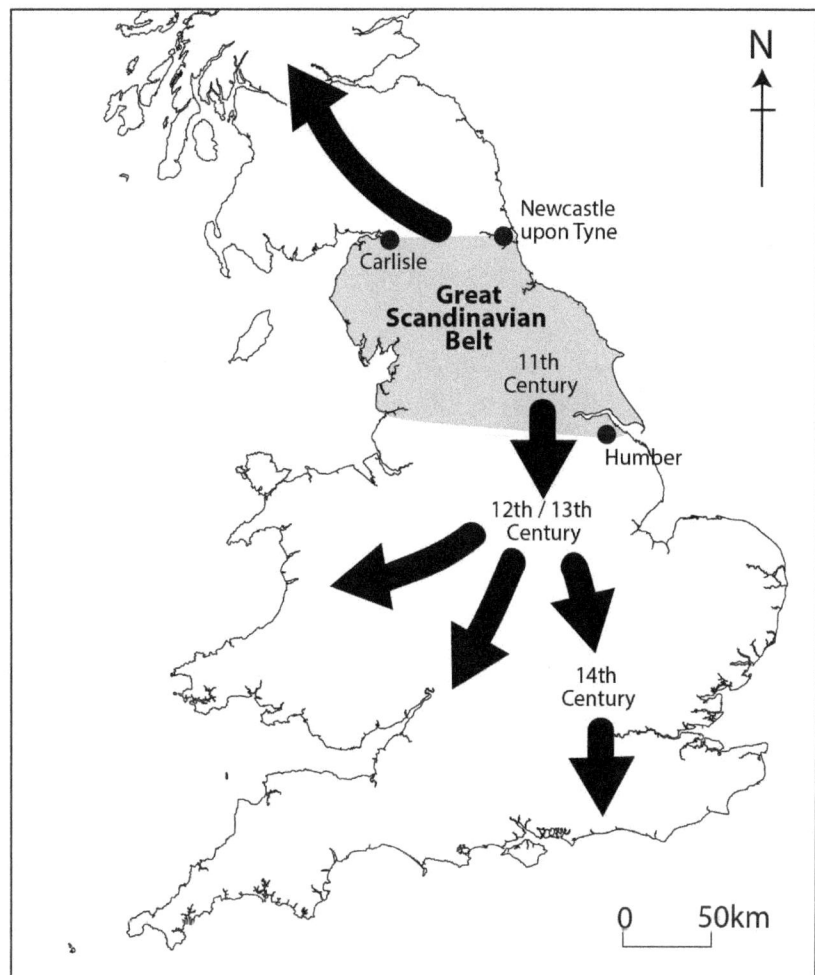

Map 6.5 The Great Scandinavian Belt.

recognised, is not accepted by the overwhelming majority of scholars on the subject, to put it mildly).

We have to ask, however, what happens when closely related languages come into contact with each other? What are the linguistic effects of people trying to understand and be understood in a situation where comprehension might be fragmentary?

In the first instance, the varieties which English and Scandinavian residents spoke had much in common with each other. The ancestral varieties had probably split completely from each other somewhat more than five centuries before. Much of the lexis would have been common to both populations, although their pronunciations would inevitably (but predictably) have been different. While the exact nature of the mutual intelligibility found between the languages has been long – and hotly – debated, at the very least, there must have been strong recognition of family relationship (for a discussion, see Eyþórsson 2002; Townend 2002). The grammatical nature of both languages was also similar, but the ways in which functions were expressed was often strikingly different. As was the case with the development of Fiji Hindi koine discussed earlier, but to a far greater extent, simplification (or rationalisation) needed to take place so that greater comprehension could become possible.

Here is an example (created by me) of how different the inflections of a simple sentence with practically the same shared vocabulary can be when comparing the two languages:

Old English: *se mann hæfde twegen suna*
Old Norse: *maðrinn [manninn] hafði tvá sǫnu*
'the man had two sons' [the distinction within Old Norse between *maðrinn* and
   mannin marks a difference between Icelandic and most Scandinavian usage at
   the time]

It is quite easy to understand why people confronted with these differences would choose to rationalise their language use towards majority patterns.

Discussion

In societies where literacy is widespread and there is relative social stability, with one grouping holding more power than the others, that group's language will remain no more than marginally affected by those also spoken in the territory (something demonstrated by the influence, or lack of influence, German has had on English in the United States, despite the considerable immigration of speakers of that language into that country, although see Chapter 2). But in the situations we are describing here, where essentially equal (adstratal) relationships pertained for most speakers of both languages, in often highly fluid political and social situations where vernacular literacy was rare, it is inevitable that new contact-driven varieties would become the norm. Did cohabitation of speakers of discrete but closely related languages affect the development of the language varieties used by their offspring, particularly when this context was regularly repeated across a territory, normally with subtle variation, and where further unions would have produced further 'simplified' koines?

Can a true distinction be made between dialect contact and (near-) language contact? To some extent, this can be done. As we have seen, the greater distance between closely related but discrete varieties than between dialects of the same language inevitably means that the former contexts often exhibit greater and more radical effects due to contact than do the latter. The guiding principles related to rationalisation and koineisation remain similar, if not actually the same, however.

6.4 Conclusion

In this chapter we have discussed what linguistic results contact between closely related varieties might have. Employing the concept of the koine, it became apparent that, to a degree, the new varieties produced were simplified (although 'made more straightforward' might be a better turn of phrase). In general, the innovations found in new varieties appear to be brought about by compromises between the input varieties, although these compromises may involve the creation of a new usage.

Contact between near relatives produces markedly different results when compared with the products of other kinds of contact. *Convergence can cause divergence; divergence can cause convergence.*

Exercises

1. A large body of literature suggests that it is the influence of Celtic second language speakers, rather than Norse, which provoked the 'great change' in English. Can the two viewpoints be brought into line?
2. Find out what you can about a 'colonial English' not covered in depth in this chapter. Do scholars differ over the origins of the particular features of a variety? Why should these disagreements come about? You may find it useful to compare a variety spoken by a large number of speakers (such as North American English) with one with far fewer speakers (such as Tristan da Cunha or Falkland Islands English).
3. Can situations of the types mentioned in this chapter be found outside the English-speaking world?
4. In seminars or individually, consider the evidence from Odda and Tyssedal in greater depth. Can you tease out more evidence for language change (in particular koineisation) in the evidence given about allegiance to different varieties of Norwegian among the inhabitants of the two settlements?

Suggested Reading

From a theoretical point of view, the nature and development of koines are best treated by Siegel (1985) and Kerswill (2001, 2013). Siegel (1987) is the classic study of how a koine develops over time in a particular place. In relation to convergence within languages, the essays in Auer, Hinskens and Kerswill (2005) represent state-of-the-art treatments.

Central to the development of the discussion of the outcomes of dialect contact is the work of Peter Trudgill (1983, 1986, 2004, 2011). Each of these works deserves a concentrated read. It should be noted that the two books from this century are contentious. The general principles on which they are based have been much debated by scholars.

Much insight can be gained from reading case studies of new dialect formation, including Kerswill (1994), Gordon et al. (2004) and Schreier (2003, 2008).

Blushes aside, Millar (2016) represents an attempt at bringing together analyses of dialect and near-relative contact, something also covered (but with differing views and outcomes) by Trudgill (1986; see also esp. Trudgill 2011).

7 Final Thoughts

In Chapter 1 we noted that linguistic contact, in one form or another, is everywhere. I hope that this truth has been given witness throughout this book. Human life, after all, has always been concerned with interaction with other humans. Not everyone you come into contact with will speak the same language as you. In the past it was likely that you would have had a regional lingua franca to hand for circumstances of this type. Whether these use languages were being spoken by native or non-native speakers must have had profound effects on the language as it moved forward through time. The presence of international lingua francas since at least the Second World War has not invalidated this observation: it has broadened the experience while also making the results much more diverse, even if interaction has often existed with a small number of languages whose speakers have hegemonic force.

I have recently been reading about the nature of First Nation alliances, connections and trading partnerships in what are now the Canadian provinces of Quebec and Ontario, along with the US states of Massachusetts down to northern Virginia, during the first century of English and French infiltration and settlement in the region (bringing with them new technologies which were attractive to most native people) (Oberg 2018: chap. 2). The dynamic complexity of ethnic identity – made particularly evident, for instance, in the Iroquois tradition of 'adopting' defeated individuals, groups and nations – must have had a profound effect on language use (including the eventual spread of English and French as lingua francas which, for many, eventually became the mother tongue). Sadly, we have at best limited evidence for the nature of these changes in the indigenous languages. We do, however, have some material from a relatively earlier period of what the English and French of the native people sounded like, albeit often presented in such a way that it reinforced racist assumptions (for some partial treatment, see Leap 1993; Gillis 2013).

Contact-inducing multilingualism is at the heart of what our discussions have involved. But the type of multilingualism in place inevitably affects the linguistic outcome of the contact. While most contacts exist in a state of societal inequality, that is far more the case when slavery is involved than is the case with an immigrant who is new to what will become their home. Both lived under a regime in which there is a considerable degree of prescription in relation to which language will be used in the new place. Compulsion is less of an issue for an immigrant than it is for an enslaved person: the first needs to learn the new language in order to compete and prosper in the new economy; the second needs to learn, and learn quickly, in order to survive. My family could have returned to the Gàidhealtachd if they had not been able at least to keep their heads above water in an urban environment. No such possibility would have been available for an enslaved Yoruba speaker forced to live in South Carolina. Both could have made use of organised groupings of their compatriots; the latter would only have alleviated somewhat the misery of the plantation: it would not have offered the potential of betterment in the new environment my ancestors might have expected.

Situations such as the latter can have quite profound effects on the language used. As we saw in Chapter 3 in particular, there is a long-standing and ongoing discussion on the origins of creoles and their relationship to pidgins. What can be said, in any event, is that the language produced, largely based on the speech forms of the 'masters' and other privileged members of the society in which enslaved people found themselves, was of a radical sort which, under the circumstances, could (but need not) have developed into what was essentially a new speech form. That these developments were at their most marked when a regional lingua franca was necessary is striking.

The languages of minorities, whether migrant or autochthonous, who had a degree of choice in relation to the course of their lives were (and are) affected by particular dominant languages as their speaker base crumbled, as was often the case. Autochthonous languages (or rather, their speakers), as we saw in Chapter 2 in particular, were more inclined to use their own materials as 'simplification' took place. The influence of the 'dying' language on the majority speech form is less tangible but is nonetheless present. (This was also the case at times with creoles, whose speech forms did influence the language use of more privileged members of the community.)

As I have already observed, convergence is at the heart of many, but not by any means all, of the changes engendered by contact described in this book. At least from one theoretical position, for instance, the post-creole continuum is an example of convergence to the standard variety in contexts where literacy is becoming commonplace; the opposing theoretical viewpoint would, of course, see the continuum as demonstrating ongoing divergence (at least in a Platonic sense: in most places, modern times have led to the omnipresence of the standard variety as the sole hegemonically acceptable form in most contexts where creole varieties are spoken and written; Haiti is a partial exception to this statement).

In other linguistic contact contexts, however, convergence is the norm. While language areas may not be considered now as somehow a unit of common distinctiveness in relation to the perceived norm, they definitely demonstrate the linguistic change which comes into place when there is long-term multilingualism in a geographical space where the specific ethnic and cultural groups have lived in essentially the same way for a considerable period. But near-dialect and near-language contact are also likely to involve convergence between the input forms. The concept of koineisation is central to this process.

In a sense, **near-relative** contact shares much in terms of outcomes with the process of pidgin and creole creation. The apparent simplification (as suggested, *rationalisation* might be a better term) of morphosyntactic features, with larger-scale patterns being strengthened at the expense of minority patterns (or, particularly with near-language contact, morphosyntactic discrepancies between the two languages being 'bred out' of their offspring), is common to both. A primary difference between the two phenomena, however, is that near-language contact and its outcomes are far more likely to be formed within an adstratal relationship where one population has essentially the same status as has the other than are pidgins and creoles.

An important point needs to be made. Often, historical linguists assume (and, to a greater extent, have assumed) that language change due to contact is a minority phenomenon, with 'normal' language change being more prevalent. This may well be the case. But, at least following the processes and analyses discussed in this book, it could be argued that change caused by contact is far more widespread than we might think. The recent re-rhoticisation of New York City Speech, as discussed by Labov (1972), would have been far less likely to have taken place if there had not been ongoing, daily contact between non-rhotic and rhotic speakers in the city (the reason why the change – or resumption – took place was due to other sociolinguistic factors at work (see Millar 2012c: 22–6), but that is not the issue at hand). The final outcomes of the English Great Vowel Shift – in particular the mainstream pronunciation of the <ee> and <ea> sets – can be described in terms of contact between speakers of somewhat different dialects with different social associations in sixteenth- and seventeenth-century London (see Millar 2012c: 35–7). It is entirely possible that changes as thoroughgoing as the First Germanic Consonant Shift – Grimm's law – were the product of contact, even if we do not know what contacts were ongoing among the speakers of the Germanic and other languages interacting at that time.

Contact is not a peripheral factor in linguistic change; it is a central (although rarely the sole) catalyst for change.

Glossary

acrolect In traditional analyses of creole development, the acrolect is the variety found on the post-creole continuum which is closest to the dominant variety and least akin to the most creole-like form of speech. It often amounts to no more than the standard variety spoken with a local accent. See Chapters 3 and 4 for further discussion.

adstratal influence When two language varieties spoken by populations which are essentially socially, economically and politically equal come into contact with each other, the influence one variety has over the other is adstratal. See Chapter 1 for further discussion.

aspect, verb Tense is not the only grammatical (and semantic) feature which can be marked on verbs (or carried through modifiers of various sorts within the verb phrase). For instance, I was told at school that French had two past tenses: the *perfect* and the *imperfect*. In fact, that language only has one past tense, but two aspects work upon it. The differences between these aspects affects our understanding of how actions and states work in relation to time. Comrie (1976: 3) observes that 'aspects are different ways of viewing the internal temporal constituency of a situation'. All languages make distinctions of these types, although which aspects are employed in which (and how) differs considerably.

attrition, linguistic In a specifically linguistic context, attrition is the process by which speakers lose the ability over their lifetimes to recall lexis, phonological patterns and structural norms in their first language, largely because their second language is dominant where they live and work. While the analysis of the process largely has roots in psycholinguistics, it has considerable applicability for our sociolinguistic understanding of linguistic change. See Chapter 2 for further discussion.

basilect In traditional analyses of creole development, the basilect is the variety found on the post-creole continuum which is least like the dominant variety and most creole-like in its nature. From the uniformitarian perspective, the basilect is a relatively recent development, as the creole has gradually diverged from other 'mainstream' varieties; other creolists would be more likely to see the basilect as the oldest speech variety, closest to the original creole. See Chapters 3 and 4 for further discussion.

borrowing, linguistic Borrowing refers to situations in language contact where elements of one language variety are transferred to the other. The most obvious kind is where lexis is borrowed. Phonological features and morphosyntactic structures can also be treated in this way. With morphosyntax in particular, concepts may be borrowed, while the 'building blocks' by which they are expressed remain native. See Chapter 1 in particular for further discussion.

case, grammatical Refers to a particular means of representing grammatical (and to some extent semantic) relationships within a language. Some grammatical cases cannot really be described as supplying fully morphosyntactic information. When we consider the Finnish case system, for instance (Mäkinen 1999–2004; see also Jaakola and Onikki 2023), it quickly becomes apparent that some of the cases (*basic cases*, as he defines them) are grammatical in nature, demonstrating syntactic relationships within the clause; the other cases essentially supply information about the noun phrase in terms of ownership, movement, stasis and so on, however. Many of these features would be expressed through the use of prepositions in English; there is, in fact, some evidence that at least some of the endings expressing non-basic case in Finnish were originally postpositions which have been *cliticised* (essentially subsumed by) the preceding noun. It should be noted that case, while a useful means of representing function, need not be used to do so. English has only remnants of its inherited case system (see Chapter 6 for further discussion); other languages, such as Vietnamese, have nothing comparable. See Chapter 1 for further discussion.

code-switching The use of elements of one language variety alongside another in the same discourse.

convergence, linguistic Traditionally, historical linguistics has concentrated on divergence as the primary means by which languages change: previously mutually intelligible varieties gradually become mutually unintelligible. Convergence represents the opposing process: previously mutually unintelligible varieties move towards each other and, at the least, may begin to share features which were previously confined only to some of the input dialects. For further discussion, see Chapters 6 and 7.

creole Until the last thirty years, defining what a creole is was relatively straightforward. Varieties of this type, demonstrating considerable 'simplification' in comparison to the lexifier, were products of the nativisation of a pidgin. Such an interpretation is now heavily contested by those who subscribe to a uniformitarian theoretical position. This school proposes the view that creoles are essentially dialects of the dominant language which, due to contact with other languages, have diverged more than other dialects. The creole exceptionalist position maintains and develops the pidgin origin hypothesis. This book suggests that both models are of considerable importance but that neither can explain fully how all creoles develop. See Chapters 3 and 4 for further discussion.

critical period hypothesis From the 1950s on, it has been the mainstream view that humans can more readily pick up a language (or languages) until the 'critical period', between the ages of eight and eleven years. After this, language acquisition becomes much more challenging.

diglossia In many places, a stable linguistic ecology prevails where a particular variety is the norm in familiar and relaxed contexts (the L 'low' variety), while another (the H 'high' variety) is used in formal and official contexts. Transgressing these boundaries in either direction is generally frowned upon within the communities involved. Good examples can be found in the Arabic-speaking world, where local L varieties would be demanded within the family and the neighbourhood. Using Modern Standard Arabic would not be acceptable in these contexts. It would be the norm, however, in, for example, news broadcasts, where local dialect use would usually be considered transgressive. Ferguson (1959) claimed that diglossia could only be verified where both the varieties involved were derived from the same language. Fishman (1967), on the other hand, demonstrated that diglossic states were also possible where two discrete languages were involved. From this viewpoint, although most English speakers in post-1066-7 England could not speak French, the former language was still the L variety in relation to the latter's H.

divergence, linguistic Divergence is considered by most historical linguists to be the mainstream and majority tendency of language change, where previously mutually intelligible varieties become mutually unintelligible. Fifteen hundred years ago, what are now English and German are likely to have been mutually intelligible; internal change (and, to a degree, contact influences) have meant that this has not been the case since. Convergence is also common, however. For more discussion, see Chapter 5.

drift As proposed by Sapir (1921), drift is an observable linguistic process whereby the same or similar changes take place within the same language as an ongoing, although apparently inexplicable, process. This book, along with several other analyses, extends this term to encompass changes which involve closely related languages. Thus *Umlaut* (otherwise 'i-mutation') took place in all of the West and North Germanic languages in the sixth to eighth centuries, some time after the two subfamilies had split and the language we now know as English had been sundered from its Continental siblings. It is almost as if a propensity for this change was present in the 'genes' of these languages.

founder effect Mufwene has postulated that the most potent influence on new varieties developing is not necessarily the earliest (or even most populous) inhabitants of a territory but rather the earlier population which is able to control the territory and its resources. Thus, while more German-speaking immigrants than English-speaking immigrants have come to what is now the United States since 1600, it is English which is dominant because English speakers have been in control of the politics and economy of the territories involved throughout (this does not rule out the influence of German upon North American English, naturally).

gender, grammatical As was true for grammatical case, a language does not have to have grammatical gender to function. Several language families, such as the Finnic languages, have, as far as we can tell, never possessed this grammatical category, while other languages, such as English and Afrikaans, have lost the category in the course of their development. These languages are in no way lacking because of this. Grammatical gender systems can, however, be a useful means of providing a more 'macro' sense of organisation than a noun class. A considerable number of nouns are contained within a particular gender class; they are therefore 'arranged', in a way, in a native speaker's mind, which will be of service to them (or so we might postulate at least).

There does seem to be a semantic basis to gender classes. Historically, the Indo-European languages (with the exception of the Anatolian subfamily) had three genders, which Greek and Roman grammarians defined as *masculine*, *feminine* and *neuter*. In those Indo-European languages which have maintained the three-way split, most nouns referring to male beings are masculine in gender, female feminine and non-human and abstract neuter. But Norwegian *barn* 'child' is neuter, while German *Stuhl* 'chair' is masculine. This move away from a semantic basis for the system is more readily visible in languages like French and Danish, in which only two genders are now employed.

Other language families which base gender assignment wholly on sex associations are more consistent in their attribution. Still other families, however, refer to different properties: *animate* versus *inanimate*, for instance, or the shapes of beings or things.

grammaticalisation Linguists theorise that there is an ongoing process in languages whereby originally fully lexical words become functional in nature: they are bleached of most of their original and intrinsic meaning. Thus English *will* and *shall* are now used primarily to mark future events. Their original senses of, respectively, volition and obligation survive only in some varieties as a 'flavouring', explaining why, for instance, many people in southern England prefer *shall* in the first person but *will* with all others. Hopper and Traugott (1993) remains the classic treatment of the phenomenon.

interference, linguistic In a sense, interference is the opposite tendency to borrowing within the study of contact influence. While definitions for the process can be quite diverse, this book takes the approach that interference occurs when contact between two or more language varieties does not involve transfer of material so much as a general movement towards simplification or convergence of structures, designed to aid both learning and comprehension. See Chapter 1 in particular for further discussion.

koineisation A process whereby previously divergent dialects come into contact with each other and converge towards a new common variety which shares much with the inputs but which has developed its own systemic unity. As part of the koineisation process, major differences between the input varieties are 'rationalised', with common features emphasised. For further discussion, see Chapter 6.

language area There are particular regions where languages appear to be converging on each other, in particular in relation to structure, even though the varieties involved are at most distantly related. Language areas are also often termed *convergence zones*. The term *Sprachbund*, German for 'language union', is still used but is, perhaps, a little archaic. For further discussion, see Chapter 5.

language bioprogram hypothesis As put forward by Derek Bickerton in the 1980s, the language bioprogram hypothesis claims that creoles come into being in the first native generation from the elementary pidgins produced by their immigrant parents. With its connection to then current Universal Grammar theories, the hypothesis was popular and influential. It is now approached cautiously even by those who support elements of the ideas involved. For further discussion, see Chapter 3.

language death takes place when speakers of a language cease to use one language in favour of another, often for complex socio-historical and economic reasons. It can also be termed *language shift*. For further discussion, see Chapter 2.

lexifier For many scholars, pidgins and creoles are created from the combination of two sources: the lexifier, normally the dominant variety in the territory, which provides the lexis, and the structure, which, depending on your view, derives either from universal rules of language formation or the local languages which the speakers also use. Scholars who subscribe to the uniformitarian hypothesis essentially deny the existence of the lexifier language as a separate entity, instead seeing creoles as the product of particularly strong but nonetheless 'natural' divergence by dialects. For further discussion, see Chapter 3.

linguistic ecology The historical, social, cultural, economic and political environment in which a language is spoken is often termed its linguistic ecology.

mesolect In traditional analyses of creole development, the mesolect is the variety which lies halfway between the basilect and the acrolect on the post-creole continuum. Speakers using this variety employ language which shares elements with both ends of the continuum. It is generally comprehensible to speakers of the dominant language variety, while still being markedly different from it at all linguistic levels. See Chapters 3 and 4 for further discussion.

near-relative language could be defined as a variety which is considered discrete on linguistic grounds from its relatives but is sufficiently close to these for some mutual intelligibility to be possible. See Chapter 6 for further discussion.

pidgin A pidgin is a use language, developed to serve the functions of basic human interaction when no other language is available. It is not a random collection of 'foreigner talk'; instead, it has internal structural logic. In its earliest and most basic form, *jargon* might better express its nature. A pidgin generally has a 'rationalised' morphosyntax and phonology, along with a relatively circumscribed lexis.

An expanded pidgin can be used to express a great many more ideas and issues than most pidgins. It can be used as a language for everyday life, even though it is no one's first language. A pidgincreole is, essentially, an expanded pidgin which has some native speakers, even though most use it as their second language (drawing a line between this state and a creole is difficult). While most pidgins cease to be spoken when their communicative purposes end, many specialists believe that some pidgins will become creoles when they acquire native speakers. For further discussion, see Chapter 3.

relexification Put in a straightforward manner, relexification is a process whereby lexis derived from one language is replaced by lexis from another within a variety. In the study of pidgins and creoles, it is often associated with the wholesale replacement of lexis from one source by material from another. Scholars who subscribe to the idea of Portuguese monogenesis would claim that the presence of some Portuguese vocabulary in creoles apparently lexified by other languages is evidence for the relexification of originally Afro-Portuguese pidgins and creoles. Other scholars would claim that the European lexis found in many pidgins and creoles replaced lexis derived from the native variety of the speakers. For more discussion, see Chapter 3.

semi-creole Also known as a creoloid and a partly restructured vernacular, a semi-creole is a variety which has creole features but which cannot be fully classified as such. For more discussion, see Chapter 4.

semi-speakers Individuals with a sound passive knowledge of a language but who are unable to produce examples of that language in ways that would satisfy the norms of forms of that language spoken by monolinguals or dominant bilinguals. A continuum exists between those semi-speakers whose abilities in the language are similar to those of fully native speakers and those who can barely produce any meaningful segments.

simplification, linguistic The process by which complex linguistic systems are 'rationalised', so that more common features are emphasised while less common ones are downplayed. This is a complex and much debated process and is discussed in some depth in Chapter 3.

sociolinguistics The study of language through the study of society. *Variationist* sociolinguistics analyses linguistic variation from a sociological viewpoint; *macrosociolinguistics*, otherwise the *sociology of language*, considers how groups use language varieties within the political, social and cultural frameworks in which they live.

substratal influence The influence exerted by a variety spoken by a population which is socially, economically and politically less powerful upon the variety spoken by the more powerful population. This influence is often more difficult to observe than is the case for superstratal influence. See Chapter 1 for further discussion.

superstratal influence The influence exerted by a variety spoken by a population which is socially, economically and politically more powerful upon the variety spoken by a less powerful population. See Chapter 1 for further discussion.

tense, verb Most languages (but not all: see Comrie 1976: 6) express distinctions between different time references through the form of their verbs. What these time references – tenses – are, and how they are expressed, can differ greatly, even within a small region. Thus French (and all the Romance languages, in fact; for a detailed discussion, see Maiden 2018) express three time references – present, past and future – through inflectional morphology, while the Germanic languages express only two – present and past ('tenses' such as 'future perfect' and 'past perfect' are related to aspect rather than time reference; for a discussion of how this confusion can come into being, see Comrie 1985). This does not mean, of course, that the Germanic languages cannot describe future events or strategies. Doing so can involve the use of adverbials, as with Modern High German *morgen sehe ich ihn* (literally, 'tomorrow see I him': 'tomorrow I will see him'), or the use of auxiliary verbs, as with *morgen werde ich ihn sehen* (literally, 'tomorrow become I him to see': 'tomorrow I will see him'; *werden*, when a fully lexical verb, means 'to become'). (English prefers the use of the modal verbs *will* and *shall*, as with *tomorrow I will/shall see him*.)

tone, lexical In English, the tone used in a particular utterance tends to be pragmatic in nature. A particular tone might imply, for example, irony, enthusiasm or a desire for haste. The words involved might be nuanced differently in terms of meaning because of this, but they do not become different words. In some languages, such as Chinese, however, the tone given to a syllable often dictates what word is being represented. While systems of this sort are generally associated primarily with East and South-East Asian languages, as well as some West African languages, they can be found (in a rather uncomplicated way) in most Swedish and Norwegian varieties. Ancient Greek also had a pitch accent system which appears to be comparable to lexical tone.

typology, linguistic Linguistic typology is, essentially, the study of similarities in structure between languages which are not (necessarily) related to each other. It is based upon precepts of types of morphosyntax which can be analysed cross-linguistically (an excellent introduction can be found in Velupillai 2012). One significant product of the field (indeed, among its earliest manifestations) is the classification of languages into various types (as Comrie 1981: 39 points out, these states have been for some time of less importance to the work of linguistic typologists themselves than they have been to, for instance, historical linguists). There is much dissent among specialists about the nature of the types about to be reviewed (for discussion, see Comrie 1981 and, more recently, Harris and Xu 2006; Iacobini 2006).

From one viewpoint, languages can be classified as being either synthetic or analytic in type. Fully synthetic languages, according to this analysis, express the morphosyntactic function of words and phrases by form. Thus, in Latin, the form *puellam* tells you both that the word means 'girl' and also that it is a feminine noun in accusative case, which generally implies that it has a direct object function. Analytic languages, on the other hand, express function through the positioning of a word or phrase in the clause. Thus English *the girl* carries with it no functional information (beyond that it is definite). Instead, the phrase needs to be placed within its syntactic context for this information to be supplied.

Another way to approach this issue is to see types as referring to the nature of the inflectional morphology (or lack thereof) employed by a language. This can be identified as demonstrating a tripartite split (although more complex schemas are possible) between agglutinative, fusional and isolating types.

Agglutinative inflections are ones in which the grammatical information is stored in the endings' morphology (in some languages, functional information is carried in prefixes, but this need not concern us here) in such a way that it is possible to peel apart the different levels of functional marking. Thus, following Comrie (1981: 41), Turkish *adam-ı* represents *adam* 'boy' in the accusative singular (hyphenation throughout is there only to point out separate inflectional morphemes; hyphens are not found in everyday writing), while *adam-lar-ı* is the plural equivalent; the dative singular is *adam-a*, while the plural equivalent is *adam-lar-a*. Extrapolating somewhat, in these contexts, each marked function is represented by a specific morpheme: *-lar-* marks plurality and always follows the stem; this itself is succeeded by an unchanging marker of function (even when this is zero, as in the case of the nominative form). These are invariant, whether in singular or plural. All functional information is carried unambiguously; conversely, the words themselves can become quite lengthy.

With fusional languages, on the other hand, functional information is carried in morphology which cannot be (entirely or at all) broken down into its constituent parts. This can be seen in the following examples (Comrie 1981: 41) from Russian, for the noun *stol* 'table': the accusative singular form is *stol*, while the plural equivalent is *stol-y*; the dative singular is *stol-u*, while its plural equivalent is *stol-am*. Similarities in functional marking certainly occur, but they are of a different order from that discussed for Turkish. For the dative case, for instance, the singular and plural case markers do not appear to be related to each other. This is made even plainer when, as Comrie does, the case endings in other noun classes are compared. The ending is meaningful of itself in a particular context but not necessarily in similar contexts with different nouns. Isolating languages follow a very different path. In their purest form, these languages do not evince functional morphology at all, as demonstrated in the following, well-known example from Vietnamese:

Khi tôi đến nhà bạn tôi, chúng tôi bắt đầu, làm bài
when I come house friend I PLURAL I begin do lessons
'When I came to my friend's house, we began to do lessons'
(Comrie 1981: 40)

Here the order of the words and phrases provides the correct analysis of the clause's structure. Indeed, every word appears also to be a single morpheme. The word *tôi* 'I' can also mean 'my'. 'We' is represented by the same pronoun, but with a (discrete) plurality marker. Verb tense is not expressed overtly; instead, it is context which tells the listener when something occurs. In a sense, therefore, both fusional and agglutinative types can be classified as synthetic, while isolating types are also analytic (there are, of course, sub-gradations recognised by specialists). Perhaps, from our point of view, the most important thing to carry away from this discussion, however, is that linguistic type is not static. While not entering into a discussion of whether the development of these typological changes can go only in one direction, it needs to be recognised, for instance, that Chinese used to be more isolating than it is today, while English is considerably more isolating now than it was a thousand years ago.

uniformitarianism The view that creoles are not new linguistic entities but rather are varieties of the dominant language, in particular in its vernacular and nonstandard forms, which have been heavily influenced by periods when many of its speakers were second language users. The hypothesis works best when discussing many of the creoles spoken in the Caribbean, Atlantic and Indian Ocean zones; it is less convincing when applied, for instance, to the Melanesian creole varieties. It is vehemently opposed to creole exceptionalism. For further discussion, see Chapter 3.

References

Aboh, E., and U. Ansaldo. 2007. 'The role of typology in language creation: A descriptive take'. In Ansaldo, Matthews and Lim (2007): 39-66.

Abondolo, Daniel. 1998a. 'Introduction'. In Abondolo (1998b): 1-42.

Abondolo, Daniel (ed.). 1998b. *The Uralic Languages.* London: Routledge.

Adamson, Sylvia, Vivian Law, Nigel Vincent and Susan Wright (eds.). 1990. *Papers from the 5th International Conference on English Historical Linguistics.* Amsterdam: John Benjamins.

Aitken, A. J. 1984. 'Scots and English in Scotland'. In Trudgill (1984): 517-32.

Ammon, U. 1989. *Status and Function of Language and Language Varieties.* Berlin: Mouton de Gruyter.

Amoamo, Maria. 2013. 'Empire and erasure: A case study of Pitcairn Island'. *Island Studies Journal* 8: 233-54.

Anderson, Benedict. 2006. *Imagined Communities: Reflections on the Origin and Spread of Nationalism.* 2nd ed. London: Verso.

Anderson, Gregory D. S. 2020. 'Form and pattern borrowing across Siberian, Turkic, Mongolic, and Tungusic languages'. In Robbeets and Savelyev (2020): 715-25.

Ansaldo, Umberto. 2009. *Contact Languages: Ecologies and Evolution in Asia.* Cambridge: Cambridge University Press.

Ansaldo, Umberto (ed.). 2012. *Pidgins and Creoles in Asia.* Amsterdam: John Benjamins.

Ansaldo, U., S. Matthews and L. Lim (eds.). 2007. *Deconstructing Creole.* Amsterdam: John Benjamins.

Ansaldo, Umberto, Stephen Matthews and Geoff Smith. 2012. 'China coast pidgin: Texts and contexts'. In Ansaldo (2012): 59-90.

Arends, J. 2017. *Language and Slavery: A Social and Linguistic History of the Suriname Creoles.* Amsterdam: John Benjamins.

Árnason, Kristján. 2011. *The Phonology of Icelandic and Faeroese.* Oxford: Oxford University Press.

Auer, Peter, Frans Hinskens and Paul Kerswill (eds.). 2005. *Dialect Change: Convergence and Divergence in European Languages.* Cambridge: Cambridge University Press.

Auer, P., F. Hinskens and K. Mattheier (eds.). 1996. 'Convergence and divergence of dialects in Europe'. Special issue. *Sociolinguistica* 10.

Ayers, Edward L. 2007. *The Promise of the New South: Life after Reconstruction.* Oxford: Oxford University Press.

Bailey, Guy. 1997. 'When did Southern American English begin?' In Schneider (1997): 255-76.

Bailey, Guy. 2001. 'The relationship between African American and white vernaculars: A sociocultural history and some phonological evidence'. In Lanehart (2001): 53-92.

Bakker, Peter. 2008. 'Pidgins versus Creoles and Pidgincreoles'. In Kouwenberg and Singler (2008): 130–57.

Bakker, Peter, and Yaron Matras (eds.). 2013. *Contact Languages: A Comprehensive Guide*. Berlin: De Gruyter Mouton.

Baladzhaeva, Liuba, and Batia Laufer. 2018. 'Is first language attrition possible without second language knowledge?' *International Review of Applied Linguistics in Language Teaching* 56: 103–86.

Ball, Martin J. (ed.). 1993. *The Celtic Languages*. London: Routledge.

Barbour, Stephen, and Cathie Carmichael (eds.). 2000. *Language and Nationalism in Europe*. Oxford: Oxford University Press.

Barme, Stefan. 2008. 'Latein – Vulgärlatein – Moselromanisch – zur Sprache der frühchristlichen Grabinschriften im Raum Trier' [Latin – Vulgar Latin – Mosel Romance – towards the language of the early Christian grave inscriptions in the Trier area]. *Zeitschrift für romanische Philologie* 124: 15–30.

Barnes, Michael P. 1998. *The Norn Language of Shetland and Orkney*. Lerwick: Shetland Times.

Barnes, Michael P. 2010. 'The study of Norn'. In Millar (2010b): 26–47.

Bartens, Angela. 2013. 'Creole languages'. In Bakker and Matras (2013): 65–158.

Baugh, Albert C., and Thomas Cable. 2018. *A History of the English Language*. 6th ed. London: Routledge.

Baxter, Tam T., and Peter Trudgill. 2019. 'On case loss and svarabhakti vowels: The sociolinguistic typology and geolinguistics of simplification in North Germanic'. *Linguistic Geography* 7: 1–13.

Bayram, Fatih, Jason Rothman, Michael Iverson, Dave Miller, Eloi Puig-Mayenco, Tanja Kupisch and Marit Westergaard. 2019. 'Differences in use without deficiencies in competence: Passives in the Turkish and German of Turkish heritage speakers in Germany'. *International Journal of Bilingual Education and Bilingualism* 22: 919–39.

Becker, Angelika, and Tonjes Veenstra. 2003. 'Creole protypes as basic varieties and inflectional morphology'. In Dimroth and Starren (2003): 235–64.

Bennett, David H. 1988. *The Party of Fear: From Nativist Movements to the New Right in American History*. Chapel Hill: University of North Carolina Press.

Bereczki, Gábor. 1993. 'The character and the scale of Turkic influence on the structure of Finno-Ugric languages'. In Broganyi and Lipp (1993): 509–19.

Berg, Kristian. 2014. 'Stability and convergence in case marking: Low and High German'. In Braunmüller, Höder and Kühl (2014): 63–75.

Bickerton, Derek. (1981) 2016. *Roots of Language*. Berlin: Language Science Press.

Bickerton, Derek. 1984. 'The language bioprogram hypothesis'. *Behavioral and Brain Sciences* 7: 173–221.

Bousquette, Joshua, and Michael T. Putnam. 2019. 'Redefining language death: Evidence from moribund grammars'. *Language Learning* 70: 188–225.

Braunmüller, Kurt, Steffen Höder and Karoline Kühl (eds.). 2014. *Stability and Divergence in Language Contact: Factors and Mechanisms.* Amsterdam: John Benjamins.

Breivik, Leiv Egil, and Ernst Håkon Jahr (eds.). 1989. *Language Change: Contributions to the Study of Its Causes.* Berlin: Mouton de Gruyter.

Brenzinger, Matthias (ed.). (1992) 2012. *Language Death: Factual and Theoretical Explorations with Special Reference to East Africa.* Berlin: Mouton de Gruyter.

Brinton, Laurel J. (ed.). 1999. *Historical Linguistics 1999: Selected Papers from the 14th International Conference on Historical Linguistics.* Amsterdam: John Benjamins.

Britain, David. 1997. 'Dialect contact and phonological reallocation: "Canadian Raising" in the English Fens'. *Language in Society* 26: 15–46.

Britain, David. 2014. 'Where North meets South? Contact, divergence, and the routinisation of the Fenland dialect boundary'. In Watt and Llamas (2014): 27–43.

Britain, David. 2015. 'Between North and South: The Fenland'. In Hickey (2015): 417–35.

Broganyi, Bela, and Reiner Lipp (eds.). 1993. *Comparative-Historical Linguistics: Indo-European and Finno-Ugric – Papers in Honor of Oswald Szemerényi III.* Amsterdam: John Benjamins.

Brown, Cecil H. 2020. 'Beck-Wichmann-Brown evaluation of lexical comparisons for the Transeurasian proposal'. In Robbeets and Savelyev (2020): 735–50.

Brown, Keith (ed.). 2006. *Encyclopedia of Language and Linguistics.* 2nd ed. Amsterdam: Elsevier.

Bucholtz, Mary. 2003. 'Sociolinguistic nostalgia and the authentication of identity'. *Journal of Sociolinguistics* 7: 398–416.

Buschfeld, Sarah, Thomas Hoffmann, Magnus Huber and Alexander Kautzsch (eds.). 2014. *The Evolution of Englishes: The Dynamic Model and Beyond.* Amsterdam: John Benjamins.

Campbell, Lyle. 2020. *Historical Linguistics: An Introduction.* 4th ed. Edinburgh: Edinburgh University Press.

Campbell, Lyle, and Martha G. Muntzel. 1989. 'The structural consequences of language death'. In Dorian (1989): 181–96.

Campbell, Lyle, and William J. Poser. 2008. *Language Classification: History and Method.* Cambridge: Cambridge University Press.

Cardoso, H. C., A. N. Baxter and N. M. Pinharanda (eds.). 2012. *Ibero-Asian Creoles: Comparative Perspectives.* Amsterdam: John Benjamins.

Carmichael, Cathie. 2000. 'Language and nationalism in the Balkans'. In Barbour and Carmichael (2000): 222–39.

Carvalho, Ana Maria. 2006. 'Nominal number marking in a variety of Spanish in contact with Portuguese'. In Face and Klee (2006): 154–66.

Castillo, Yolanda Rivera, and Nicholas Faraclas. 2006. 'The emergence of systems of lexical and grammatical tone and stress in Caribbean and West African

Creoles'. *Language Typology and Universals* 59: 148–69.

Ceolin, Andrea. 2019. 'Significance testing of the Altaic family'. *Diachronica* 36: 299–336.

Chambers, J. K., and N. Schilling (eds.). 2013. *The Handbook of Language Variation and Change*. 2nd ed. Chichester: Wiley.

Chambers, J. K., P. Trudgill and N. Schilling-Estes (eds.). 2001. *The Handbook of Language Variation and Change*. Oxford: Blackwell.

Chaudenson, Robert. 1974. *La lexique du parler Créole de la Réunion* [The lexis of the Creole dialect of Réunion]. 2 vols. Paris: Champion.

Chaudenson, Robert. (1992) 2012. *Des iles, des hommes, des langues* [About the islands, the people, the languages]. Paris: L'Harmatian.

Chaudenson, Robert. 2001. *Creolization of Language and Culture*. London: Routledge.

Chaudenson, Robert. 2003. *La créolisation: Théorie, applications, implications* [Creolisation: theory, applications, implications]. Paris: L'Harmatian.

Chesterman, Andrew. 1991. *On Definiteness: A Study with Special Reference to English and Finnish*. Cambridge: Cambridge University Press.

Clackson, James, Patrick Jones, Katherine McDonald and Livia Tagliapietra (eds.). 2020. *Migration, Mobility and Language Contact around the Ancient Mediterranean*. Cambridge: Cambridge University Press.

Clayton, Ian. 2018. 'Revisiting Hebrides English'. *English World-Wide* 39: 157–89.

Clemens, Lukas. 2014. 'Trier in Umbruch – die Stadt während des 5. bis 9. Jahrhunderts n.Chr' [Trier in upheaval – the city during the fifth to ninth centuries CE]. In Landesmuseum Württemberg and Rheinisches Landesmuseum (2014): 328–35.

Clyne, Michael (ed.). (1992) 2012. *Pluricentric Languages: Differing Norms in Different Nations*. Berlin: Mouton de Gruyter.

Clyne, Michael. 2003. *Dynamics of Language Contact: English and Immigrant Languages*. Cambridge: Cambridge University Press.

Cole, Beth. 2015. 'Morphosyntactic variation in Uist Gaelic: A case of language shift?' Unpublished doctoral dissertation, University of Aberdeen.

Coleman, Julie. 1995. 'The chronology of French and Latin loan words in English'. *Transactions of the Philological Society* 9: 95–124.

Collins, James T. 2022. 'The geographic and demographic expansion of Malay'. In Mufwene and Escobar (2022): 1:327–57.

Combrink, Johan. 1978. 'Afrikaans: Its origins and development'. In Dutton and Prinsloo (1978): 69–95.

Comrie, Bernard. 1976. *Aspect*. Cambridge: Cambridge University Press.

Comrie, Bernard. 1981. *Language Universals and Linguistic Typology*. Oxford: Basil Blackwell.

Comrie, Bernard. 1985. *Tense*. Cambridge: Cambridge University Press.

Cook, Eung-Do. 1995. 'Is there a convergence in language death? Evidence from Chipewyan and Stoney'. *Journal of Linguistic Anthropology* 5: 217–31.

Cook, Vivian (ed.). 2003. *Effects of the Second Language on the First.* Clevedon: Multilingual Matters.

Corne, Chris. 1999. *From French to Creole.* London: University of Westminster Press.

Dahl, Östen. 2001. 'The origin of the Scandinavian languages'. In Dahl and Koptjevskaja-Tamm (2001): 215–35.

Dahl, Östen. 2004. *The Growth and Maintenance of Linguistic Complexity.* Amsterdam: John Benjamins.

Dahl, Östen, and Maria Koptjevskaja-Tamm (eds.). 2001. *Circum-Baltic Languages.* Amsterdam: John Benjamins.

Dahlberg, T. (1954–6). 'Das Niederdeutsche im skandinavischen Raum' [Low German in the Scandinavian area]. *Wirkendes Wort* 6: 193–9.

Damousi, Joy. 2010. *Colonial Voices: A Cultural History of English in Australia 1840–1940.* Cambridge: Cambridge University Press.

Dawkins, Richard M. 1916. *Modern Greek in Asia Minor.* Cambridge: Cambridge University Press.

de Boer, Cornelis, Jacobus van Ginneken and Anton G. van Hamel (eds.). 1930. *Actes du Premier Congrès International des Linguistes à La Haye, du 10–15 Avril 1928* [Acts of the First International Congress of Linguists at The Hague, 10–15 April 1928]. Leiden: A. W. Sijthoff.

Decamp, David. 1971. 'Introduction: The study of pidgin and creole languages'. In Hymes (1971): 13–43.

De Fréine, Seán. 1965. *The Great Silence.* Dublin: Foilseachain Naisiunta Teoranta.

De Graff, M. 2005. 'Linguists' most dangerous myth: The fallacy of creole exceptionalism'. *Language in Society* 34: 533–91.

Deumert, Ana. 2001. 'Language variation and standardization at the Cape (1880–1922): A contribution to Afrikaans sociohistorical linguistics'. *Journal of Germanic Linguistics* 13: 301–52.

Deumert, Ana. 2004. *Language Standardization and Language Change: The Dynamics of Cape Dutch.* Amsterdam: John Benjamins.

Devine, T. M. 2018. *The Scottish Clearances: A History of the Dispossessed, 1600–1900.* Harmondsworth: Penguin.

Dickson, Neil T. R. 2002. *Brethren in Scotland 1838–2000: A Social Study of an Evangelical Movement.* Bletchley: Paternoster.

Dimroth, Christine, and Marianne Starren (eds.). 2003. *Information Structure and the Dynamics of Language Acquisition.* Amsterdam: John Benjamins.

Dixon, R. W. 1997. *The Rise and Fall of Languages.* Cambridge: Cambridge University Press.

Donaldson, Gordon. 1983. 'The Scots settlement in Shetland'. In Withrington (1983): 8–19.

Dorian, Nancy C. 1977. 'The problem of the semi-speaker in language death'. *Linguistics* 15: 23–32.

Dorian, Nancy C. 1978. 'The fate of morphological complexity in language death: Evidence from East Sutherland Gaelic'. *Language* 54: 590–609.

Dorian, Nancy C. 1981. *Language Death: The Life Cycle of a Scottish Gaelic*

Dialect. Philadelphia: University of Pennsylvania Press.

Dossena, Marina. 2005. *Scotticisms in Grammar and Vocabulary*. Edinburgh: John Donald.

Dossena, Marina, and Roger Lass (eds.). 2009. *Studies in English and European Historical Dialectology*. Bern: Peter Lang.

Drechsel, Emanuel J. 2014. *Language Contact in the Early Colonial Pacific*. Cambridge: Cambridge University Press.

Dressler, Wolfgang U. 1983. 'On the predictiveness of natural morphology'. *Journal of Linguistics* 21: 321–37.

Dressler, Wolfgang U. 1985. *Morphonology*. Ann Arbor: Karoma.

Dutton, L., and K. Prinsloo (eds.). 1978. *Language and Communication Studies in South Africa*. Oxford: Oxford University Press.

Ejerhed, E., and I. Henrysson (eds). 1980. *Tvåspråkighet: Föredrag från tredje nordiska tvåspråkighetsymposiet 4–5 juni 1980, Umeå universitet* [Bilingualism: Proceedings from the third Nordic bilingualism symposium 4–5 June 1980, Umeå University]. Umeå: Umeå University.

Elder, Olivia. 2020. 'Population migration and language in the city of Rome'. In Clackson et al. (2020): 268–95.

Emonds, Joseph Embley. 2011. 'English as a North Germanic language: From the Norman Conquest to the present'. In Trušník, Nemčoková and Bell (2011): 13–26.

Emonds, Joseph Embley, and Jan Terje Faarlund. 2014. *English: The Language of the Vikings*. Olomouc: Palacký University. http://anglistika.upol.cz/vikings2014.

Eska, Joseph F. 2006. 'Galatian language'. In Koch (2006): 3:378.

Ewing, Michael C. 2020. 'Features of Indonesian in Bandung'. *Nusa* 68: 51–66.

Eyþórsson, Þórhallur. 2002. 'Hvaða mál talaði Egill Skalla-Grímsson á Englandi?' [What language did Egill Skalla-Grímsson speak in England?]. *Málfríður* 18: 21–6.

Face, Timothy I., and Carol I. Klee (eds.). 2006. *Selected Proceedings of the 8th Hispanic Linguistics Symposium*. Somerville: Cascadilla Proceedings Project.

Falck, P. T. 1881. *Die Oberpahlische Freundschaft* [The Oberpahlish fellowship]. Leipzig.

Fasold, Ralph. 1987. *The Sociolinguistics of Society*. Oxford: Blackwell.

Feagin, Crawford. 1979. *Variation and Change in Alabama English: A Sociolinguistic Study of the White Community*. Washington, DC: Georgetown University Press.

Fenton, Alexander. 1968-9. 'The Tabu language of the fishermen of Orkney and Shetland'. *Ethnologia Europaea* 2-3: 118–22.

Fenton, Alexander. 1978. *The Northern Isles: Orkney and Shetland*. Edinburgh: Donald.

Ferguson, Charles. 1959. 'Diglossia'. *Word* 15: 325–40.

Fishman, Joshua A. 1967. 'Bilingualism with and without diglossia; diglossia with and without bilingualism'. *Journal of Social Issues* 23: 29–38.

Fishman, Joshua A. 1991. *Reversing Language Shift: Theoretical and Empirical Foundations of Assistance to Threatened Languages*. Clevedon: Multilingual Matters.

Fletcher, Richard. 1997. *The Conversion of Europe: From Paganism to Christianity 371–1386*. London: HarperCollins.

Friedman, Victor A., and Brian D. Joseph. 2017. 'Reassessing Sprachbunds: a view from the Balkans'. In Hickey (2017): 55–87.

Friedrich, Svetlana. 2009. *Definitheit im Russischen* [Definiteness in Russian]. Frankfurt am Main: Peter Lang.

Fritz, Matthias, and Michael Meier-Brügger. 2021. *Indo-Germanische Sprachwissenschaft* [Indo-European linguistics]. 10th ed. Berlin: De Gruyter.

Gabaccia, Donna R. 2013. *Italy's Many Diasporas*. London: Routledge.

Gal, Susan. 1978. 'Peasant men can't get wives: language change and sex roles in a bilingual community'. *Language in Society* 7: 1–16.

Gal, Susan. 1979. *Language Shift: Social Determinants of Linguistic Change in Bilingual Austria*. New York: Academic Press.

Giglioli, Pier Paolo (ed.). 1972. *Language and Social Context*. Harmondsworth: Penguin.

Gilles, Peter. 2023. 'Luxembourgish'. In Kürscher and Dammel (2023).

Gillies, William. 1993. 'Scottish Gaelic'. In Ball (1993): 145–227.

Gillis, Brian. 2013. 'Red English: Language and American Indian English'. In Lawson (2013): 180–86.

Githiora, Chege. 2002. 'Sheng: Peer language, Swahili dialect or emerging Creole'. *Journal of African Cultural Studies* 15: 159–81.

Goldman, David. 2021. *Immortal*. London: Academic Press.

Good, Jeff. 2009. 'A twice-mixed creole? Tracing the history of a prosodic split in the Saramaccan lexicon'. *Studies in Language* 33: 459–98.

Good, Jeff. n.d. 'Loanwords in Saramaccan, an English-based Atlantic creole of Suriname'.

Gordon, Elizabeth, Lyle Campbell, Jennifer Hay, Margaret Maclagan, Andrea Sudbury and Peter Trudgill. 2004. *New Zealand English: Its Origins and Evolution*. Cambridge: Cambridge University Press.

Gregory, James N. 2005. *The Southern Diaspora: How the Great Migration of Black and White Southerners Transformed America*. Chapel Hill: University of North Carolina Press.

Gumperz, John J. 1982. *Discourse Strategies*. Cambridge: Cambridge University Press.

Gumperz, J., and R. Wilson. 1971. 'Convergence and creolization: A case from the Indo-Aryan /Dravidian border in India'. In Hymes (1971): 151–67.

Gzella, Holger. 2021. *Aramaic: A History of the First World Language*. Translated by Benjamin D. Suchard. Grand Rapids: William B. Erdmans.

Hall, Robert A. 1966. *Pidgin and Creole Languages*. Ithaca, NY: Cornell University Press.

Hancock, I. F., E. Polomé, M. Goodman and B. Heine (eds.). 1979. *Readings in Creole Studies*. Ghent: E. Story-Scientia.

Harris, A., and Z. Zu. 2006. 'Diachronic morphological typology'. In Brown (2006): 8:1–7.

Haugen, Einar. 1976. *The Scandinavian Languages: An Introduction*. London: Faber and Faber.

Hay, Jeniffer, Margaret Maclagan and Elizabeth Gordon. 2008. *New*

Zealand English. Edinburgh: Edinburgh University Press.

Heddle, Donna. 2010. 'The Norse element in the Orkney dialect'. In Millar (2010b): 48–57.

Heine, B. 1979. 'Some linguistic characteristics of African-based pidgins'. In Hancock et al. (1979): 89–98.

Hernàndez-Campoy, Juan M., and J. Camilo Conde-Silvestre (eds.). 2012. *The Handbook of Historical Sociolinguistics*. Oxford: Wiley-Blackwell.

Hickey, Raymond. 2007. *Irish English: History and Present-Day Forms*. Cambridge: Cambridge University Press.

Hickey, Raymond (ed.). 2015. *Researching Northern English*. Amsterdam: John Benjamins.

Hickey, Raymond (ed.). 2017. *The Cambridge Handbook of Areal Linguistics*. Cambridge: Cambridge University Press.

Hickey, Raymond (ed.) 2020. The Handbook of Language Contact. Second edition. Malden, MA: Wiley-Blackwell.

Hock, Hans Heinrich. 1991. *Principles of Historical Linguistics*. Berlin: Mouton de Gruyter.

Hock, Hans Heinrich, and Brian D. Joseph. 2019. *Language History, Language Change, and Language Relationship*. Berlin: De Gruyter.

Holm, John. 1988-9. *Pidgins and Creoles*. 2 vols. Cambridge: Cambridge University Press.

Holm, John. 2004. *Languages in Contact: The Partial Restructuring of Vernaculars*. Cambridge: Cambridge University Press.

Holm, John. 2014. 'An 18th-century novel from the Miskito Coast: what was creolized?' *English World-Wide* 35: 52–67.

Holmes, Janet. 1997. 'Maori and Pakeha English: Some New Zealand social dialect data'. *Language in Society* 26: 65–101.

Honti, László. 1998. 'ObUgrian'. In Abondolo (1998b): 327–57.

Hopper, Paul J., and Elizabeth Closs Traugott. 1993. *Grammaticalization*. 2nd ed. Cambridge: Cambridge University Press.

Horrocks, Geoffrey. 1997. *Greek: A History of the Language and Its Speakers*. London: Longman.

Hunter, James. 2015. *Set Adrift on the World: The Sutherland Clearances*. Edinburgh: Birlinn.

Hupe, Joachim. 2014. 'Topographie und Stadtentwicklung der colonia Augusta Trevorum' [The topography and urban development of *colonia Augusta Trevorum*]. In Landesmuseum Württemberg and Rheinisches Landesmuseum (2014): 96–111.

Hutchinson, Mark, and John Wolffe. 2012. *A Short History of Global Evangelicalism*. Cambridge: Cambridge University Press.

Hymes, Dell H. (ed.). 1971. *Pidginization and Creolization of Languages*. Cambridge: Cambridge University Press.

Iacobini, Claudio. 2006. 'Morphological typology'. In Brown (2006): 8:278–82.

Jaakola, Minna, and Tiina Onikki (eds.). 2023. *The Finnish Case System: Cognitive Linguistic Perspectives*. Helsinki: Finnish Literature Society.

Jahr, Ernst Håkon (ed.). 1995. *Nordisk og Nedertysk: Språkkontakt og språkutvikling i Norden i seinmellomalderen* [Nordic and Low German: language contact and language development in the north in the late Middle Ages]. Oslo: Novus.

Junttila, Santeri. 2012. 'The prehistoric context of the oldest contacts between Baltic and Finnic languages'. In *A Linguistic Map of Prehistoric Northern Europe*, 261–96. Helsinki: Suomalais-Ugrilaisen Seuran Toimituksia.

Karlsson, Fred. 2018. *Finnish: A Comprehensive Grammar*. London: Routledge.

Kautsch, Alexander. 2002. *The Historical Evolution of Earlier African American English: An Empirical Comparison of Early Sources*. Berlin: Mouton de Gruyter.

Keesing, Roger M. 1991. 'The expansion of Melanesian pidgin: Further early evidence from the Solomons'. *Journal of Pidgin and Creole Languages* 6: 215–29.

Keller, Rudi. 1994. *On Language Change: The Invisible Hand in Language Change*. London: Routledge.

Kerswill, Paul. 1994. *Dialect Convergence: Rural Speech in Urban Norway*. Oxford: Clarendon Press.

Kerswill, Paul. 2001. 'Koineization and accommodation'. In Chambers, Trudgill and Schilling-Estes (2001): 669–701.

Kerswill, Paul, and Ann Williams. 2000. 'Creating a New Town koiné: Children and language change in Milton Keynes'. *Language in Society* 29: 65–115.

Kim, Ronald I. 2008. 'California Chinese Pidgin English and its connections: preliminary remarks'. *Journal of Pidgin and Creole Languages* 23: 329–44.

Klein, Thomas B., and Michael Adams. 2017. 'Continuity versus English influence in the West African Lexicon of Gullah'. *American Speech* 92: 107–50.

Knooihuizen, Remco. 2006. 'The Norn to Scots language shift: Another look at the evidence'. *Northern Studies* 39: 5–16.

Knooihuizen, Remco. 2007. 'Fishing for words: The taboo language of Shetland fishermen and the dating of Norn language death'. *Transactions of the Philological Society* 106: 100–113.

Knooihuizen, Remco. 2009. 'Shetland Scots as a new dialect: Phonetic and phonological considerations'. *English Language and Linguistics* 13: 483–501.

Koch, Harold. 2011. 'Substrate influences on New South Wales Pidgin'. In Lefebvre (2011): 489–512.

Koch, John T. (ed.). 2006. *Celtic Culture: A Historical Encyclopedia*. Santa Barbara: ABC-CLIO.

Kopitar, Jernej. 1829. 'Albanische, walachische und bulgarische Sprache' [Albanian, Walachian and Bulgarian language]. *Jahrbücher der Literatur* 46: 59–106.

Kotzoglou, G., K. Nikolou, E. Karantzola, K. Frantzi, I. Galantomos, M. Georgalidou, V. Kourti-Kazoullis, C. Papadopoulou and E. Vlachou (eds.). 2014. *Selected Papers of the 11th International Conference on Greek Linguistics (Rhodes, 26–29 September, 2013)*. Rhodes: Laboratory of Linguistics of the Southeastern Mediterranean.

Kouwenberg, Silvia, and John Victor Singler (eds.). 2008. *The Handbook of Pidgin and Creole Studies*. Chichester: Wiley-Blackwell.

Kürscher, Sebastian, and Antje Dammel (eds.). 2023. *The Oxford Encyclopedia of Germanic Linguistics*. Oxford: Oxford University Press.

Kusters, Wouter. 2003. *Linguistic Complexity: The Influence of Social Change on Verbal Inflection*. Utrecht: LOT.

Laakso, Johanna. 2001. 'The Finnic languages'. In Dahl and Koptjevskaja-Tamm (2001): 179–212.

Labov, William. (1969) 1972. 'The logic of Nonstandard English'. In Giglioli (1972): 179–215.

Labov, William. 1972. *Sociolinguistic Patterns*. Philadelphia: University of Pennsylvania Press.

Laing, Margaret (ed.). 1989. *Middle English Dialectology: Essays on Some Principles and Problems by Angus McIntosh, M L Samuels and Margaret Laing*. Aberdeen: Aberdeen University Press.

Landesmuseum Württemberg and Rheinisches Landesmuseum (eds.). 2014. *Ein Traum von Rom: Stadtleben im Römischen Deutschland* [A dream of Rome: city life in Roman Germany]. Stuttgart: Konrad Theiss.

Lanehart, S. L. (ed.). 2001. *Sociocultural and Historical Contexts of African American English*. Amsterdam: John Benjamins.

Lanehart, Sonja L. (ed.). 2015. *The Oxford Handbook of African American Language*. Oxford: Oxford University Press.

Lang, Valter. 2020. *Homo Fennicus: Itämerensuomalaisten etnohistoria* [Homo Fennicus: the ethnohistory of the Baltic Finns]. Helsinki: Suomalaisen Kirjallisuuden Seura.

Larsson, Lars-Gunnar. 2001. 'Baltic influence on Finnic languages'. In Dahl and Koptjevskaja-Tamm (2001): 237–54.

Lass, Roger. 1987. 'How reliable is Goldswain? On the credibility of an early South African English source'. *African Studies* 46: 155–62.

Lass, Roger. 1990. 'Where do extraterritorial Englishes come from? Dialect input and recodification in transported Englishes'. In Adamson et al. (1990): 245–8.

Lass, Roger. 1995. 'South African English'. In Mesthrie (1995): 89–106.

Lass, Roger. 2004. 'South African English'. In Hickey (2004b): 363–86.

Lawson, Russell M. (ed.). 2013. *Encyclopedia of American Issues Today*. Santa Barbara: Greenwood.

Laycock, D. 1989. 'The status of Pitcairn-Norfolk: Creole, dialect, or cant?' In Ammon (1989): 608–29.

Leap, William L. 1993. *American Indian English*. Salt Lake City: University of Utah Press.

Lefebvre, Claire (ed.). 2011. *Creoles, Their Substrates and Language Typology*. Amsterdam: John Benjamins.

Lehiste, Ilse. 1965. 'A poem in Halbdeutsch and some questions concerning substratum'. *Word* 21: 55–69.

Lehiste, I., and J. Ross (eds.). 1997. *Estonian Prosody: Papers from a Symposium*. Tallinn: Institute of Estonian Language.

Leinonen, Marja. 1982. *Russian Aspect, "Temporal'naja Lokalizacija" and*

Definiteness/ Indefiniteness. Helsinki: Neuvostoliittoinstituutti.

Leith, Dick. (1983) 1997. *A Social History of English.* London: Routledge.

Liosis, N. 2014. 'Language varieties of the Peloponnese: Contact in diachrony'. In Kotzoglou et al. (2014): 884–94.

Lippi-Green, Rosina. 1997. *English with an Accent: Language, Ideology, and Discrimination in the United States.* London: Routledge.

Ljosland, Ragnhild. 2013. '"I'll cross dat brig whin I come til him": Grammatical gender in the Orkney and Shetland dialects of Scots'. *Scottish Language* 31/32: 29–58.

Ljosland, Ragnhild. 2016. 'The be-perfect in transitive constructions in Orkney and Shetland Scots: Influenced by Norn or not?' In Millar and Cruickshank (2016): 107–27.

McCormick, Eric Hall. 2013. *Omai: Pacific Envoy.* Auckland: Auckland University Press.

McWhorter, John H. 2007. *Language Interrupted: Signs of Non-Native Acquisition in Standard Language Grammars.* Oxford: Oxford University Press.

McWhorter, John H. 2018. *The Creole Debate.* Cambridge: Cambridge University Press.

Maiden, Martin. 2018. *The Romance Verb: Morphemic Structure and Diachrony.* Oxford: Oxford University Press.

Mäkinen, Panu. 1999–2004. 'Suomen kielioppi. Finnish grammar. Finnische grammatik'. http://users.jyu.fi/~pamakine/kieli/suomi/.

Malkiel, Yakov. 1981. 'Drift, slope and slant: Background of, and variations upon, a Sapirian theme'. *Language* 57: 535–70.

Marcantonio, Angela. 2002. *The Uralic Language Family: Facts, Myths and Statistics.* Oxford: Blackwell.

Marten, Lutz. 2012. 'Bantu and Bantoid'. In Vossen and Dimmendaal (2020): 205–19.

Matras, Yaron. 1999. 'The state of present-day Domari in Jerusalem'. *Mediterranean Language Review* 11: 1–58.

Matras, Yaron. 2002. *Romani: A Linguistic Introduction.* Cambridge: Cambridge University Press.

Matras, Yaron. 2010. *Language Contact.* Cambridge: Cambridge University Press.

Matras, Yaron. 2013. 'Contact, convergence, and typology'. In Hickey (2013): 66–85.

Mattheier, K. 1996. 'Varietätenkonvergenz. Überlegungen zu einem Baustein einer Theorie der Sprachvariation' [Convergence of varieties. Considerations for a building block for a theory of language variation]. In Auer, Hinskens and Mattheier (1996): 31–52.

Matthews, Stephen, and Michelle Li. 2012. 'Portuguese pidgin and Chinese Pidgin English in the Canton trade'. In Cardoso, Baxter and Pinharanda (2012): 263–87.

Mazrui, Alamin. 2022. 'The geographic and demographic spread of Swahili'. In Mufwene and Escobar (2022): 1:359–81.

Meisel, J. (ed.). 1977. *Langues en contact – pidgins – creoles* [Languages in contact – pidgins – creoles]. Tübingen: Narr.

Melchers, Gunnel. 1980. 'The Norn element in Shetland dialect today – a case of "never accepted" language death'. In Ejerhed and Henrysson (1980): 254–61.

Menn, Lise. 1989. 'Comparing approaches to comparative aphasiology'. *Aphasiology* 3: 143–50.

Mermin Feinsilver, Lilian. 1962. 'Yiddish idioms in American English'. *American Speech* 37: 200–206.

Mesthrie, Rajend (ed.). 1995. *Language and Social History: Studies in South African Sociolinguistics*. Claremont: David Philip.

Mesthrie, Rajend (ed.). 2004. *Language in South Africa*. Cambridge: Cambridge University Press.

Meyer, Robin. 2023. *Iranian Syntax in Classical Armenian*. Oxford: Oxford University Press.

Meyerhoff, Miriam. 2008. 'Forging pidgin and creole syntax: Substrate, discourse, and inherent variability'. In Kouwenberg and Singler (2008): 48–73.

Miethaner, Ulrich. 2014. 'Innovation in pre-World War II African American English? Evidence from BLUR'. In Buschfeld et al. (2014): 365–85.

Migge, Bettina. 2003. *Creole Formation as Language Contact: The Case of the Surinamese Creoles*. Amsterdam: John Benjamins.

Millar, Robert McColl. 1996. 'Gaelic-influenced Scots in pre-Revolutionary Maryland'. In Ureland and Clarkson (1996): 387–410.

Millar, Robert McColl. 2000. *System Collapse, System Rebirth: The Demonstrative Systems of English 900–1350 and the Birth of the Definite Article*. Bern: Peter Lang.

Millar, Robert McColl. 2005. *Language, Nation and Power*. Basingstoke: Palgrave Macmillan.

Millar, Robert McColl. 2007. *Northern and Insular Scots*. Edinburgh: Edinburgh University Press.

Millar, Robert McColl. 2008. 'The origins and development of Shetland dialect in light of dialect contact theories'. *English World-Wide* 29: 237–67.

Millar, Robert McColl. 2009. 'The origins of the northern Scots dialects'. In Dossena and Lass (2009): 191–208.

Millar, Robert McColl. 2010a. 'Linguistic marginality in Scotland: Scots and the Celtic languages'. In Millar (2010b): 5–17.

Millar, Robert McColl (ed.). 2010b. *Marginal Dialects: Scotland, Ireland and Beyond*. Aberdeen: Forum for Research on the Languages of Scotland and Ireland.

Millar, Robert McColl (ed.). 2010c. *Northern Lights, Northern Words: Selected Papers from the FRLSU Conference, Kirkwall 2009*. Aberdeen: Forum for Research on the Languages of Scotland and Ulster.

Millar, Robert McColl. 2012a. 'The death of Orkney Norn and the genesis of Orkney Scots'. *Scottish Language* 29: 16–36.

Millar, Robert McColl. 2012b. *English Historical Sociolinguistics*. Edinburgh: Edinburgh University Press.

Millar, Robert McColl. 2012c. 'Social history and the sociology of language'. In Hernàndez-Campoy and Conde-Silvestre (2012): 42–59.

Millar, Robert McColl. 2016. *Contact: The Interaction of Closely Related Linguistic Varieties and the History of English*. Edinburgh: Edinburgh University Press.

Millar, Robert McColl. 2018. *Modern Scots: An Analytical Survey*.

Millar, Robert McColl. 2020. *A Sociolinguistic History of Scotland*. Edinburgh: Edinburgh University Press.

Millar, Robert McColl. 2023. *A History of the Scots Language*. Oxford: Oxford University Press.

Millar, Robert McColl, William Barras, and Lisa Marie Bonnici. 2014. *Lexical Variation and Attrition in the Scottish Fishing Communities*. Edinburgh: Edinburgh University Press.

Millar, Robert McColl, and Janet Cruickshank (eds.). 2016. *Before the Storm: Selected Papers from the FRLSU Conference, Ayr 2015*. Aberdeen: Forum for Research on the Languages of Scotland and Ulster.

Millar, Robert McColl, and Alex Nicholls. 1997. 'Ælfric's De Initio Creaturae and London, British Library, Cotton Vespasian A.xxii: Omission, addition, retention and innovation'. In Szarmach and Rosenthal (1997): 431–64.

Millar, Robert McColl, and R. L. Trask. 2023. *Trask's Historical Linguistics*. 4th ed. London: Routledge.

Miller, David B. 2007. 'The many frontiers of pre-Mongol Rus'. In Shepard (2007): 221–60.

Miller, D. Gary. 2012. *External Influences on English: From Its Beginnings to the Renaissance*. Oxford: Oxford University Press.

Miller, Roy Andrew. 1980. *Origins of the Japanese Language: Lectures in Japan during the Academic Year 1977–78*. Seattle: University of Washington Press.

Mišeska Tomić, Olga. (1992) 2012. 'Macedonian as an Ausbau language'. In Clyne ((1992) 2012): 437–54.

Mišeska Tomić, Olga. 2006. *Balkan Sprachbund Morpho-syntactic Features*. Dordrecht: Springer.

Momma, Haruko, and Michael Matto (eds.). 2008. *A Companion to the History of the English Language*. Chichester, Wiley-Blackwell.

Morgan, Philip D England. 1998. *Slave Counterpoint: Black Culture in the Eighteenth Century Chesapeake and Lowcountry*. Chapel Hill: University of North Carolina.

Mougeon, Raymond, and Édouard Beniak (eds.). 1994. *Les origines du français québécois* [The origins of Quebec French]. Sainte-Foy: Les Presses de l'Université Laval.

Mous, Maarten. 2019. 'Language contact'. In Van der Velde et al. (2019): 355–80.

Mufwene, Salikoko S. (ed.). 1993. *Africanisms in Afro-American Language Varieties*. Athens: University of Georgia Press.

Mufwene, Salikoko S. 1997. 'Jargons, pidgins, creoles, and koines: What are they?' In Spears and Winford (1997): 35–70.

Mufwene, Salikoko S. 2001. *The Ecology of Language Evolution*. Cambridge: Cambridge University Press.

Mufwene, Salikoko S. 2008. *Language Evolution: Contact, Competition and Change*. London: Continuum.

Mufwene, Salikoko S. 2013. 'Driving forces in English contact linguistics'. In Schreier and Hundt (2013): 204–21.

Mufwene, Salikoko S. 2014a. 'The English origins of African American Vernacular English: What Edgar W. Schneider has taught us'. In Buschfeld et al. (2014): 349–64.

Mufwene, Salikoko S. (ed.). 2014b. *Iberian Imperialism and Language Evolution in Latin America*. Chicago: University of Chicago Press.

Mufwene, Salikoko S. 2015. 'The emergence of African American English: Monogenetic or polygenetic with or without "decreolization" – under how much substrate influence?' In Lanehart (2015): 57–84.

Mufwene, Salikoko S., Christophe Coupé, and François Pellegrino. 2017. 'Complexity in language: A multifaceted phenomenon'. In Mufwene, Pellegrino and Coupé (2017): 1–29.

Mufwene, Salikoko S., and Anna Maria Escobar (eds.). 2022. *The Cambridge Handbook of Language Contact*. 2 vols. Cambridge: Cambridge University Press.

Mufwene, Salikoko S., François Pellegrino and Christophe Coupé (eds.). 2017. *Complexity in Language: Developmental and Evolutionary Perspectives*. Cambridge: Cambridge University Press.

Mühlhäusler, Peter. 1986. *Pidgin and Creole Linguistics*. Oxford: Basil Blackwell.

Mühlhäusler, Peter. 1990. 'Tok Pisin: Model or special case?' In Verhaar (1990): 171–86.

Mühlhäusler, Peter. 2007. 'The Pitkern-Norf'k language and education'. *English World-Wide* 28: 215–47.

Mühlhäusler, Peter. 2020. *Pitkern-Norf'k: The Language of Pitcairn Island and Norfolk Island*. Berlin: De Gruyter Mouton.

Mühlhäusler, Peter, Thomas E. Dutton and Suzanne Romaine. 2003. *Tok Pisin Texts: From the Beginning to the Present*. Amsterdam: John Benjamins.

Muysken, Peter, and Norval Smith (eds.). 2015. *Surviving the Middle Passage: The West African–Surinam Sprachbund*. Berlin: De Gruyter Mouton.

Myers-Scotton, Carol. 2002. *Contact Linguistics: Bilingual Encounters and Grammatical Outcomes*. Oxford: Oxford University Press.

Naro, Anthony J. 1978. 'A study on the origins of pidginization'. *Language* 54: 314–47.

Nelde, Peter H., P. Sture Ureland and Iain Clarkson (eds.). 1986. *Language Contact in Europe*. Tübingen: Niemeyer.

Neteland, Randi. 2019. *Koine Formation and Society: A Sociolinguistic Study of Migration, Dialects, and Norms in Norwegian Industrial Towns*. Lanham: Lexington Books.

Newmark, Kalina, Nacole Walker and James Stanford. 2016. '"The rez accent knows no borders": Native American ethnic identity expressed through English prosody'. *Language in Society* 45: 633–64.

Nichols, Johanna. 2009. 'Linguistic complexity: A comprehensive definition and survey'. In Sampson, Gil and Trudgill (2009): 110–25.

Oberg, Michael Leroy. 2018. *Native America: A History*. 2nd ed. Malden: Wiley Blackwell.

Opitz, Conny. 2019. 'A complex dynamic systems perspective on personal background variables in L1 attrition'. In Schmid and Köpke (2019): 49–60.

Ostler, Nicholas. 2022. 'The emergence of lingua francas'. In Mufwene and Escobar (2022): II, 403–28.

Owens, Jonathan. 2022. 'Arabic language contact'. In Mufwene and Escobar (2002): 1: 382–424.

Pallier, Christophe. 2007. 'Critical periods in language acquisition and language attrition'. In Schmid et al. (2007): 155–68.

Parkvall, Mikael, and Peter Bakker. 2013. 'Pidgins'. In Bakker and Matras (2013): 15–64.

Peters, Pam. 2008. 'Australian and New Zealand English'. In Momma and Matto (2008): 389–99.

Polinsky, Maria. 2018. *Heritage Languages and Their Speakers*. Cambridge: Cambridge University Press.

Poplack, Shana (ed.). 2000. *The English History of African American English*. Oxford: Blackwell.

Poplack, Shana, and David Sankoff. 1987. 'The Philadelphia story in the Spanish Caribbean'. *American Speech* 62: 291–314.

Poplack, Shana, and Sali A. Tagliamonte. 2001. *African American English in the Diaspora*. Oxford: Blackwell.

Raine, Thomas. 1824. 'Narrative of visit to Pitcairn's Island, in the ship Surrey, 1821'. *Literary Chronicle and Weekly Review* 268: 425–68.

Rendboe, Laurits. 1984. 'How "worn out" or "corrupted" was Shetland Norn in its final stage?' *NOWELE* 3: 53–88.

Rendboe, Laurits. 1987. *Det gamle shetlandske sprog: George Low's ordliste fra 1774* [The old Shetland language: George Low's wordlist from 1774]. *NOWELE* 3 (suppl.).

Rickford, John R. 2015. 'The creole origins hypothesis'. In Lanehart (2015): 35–56.

Riehl, Claudia Maria. 2019. 'Language contact and language attrition'. In Schmid and Köpke (2019): 314–28.

Robbeets, Martine. 2005. *Is Japanese Related to Korean, Tungusic, Mongolic and Turkic?* Wiesbaden: Harrassowitz.

Robbeets, Martine. 2015. *Diachrony of Verb Morphology: Japanese and the Transeurasian Languages*. Berlin: De Gruyter Mouton.

Robbeets, Martine. 2017. 'The language of the Transeurasian farmers'. In Robbeets and Savelyev (2017): 93–122.

Robbeets, Martine. 2020a. 'Basic vocabulary in the Transeurasian languages'. In Robbeets and Savelyev (2020): 511–21.

Robbeets, Martine. 2020b. 'The classification of the Transeurasian languages'. In Robbeets and Savelyev (2020): 31–9.

Robbeets, Martine. 2020c. 'The typological heritage of the Transeurasian languages'. In Robbeets and Savelyev (2020): 127–44.

Robbeets, Martine, and Alexander Savelyev (eds.). 2017. *Language Dispersal beyond Farming*. Amsterdam: John Benjamins.

Robbeets, Martine, and Alexander Savelyev (eds.). 2020. *The Oxford Guide to the Transeurasian Languages*. Oxford: Oxford University Press.

Rountree, S. C., and N. Glock. 1982. *Saramaccan for Beginners: A Pedagogical Grammar of the Saramaccan Language*. Paramaribo: Summer Institute of Linguistics.

Ryckeboer, Hugo. 2000. 'The role of political borders in the millennial retreat of Dutch (Flemish) in the north of France'. *International Journal of the Sociology of Language* 145: 79–108.

Salminen, Tapani. 1998. 'Pohjoisten itämorensuomalaisten kielten luokittelun ongelmia' [Problems in the classification of the northern Baltic Finnic languages]. *Mémoires de la Société Finno-Ougrienne* 228: 390–406.

Sampson, Geoffrey, David Gil and Peter Trudgill (eds.). 2009. *Language Complexity as an Evolving Variable*. Oxford: Oxford University Press.

Samuels, M. L. 1989a. 'Chaucerian final -e'. In Smith (1989): 7–12.

Samuels, M. L. 1989b. 'The Great Scandinavian Belt'. In Laing (1989): 106–15.

Samuels, M. L. 1989c. 'Some applications of Middle English dialectology'. In Laing (1989): 64–80.

Sandve, B. H. 1976. 'Om talemålet i industristatene Odda og Tyssedal: Generasjonsskilnad og tilnærmind mellom de to målfora' [On the spoken language in the industrial towns Odda and Tyssedal: generational differences and convergence between the two dialects]. Unpublished dissertation, University of Bergen.

Sapir, Edward. 1921. *Language*. New York: Harcourt, Brace and World.

Sasse, Hans-Jürgen. (1992) 2012a. 'Language decay and contact-induced change: similarities and differences'. In Brenzinger ((1992) 2012): 59–82.

Sasse, Hans-Jürgen. (1992) 2012b. 'Theory of language death'. In Brenzinger ((1992) 2012): 7–30.

Sayahi, Lotfi. 2014. *Diglossia and Language Contact: Language Variation and Change in North Africa*. Cambridge: Cambridge University Press.

Schmid, Monika. 2002. *First Language Attrition, Use and Maintenance: The Case of German Jews in Anglophone Countries*. Amsterdam: John Benjamins.

Schmid, Monika S. 2007. 'The role of L2 use for L1 attrition'. In Schmid et al. (2007): 135–53.

Schmid, Monika S. 2011. *Language Attrition*. Cambridge: Cambridge University Press.

Schmid, Monika S., and Scott Jarvis. 2014. 'Lexical access and lexical diversity in first language attrition'. *Bilingualism: Language and Cognition* 17: 729–48.

Schmid, Monika S., and Tuğba Karayayla. 2020. 'The roles of age, attitude, and use in first language development and attrition of Turkish-English bilinguals'. *Language Learning* 70: 54–84.

Schmid, Monika S., and Barbara Köpke (eds.). 2019. *The Oxford Handbook of Language Attrition*. Oxford: Oxford University Press.

Schmid, Monika S., Barbara Köpke, Merel Keijzer and Lina Weilemar (eds.). 2007. *Language Attrition: Theoretical Perspectives*. Amsterdam: John Benjamins.

Schmidt, A. 1985. *Young Person's Dyirbal: An Example of Language Death from Australia*. Cambridge: Cambridge University Press.

Schneider, Edgar (ed.). 1997. *Englishes around the World: Vol. 1. General Studies, British Isles, North America*. Amsterdam: John Benjamins.

Schneider, Edgar W. 2015. 'Documenting the history of African American Vernacular English: A survey and assessment of sources and results'. In Lanehart (2001): 125–39.

Scholtmeijer, Harrie. 1999. 'Taalontwikkeling in een nieuwe polder' [Language development in a new polder]. *Cultuur-historisch Jahrboek voor Flevoland* 9: 71–83.

Schreier, Daniel. 2003. *Isolation and Language Change: Contemporary and Sociohistorical Evidence from Tristan da Cunha English*. Basingstoke: Palgrave Macmillan.

Schreier, Daniel. 2008. *St Helenian English: Origins, Evolution and Variation*. Amsterdam: John Benjamins.

Schreier, Daniel, and Marianne Hundt (eds.). 2013. *English as a Contact Language*. Cambridge: Cambridge University Press.

Schwindler, Lothar. 2014. 'Menschen im römischen Trier – zum Bevölkerungsstruktur der colonia Augusta Treverorum' [Humans in Roman Trier – towards a demography of colonia Augusta Treverorum]. In Landesmuseum Württemberg and Rheinisches Landesmuseum (2014): 184–93.

Scodari, Christina. 2018. *Alternate Roots: Ethnicity, Race, and Identity in Genealogy Media*. Jackson: University Press of Mississippi.

Shepard, Jonathan (ed.). 2007. *The Expansion of Orthodox Europe: Byzantium, the Balkans and Russia*. Aldershot: Ashgate Variorum.

Sick, Bastian. 2016. *Der Dativ ist dem Genitiv sein Tod: Ein Wegweiser durch den Irrgaarten der deutschen Sprache* [The dative is the genitive's death: a guide through the maze of the German language]. Cologne: Kiepenheuer & Witsch.

Siegel, Jeff. 1985. 'Koinés and koinéisation'. *Language in Society* 14: 357–78.

Siegel, Jeff. 1987. *Language Contact in a Plantation Environment*. Cambridge: Cambridge University Press.

Siegel, Jeff. 1998. 'Substrate reinforcement and dialectal differences in Melanesian Pidgin'. *Journal of Sociolinguistics* 2: 347–73.

Siegel, Jeff. 2001. 'Koine formation and creole genesis'. In Smith (2001): 175–97.

Siegel, Jeff. 2008a. *The Emergence of Pidgin and Creole Languages*. Oxford: Oxford University Press.

Siegel, Jeff. 2008b. 'Pidgins/creoles and second language acquisition'. In Kouwenberg and Singler (2008): 189–218.

Siegel, Jeff. 2010. *Second Dialect Acquisition*. Cambridge: Cambridge University Press.

Simpson, W. Douglas (ed.). 1954. *The Viking Congress Lerwick, July 1950*. Edinburgh: Oliver and Boyd.

Singler, John Victor. 2008. 'The sociohistorical context of creole genesis'. In Kouwenberg and Singler (2008): 332–58.

Smith, Jeremy J. (ed.). 1989. *The English of Chaucer and His Contemporaries: Essays by M. L. Samuels and J. J. Smith*. Aberdeen: Aberdeen University Press.

Smith, Norval (ed.). 2001. *Creolization and Contact*. Amsterdam: John Benjamins.

Smith, Norval. 2015. 'A preliminary list of probable KiKongo (KiKoongo) lexical items in the Surinam creoles'. In Muysken and Smith (2015): 417–62.

Spears, Arthur K., and Donald Winford (eds.). 1997. *The Structure and Status of Pidgins and Creoles*. Amsterdam: John Benjamins.

Stammler, Wolfgang. 1922. 'Das "Halbdeutsch" der Esten' [The "Half German" of the Ests/Estonians]. *Zeitschrift für Deutsche Mundarten* 17: 160–72.

Stegmann, Kurt von Pritzwald. 1952. 'Das baltische Deutsch als Standessprache' [Baltic German as a class language]. *Zeitschrift für Ostforschung* 1: 407–22.

Steinmetz, Sol. 2001. *Yiddish and English: The Story of Yiddish in America*. Tuscaloosa: University of Alabama Press.

Sutcliffe, David. 2001. 'The voice of the ancestors: New evidence on 19th-century precursors to 20th-century African American English'. In Lanehart (2001): 130–63.

Szarmach, Paul C., and Joel T. Rosenthal (eds.). 1997. *The Preservation and Transmission of Anglo-Saxon Culture*. Kalamazoo: Publications of the Center for Medieval Studies.

Thomason, Sarah G. (ed.). 1997a. *Contact Languages: A Wider Perspective*. Amsterdam: John Benjamins.

Thomason, Sarah G. 1997b. 'Mednyj Aleut'. In Thomason (1997a): 449–68.

Thomason, Sarah G. 2001. *Language Contact: An Introduction*. Edinburgh: Edinburgh University Press.

Thomason, Sarah Grey, and Terrence Kaufman. 1988. *Language Contact, Creolization, and Genetic Linguistics*. Berkeley: University of California Press.

Thompson, Paul, with Tony Wailey and Trevor Lummis. 1983. *Living the Fishing*. London: Routledge and Kegan Paul.

Thorsen, Per. 1954. 'The third Norn dialect – that of Caithness'. In Simpson (1954): 230–54.

Townend, Matthew. 2002. *Language and History in Viking Age England: Linguistic Relations between Speakers of Old Norse and Old English*. Turnhout: Brepols.

Trubetzkoy, Nikolai S. 1923. 'Vavilonskaja bašnja i smešenie jazykov' [The tower of Babel and the confusion of languages]. *Evrazijskij vremennik* 3: 197–24.

Trubetzkoy, Nikolai S. 1930. 'Proposition 16'. In de Boer, van Ginneken and van Hamel (1930): 17–18.

Trudgill, Peter. 1983. *On Dialect: Social and Geographical Perspectives*. Oxford: Blackwell.

Trudgill, Peter (ed.). 1984. *Language in the British Isles*. Cambridge: Cambridge University Press.

Trudgill, Peter. 1986. *Dialects in Contact*. Oxford: Blackwell.

Trudgill, Peter. 1988. 'Norwich revisited: Recent changes in an English urban dialect'. *English World-Wide* 9: 33–49.

Trudgill, Peter. 2002. *Sociolinguistic Variation and Change*. Edinburgh: Edinburgh University Press.

Trudgill, Peter. 2004. *New-Dialect Formation: The Inevitability of*

Colonial Englishes. Edinburgh: Edinburgh University Press.

Trudgill, Peter. 2008. 'Colonial dialect contact is the history of European languages: On the irrelevance of identity to new-dialect formation'. *Language in Society* 37: 241–50.

Trudgill, Peter. 2010. *Investigations in Sociohistorical Linguistics: Stories of Colonisation and Contact*. Cambridge: Cambridge University Press.

Trudgill, Peter. 2011. *Sociolinguistic Typology: Social Determinants of Linguistic Complexity*. Oxford: Oxford University Press.

Trušník, Roman, Katarína Nemčoková and Gregory Jason Bell (eds.). 2011. *Proceedings of the Third International Conference on Anglophone Studies September 7–8, 2011 Tomas Bata University in Zlín, Czech Republic*. Zlin: Univerzita Tomáše Bati ve Zlíně.

Turner, L. D. 1949. *Africanisms in the Gullah Dialect*. Ann Arbor: University of Michigan Press.

Udolph, Jürgen. 1994. *Namenkundliche Studien zum Germanenproblem* [Onomastic studies related to the problem of the Germanic peoples]. Berlin: Walter de Gruyter.

Ureland, P. Sture. 1986. 'Some contact-linguistic structures in Scandinavian languages'. In Nelde, Ureland and Clarkson (1986): 31–79.

Ureland, P. Sture. 1989. 'Some contact structures in Scandinavian, Dutch and Raeto-Romansch: Inner-linguistic and/or contact causes of language change'. In Breivik and Jahr (1989): 239–76.

Ureland, P. Sture, and Iain Clarkson (eds.). 1996. *Language Contact across the North Atlantic*. Tübingen: Niemeyer.

Vajda, Edward. 2020. 'Transeurasian as a continuum of diffusion'. In Robbeets and Savelyev (2020): 726–34.

Valkhoff, M. F. 1966. *Studies in Portuguese and Creole with Special Reference to South Africa*. Johannesburg: Witwatersrand University Press.

Van der Velde, Mark, Koen Bostoen, Derek Nurse and Gérard Philippson (eds.). 2019. *The Bantu Languages*. London: Routledge.

Van Herk, Gerard. 2015. 'The English origins hypothesis'. In Lanehart (2015): 23–34.

Veenstra, Tonjes. 2008. 'Creole genesis: The impact of the language bioprogram hypothesis'. In Kouwenberg and Singler (2008): 219–42.

Velupillai, Viveka. 2012. *An Introduction to Linguistic Typology*. Amsterdam: John Benjamins.

Velupillai, Viveka. 2019. 'Gendered inanimates in Shetland dialect: Comparing pre-oil and contemporary speech'. *English World-Wide* 40: 269–98.

Verhaar, John W. M. (ed.). 1990. *Melanesian Pidgin and Tok Pisin: Proceedings of the First International Conference of Pidgins and Creoles in Melanesia*. Amsterdam: John Benjamins.

Viitso, T. R. 1997. 'The prosodic system of Estonian in the Finnic space'. In Lehiste and Ross (1997): 222–34.

Voorhoeve, J. 1962. *Sranan Syntax*. Amsterdam: North-Holland.

Vossen, Rainer, and Gerrit J. Dimmendaal (eds.). 2020. *The Oxford Handbook of African Languages*. Oxford: Oxford University Press.

Vovin, Alexander. 2005. 'The end of the Altaic controversy: In memory of Gerhard Doerfer'. *Central Asiatic Journal* 49: 71–132.

Vovin, Alexander. 2017. 'Origins of the Japanese language'. In *Oxford Research Encyclopedia of Linguistics*. https://oxfordre.com/linguistics.

Wallis, Jim. 2016. *America's Original Sin: Racism, White Privilege, and the Bridge to a New America*. Grand Rapids: Brazos Press.

Warren, Meralda (ed.). 2008. *Mi bas side orn Pitcairn*. Norfolk Island: Pitcairn Island School.

Watt, Dominic, and Carmen Llamas (eds.). 2014. *Languages, Borders and Identity*. Edinburgh: Edinburgh University Press.

Weinreich, Uriel. 1953. *Languages in Contact: Findings and Problems*. New York: Linguistic Circle of New York.

Weldon, Tracey L., and Simanique Moody. 2015. 'The place of Gullah in the African American linguistic continuum'. In Lanehart (2015): 163–80.

Wilkerson, Isabel. 2020. *The Warmth of Other Suns: The Epic Story of America's Great Migration*. Harmondsworth: Penguin.

Winford, Donald. 2003. *An Introduction to Contact Linguistics*. Oxford: Blackwell.

Winford, Donald. 2015. 'The origins of African American Vernacular English'. In Lanehart (2015): 85–104.

Withrington, Donald J. (ed.). 1983. *Shetland and the Outside World 1469–1969*. Oxford: Oxford University Press.

Wolfram, Walt. 1974. 'The relationship of white southern speech to Vernacular Black English'. *Language* 50: 498–527.

Wührer, K. 1954. 'Der Einfluss des Deutschen auf die skandinavischen Sprachen' [The influence of German on the Scandinavian languages]. *Muttersprache: Zeitschrift zur Pflege und Erforschung der deutschen Sprache* 1: 448–59.

Yerastov, Yuri. 2010. 'Done, finished and started as reflexes of the Scottish transitive be perfect in North America: Their synchrony, diachrony and current marginalisation'. In Millar (2010b): 19–52.

Index

abandoned language, 22, 32, 34–35, 41, 43–44, 53, 87, 137, 184
Aberdeen, 1, 31–32
acrolect, 81–83, 87, 112, 170, 174
adstratum, 12, 29, 164, 169–170
Aegean islands, 148
Ælfric, 161
Afghanistan, 147
Africa, 8, 57, 59, 67, 69, 71, 88, 90, 93, 99, 107, 110, 115, 120, 123–125
  central, 76
  East, 70, 117
  North, 8
  southern, 113–114, 143
  sub-Saharan, 8
  West, 70, 110, 120
African American, 67, 88, 119, 121–125
African American Vernacular English, 97, 123
African languages, 88, 90, 103
Afrikaans, 60, 106, 113–114, 116, 118–119, 126, 134, 137, 143, 147, 158, 173
  Cape Coloured, 114, 116
  Fly-Taal, 115
  Orange River, 114, 119
  poor rural whites, 114
  Standard, 115–116
Afrikaners, 115, 118
Afro-Asiatic languages, 145
agglutinative typology, 19–20, 25, 130, 140, 177–178
Åland Islands, 18
Albania, 147
Albanian, 38, 136–137
Aleut
  Mednj (Copper Island), 29
  Medny (Copper Island), 21
Algonquian languages, 11
Altaic languages, 140–141, 145
analytic typoloogy, 177–178
Anatolian languages, 173
Angola, 120

Antarctica, 30
anterior aspect, 66–69, 99–100
apartheid, 115, 118
Arabic, 22, 70, 117, 129, 172
  Modern Standard, 172
Arawak languages, 99
Armenian, 19–20, 25, 129–130
  Modern, 19–20, 25
  Old, 19–20
Arnhem Land, 23
Arumanian, 136
Arvantika, 38
Asia, 8, 140
  central, 141
  East, 18, 65, 102, 130, 132–133, 148, 176
  south, 73–74, 117, 128, 149
  South-East, 65, 148, 176
  south-west, 22, 29, 148
Asia Minor, 7, 23
Athens, 147
Atlantic Ocean, 46, 65, 67–69, 88, 95, 98, 110–112, 120, 151, 178
Atlantic-Caribbean
  region, 65, 111
  varieties of pidgins and creoles, 65
Australia, 23, 41, 43, 60, 70, 72, 96, 102, 108, 112, 155
Austria, 33–34, 38, 53
Austronesian languages, 62, 145, 149
  Polynesian, 2, 62
  Western Oceanic, 62
autochthonous languages, 11, 30, 33, 38–40, 43, 45, 53, 62, 81, 168
Azeri, 20

baby talk, 77
Babylonian Empire, 148
Balkan Language Area, 23–24, 134–135, 137, 140, 142
Balkans, 136–137
Balmoral Castle, 31
Baltic languages, 17, 20–21, 25–26, 30, 133
Baltic Sea, 17, 139, 158–159

Baltic territories, 26
Bangladesh, 150
Bantu languages, 59, 118, 138
Barbados, 24
basilect, 72, 81–83, 86–87, 95, 104, 112–113, 123, 126, 170, 174
Basque, 136
Belarus, 13
Belgium, 114, 116, 143
Bergen, 151, 158
Berlin, 7
Berlin, Irving, 119
Bickerton, Derek, 57, 84–88, 90–92, 96, 104, 174
bilingualism, 13, 15, 17, 21–22, 24–26, 28–29, 36–37, 40–41, 49, 142, 159–161, 175
Bislama (Vanuatu), 75
Bolivia, 39
borrowing, linguistic, 8–9, 12–13, 15–17, 19, 21, 23–27, 31, 42, 48, 51, 65, 89, 100, 130, 137, 146, 170, 173
Boston, 14
Botswana, 59
Brazil, 98, 101
Britain, Island of, 133
British Columbia, 70
British Empire, 118, 149, 157
Bulgaria, 136–137, 142

Caithness, 36, 48, 51
Californian Chinese Pidgin English, 64
Canada, 5, 12, 32, 36, 41, 53, 124, 167
Cape Breton, 53
Cape Colony, 118
Cape of Good Hope, 110, 117–119, 147
Cape Town, 117–118
Carbbean Atlantic pidgins and creoles, 69
Carib languages, 99
Caribbean islands, British, 68
Carinthia, 33–34

case, grammatical, 14, 19–21, 25, 27–28, 36, 44, 46–47, 50, 57, 85, 94, 100, 114–115, 121, 133, 136–137, 142–144, 160–162, 164, 166, 171–172, 177
Caucasus linguistic area, 144
Celtic languages, 7, 165
    P-Celtic, 31
    Q-Celtic, 32
Chaucer, Geoffrey, 16, 161
Chaudenson, Robert, 81, 86, 93–94, 105
cherry-picking, 92
Chicago, 14
China, 63–65, 70, 86, 140
China Coast Pidgin, 63–65, 73, 86
Chinese, 57, 65, 73, 86, 140, 148, 176, 178
    Cantonese, 65
    Wutun dialect, 23
Chinese Pidgin English. *See* China Coast Pidgin
Chinook Jargon, 70, 76
Choctaw, 11
Chomsky, Noam, 84
Christianity, 13, 31, 66, 101, 139, 149
Christianity, evangelical, 36, 108
Clearances, Highland, 36
clicks, phonological, 59
closely related varieties, 146
Clyne, Michael, 41, 43, 54, 182
code-switching, 9, 171
Cologne, 7
colonisation, 4, 102, 104, 110, 157
Congo, River, 99, 120
Conquest, Norman, 10, 16
contact
    close relative, 56, 134, 142, 150, 158
    near relative, 128, 165
convergence, linguistic, 23, 43, 82, 128–130, 134–135, 137–138, 140–142, 144, 146, 154–155, 165, 168, 171–174
Cree, 12
creole class, 82
creole exceptionalism, 55, 57, 80–83, 86, 90–92, 94–97, 104–105, 123, 171

creole genesis, 56, 72, 75, 79–81, 83, 91, 93, 98, 106, 149, 170, 174
creole origin, 80
creole prototype, 92–93
creoles, 24–25, 29, 39, 55–60, 63, 65–73, 75, 79–106, 109, 111–114, 116, 118–127, 131, 147, 149, 155, 168–171, 174–175, 178
creoles, exogenous, 81
creoles, indigenous, 80
creolisation, 58, 70, 84, 88–89, 91–92, 94, 97–98, 106–107, 113, 124, 126, 149
creoloids, 106

Danish, 46, 52, 133, 152, 160, 173
Danube, River, 13, 139–140
De Graff, Michel, 94, 105
De Initio Creaturae, 161
Decamp, David, 72, 75, 80–81
Dee, River, 31
Delaware Jargon, 76, 104
Delhi, 128
Dhaka, 150
dialect continuum, 131, 133–134, 137, 150
dialectology, 39
dialects, traditional, 82, 155
diglossia, 34, 172
divergence, linguistic, 43, 65, 68, 95, 102, 116, 128, 154, 158, 165, 168, 171–172, 174
Domari, 22
Dominican Republic, 124
Don, River, 31
Dorian, Nancy, 35, 37–38, 42, 54
Dornoch, 36
Dravidian languages, 23, 128
Dublin, 68
Dunkirk, 5
Dutch, 5–6, 27, 35, 60, 67, 99–103, 110, 113–119, 132–134, 136–137, 143, 147–148, 158
    broken, 118–119
    dialectal, 119
    Netherlandic, 115–116
    Standard, 115–116, 134
Dutch Reformed Church, 101

Early Melanesian Pidgin, 60

early modern period, 65, 77, 94, 139, 158, 160
East India Company, British, 110, 130
East India Company, Dutch, 117
East Sutherland, 35–37, 42
education, ix, 5, 39, 82–83, 88, 101, 111, 113, 155
Empire
    British, 126
    Portuguese, 117
England, 1, 4, 10, 16, 62–63, 68, 70, 100, 102, 109, 111, 120, 156–157, 162, 172
    East Anglia, 157
    eastern, 148
    north, 12
    northern, 162
    south-east, 155–156, 162
    southern, 155, 173
English, 1, 2–5, 7–8, 10–16, 21, 23–25, 27–28, 31, 36–37, 40, 42–45, 47, 49–51, 53, 57, 59–60, 62–69, 71, 73, 75–76, 86, 88–90, 93, 95, 97, 99–104, 106–114, 116–119, 121–127, 130–134, 136–137, 139, 142–143, 147, 149, 155–157, 160–163, 165, 167, 171–173, 176–178, 187
    Scottish, Standard, 10–11
    African American Vernacular, 68, 88, 106, 111, 119–126
    Australian, 102, 155–157
    British, 35, 116
    Caribbean varieties, 65, 68–71, 88, 90, 92, 95–96, 101, 111, 119, 125, 178
    Celtic, 69
    Cockney, 155–156
    dialects, 1
    Falkland Islands, 165
    General American, 1
    Highland and Islands, 45, 53, 67
    Irish, 4, 24, 67
    Italian American, 14
    Jamaican, 121, 126
    London, 161
    Māori, 11
    Middle, 162

New York City, 169
New Zealand, 11, 102,
    112-113, 156-158
North American, 11, 24, 35,
    88, 102-103, 116, 122,
    164-165, 172
Old, 25, 160, 162-164
Pitcairn (and Norfok) Island
    Vernacular, 106, 108,
    126
Received Pronunciation
    (RP), 1, 155
Scottish Standard, 4
South African, 113, 156
south-east England, 11, 68,
    111, 156-157
southern England, 112
Southern Hemisphere, 11,
    63, 102, 110-112,
    154-156
Southern White Vernacular,
    63, 68, 102, 110-111,
    122-124
St Helena, 68, 106, 110-111,
    113, 126, 154
    Vernacular, 106
Standard, 10-11, 48, 60, 64,
    108-109, 111
Tristan da Cunha, 112-113,
    165
West Saxon Schriftsprache,
    161
Yorkshire, 111
English, Early Modern, 23
English, Standard, 81
Estonia, 18, 26-27
Estonian, 18, 26-28, 138-139
Eurasia, 140
Europe
    east central, 13
    eastern, 13
    southern, 8, 14
Evenki, 140
evolutionary theory
    Darwinian, 131, 141
    Lamarckian, 131, 141
    sub-Darwinian, 131
expanded pidgin, 60, 71, 95,
    175

Faeroe Islands, 46, 49
Faeroese, 47, 49-50, 52, 133,
    143, 152, 159
Fanagalo, 59
Fenland, 148
Ferguson, Charles, 34, 172
Fiji, 73, 149-151
Fiji Hindi, 73, 128, 149, 164

Fijian, 73, 149
Finland, 18
    Gulf of, 18
Finnic
    Baltic, 17-21, 27, 139
Finnic languages, 30, 138-140,
    173
Finnish, 17-18, 27, 53, 57,
    138-139, 142, 171
Finno-Ugric, 138-140, 142
First Germanic Consonant
    Shift (Grimm's Law),
    169
first language, 9, 16, 26,
    32-33, 36, 41-45, 50,
    57, 66-67, 69, 71, 77,
    79, 83-85, 88, 95, 97,
    114, 117, 119, 124,
    147-148, 154, 170,
    173, 175
Fishman, Joshua A., 32, 34,
    172
Flanders
    French, 5
foreigner talk, 28, 76-77, 96,
    174
Foula, 50
founder effect, 83, 158, 172
France, 5, 8, 16, 39, 101
French, 5-12, 16, 21, 23, 39,
    44-45, 57, 69, 76-77,
    86, 89, 93, 97-98, 101,
    117, 126, 143, 140, 160,
    167, 170, 172-173, 176
    Anglo-Norman, 16, 24
    Norman, 10
    Québec, 148
French territories, central
    Indian Ocean, 71
Frisian, 132-134
fusional typology, 19, 25, 130,
    177-178

Gaelic, 1-4, 11, 31-32, 35-38,
    42, 45, 53, 144
Gàidhealtachd, 168, See Gaelic
Gal, Susan, 38, 54
Galatians, 7
Ganges/Ganga, River, 150
Gangetic plain, 128, 150
gender, grammatical, 22,
    27-28, 44, 48, 50,
    114-116, 160-162,
    172-173
Georgia, 67, 121
German, 6-9, 15, 23, 26-28,
    33-35, 38, 41, 43-44,
    49, 53, 76, 116-117,

130, 132-134,
136-137, 139,
142-143, 164,
172-174, 176
    Australian, 43-44
    Bavarian, 27
    Frankish, 8, 134
    Halbdeutsch, 26-28
    Low, 26-28, 132-134,
        158-162
    Old High, 160
    Rhine-Mosel, 9
    Standard High, 26-27,
        43-44, 143
    Swiss, 134
    Trier dialect, 8-9
Germanic
    North Sea, 133
    West Continental, 116
Germanic langauges, 2, 7, 13,
    17-18, 27, 95,
    115-116, 131-132,
    134, 140, 142-143,
    158, 160-161, 169, 176
    North, 47-51, 63, 132-133,
        161, 162, 172
    East, 132
    Proto-North West, 132
    runes, 132
    South, 133
    West, 50, 63, 133-134, 172
Germanic Languages,
    runic, 132
Germany, 6, 8, 41, 46,
    133-134, 188
globalisation, 5, 32, 39
Gothic, 131-132
Gotland, 159
    traditional dialects, 133
grammaticalisation, 63, 173
Great Migration, 121
Great Scandinavian Belt,
    162-163
Great Vowel Shift, English, 169
Greece, 38, 136
Greek, 7, 13, 23, 89, 129-130,
    136-137, 147-148,
    173, 176
    Attic, 147-148
    Ionic, 147-148
    Tsakonian, 148
Grimm, Jacob, 130
Guiane, 98
Gujarati, 128
Gullah, 67-69, 93, 111, 121
Guyana, 98

Haiti, 86, 168

Hall, Robert A., jr, 57, 65, 74, 77, 80
Hanseatic League, 158–159
Hardanger fjord, 151
Harlem, 122
Hawai'i, 88, 92, 96, 100
Hawai'ian Pidgin English, 74, 88, 96
Hebrew, Israeli, 44
Hellenism, 147–148
Henry, William, 50
heritage languages, 43–45, 88
Hildina Ballad, 50
Hindi, 128, 150
    Awadhi, 150
    Bhojpuri, 150
    Braj, 150
    Fiji, 151, 155
Hinduism, 128, 149
historical linguistics, 1, 171
history of English
    emigration and spread of speakers
    New Zealand, 11
HMS *Bounty*, 107
Holocaust, The, 41
homestead period, 94, 121
homestead phase, 82, 100, 124–125
Honduras, 68
Hungarian, 38, 137–139
Hungary, 139
Hunnish, 8

Iceland, 46
Icelandic, 13, 47, 49, 133, 143, 152, 159, 164
Icelandic Pidgin Basque, 76
imperialism, 5, 11, 32, 39, 57, 67, 71, 73, 77, 82, 94, 99, 117, 167
indentured servants, 93–94, 149
India, 75, 118, 128–130
    southern, 23
Indian Ocean, 69, 71, 86, 95, 97, 118, 178
Indic languages, 22
Indies, East, 75
Indies, West, 107
Indo-European, 21
    Baltic, 17–21, 25, 139
    ProtoBaltic, 17
Indo-European languages, 19–21, 25, 128, 130, 132, 138–141, 145, 149, 173

Indic, 128
Indonesia, 78, 98, 117
industrialisation, 39
interference, linguistic, 22–26, 40, 44–45, 52, 86, 103, 119, 137, 173
invisible hand, 98
Iran, 22
Iranian languages, 8, 20, 129
Ireland, 4, 68, 157
    Co. Cork, 4
    Forth and Bargy, 4
    south-east, 4
Irish, 4, 14, 24
Irish Sea, 32
Iroquois, 167
isiZulu, 59
Islam, 78, 117, 128, 140, 149
isolating typology, 177
Italian, 13–15, 142

Jainism, 128
Jakobsen, Jakob, 50–52
Jamaica, 69, 81, 83, 103, 123
Japan, 89
Japanese, 86, 89, 141, 191
Jargon, 72, 77–78, 174
Java, 117
Jerome, St, 7
Jerusalem, 22
Jewish immigrants to North America, 41
Jews, Sephardic, 101
Jim Crow laws, 121

Kalinago people, 24
Kannada, 128–129
Karelian, 139
Kerswill, Paul, 148, 151, 165–166
Khanty, 139
Khazar Empire, 140
Khoikhoi languages, 117
Khoikhoi people, 117
Khoisan languages, 59, 145
Kincardineshire, 50
kiSwahili, 70
koine, 25, 74, 113, 126, 146–149, 158, 161, 164–165
koine glossa, 147–148
koineisation, 102, 126, 147, 149, 151, 164–165, 168, 173
koines, 91, 95, 147–149, 164–165
Korean, 141

Kupwar, 23, 128–130, 144

Labov, William, 123, 169
Lahore, 150
Lancashire, 49
language area, 128, 135, 144, 168, 174
Language attrition, x, 30, 40–42
language bioprogram hypothesis, 84, 91
language death, x, 16, 30, 32–33, 42–43, 174, 194
language maintenance, 23
language of recent immigration, 8, 39
languages of wider communication, 33
languages, pre-Columbian, 11
Latin, 7–8, 13, 16, 23, 76, 89, 142, 144, 177
Latvia, 18–19, 26–27
Latvian, 21, 26
lexicalisation, 92
lexicostatistics, 141
lexifier language, 58–59, 69, 76, 81–83, 85–86, 90–93, 95–97, 100, 104, 106–107, 127, 147, 171, 174
Liberia, 124
Lingua Franca, 24, 71, 75, 167
lingua franca (common language), 62, 77–78, 84, 87, 99, 167–168
lingua francas,
Lingua Geral, 104
linguistic attrition, 40–42, 44, 54, 170
linguistic bioprogram hypothesis, 84, 87–88, 104, 174
linguistic drift, 43, 58, 98, 143, 156, 172
linguistic family tree, 102, 130, 132, 138–139, 142, 158
literacy, 10, 31, 43, 81, 83, 92–94, 103, 107–109, 134, 150, 164, 168
Lithuanian, 21, 139
Liverpool, 68
Livonian, 19, 27, 139
Lorraine, 8
Los Angeles, 53
Louisiana, 16
Low, Reverend Mr George, 50
Luxembourg, 9

northern, 9
Luxembourg City, 9
Luxembourgish, 9, 27, 29, 134, 143

Macao, 65
Macedonian, 136–137, 142
Macedonian kings, 147
Madagascar, 110, 117
Magyar. *See* Hungarian
Magyars, 139
Malagasy, 110, 117
Malay, 65, 77
Malayalam, 128
Malmö, 158
Man, Isle of, 32
Manchu, 140
Manchuria, 140
Manhattan, 30
Manitoba, 12
Mansi, 139
Manx, 32
Māori, 11, 72
Marathi, 128–129
Maroons, 66, 101, 103
Massachusett, 11
Massachusetts, 167
Matras, Yaron, 22, 29, 130, 180
McWhorter, John H, 71, 80, 91–94, 97–98, 100, 103–105
Mediterranean Sea, 8, 75, 148
Melanesia, 70, 90
Melanesian pidgins and creoles, 60, 62, 71, 75, 83, 86, 90–91, 93, 96–97, 104, 178
mesolect, 81–83, 87, 123, 174
Meyerhoff, Miriam, 90
Michif, 12, 21, 131, 161
Middle Ages, 2, 10, 16, 26, 48, 132–134, 156, 158, 160
migration, 3, 13–14, 26, 38–39, 86, 98, 108, 119, 125
Miskito Coast Creole English, 68–69
Miskito Coast Crole English,
Mississippi, River, 11, 102
Mongol languages, 140–141
monogenesis, 75–76
monolingualism, 5–6, 35, 39, 42, 46, 48, 57, 104
Moravian Brethren, 66, 101
Moray Firth, 37
Mordva, 138
Moscow, 30, 138
Mosel/Moselle, River, 6–8

Mufwene, Salikoko S., 57, 84–85, 89, 92–96, 98, 105–106, 123, 125, 172
Mühlhäusler, Peter, 60, 62, 71–72, 76, 78, 81–82, 100, 107–109
multilingualism, x, 1–6, 8, 23, 41, 55, 90, 118, 130, 148, 167–168
Munsee, 30
Myers-Scotton, Carol, 9

Nama, 59
Namibia, 59, 114
Narrangansett, 11
Native American languages, 11
native language
 nativisation, 80
nativisation, 4, 79–80, 171
natural morphology, 45, 58
Nazism, 41
near-relative language, 174
neogrammarian hypothesis, 1, 131
Netherlands, The, 7, 46, 100–101, 114–116, 119, 134, 143
New Britain, 23
New Guinea, 23, *See* Papua New Guinea
New Ireland, 60, 62
New Jersey, 14, 120
New South Wales, 108
new variety formation, 154
New York, 30, 120
New York City, 14, 68, 122
New Zealand, 11, 72, 102, 112–113, 156–157
Nicaragua, 68
Nigeria, 89
Nigerian Pidgin, 71, 79, 81, 86
Norf'k. *See* English, Pitcain (and Norfolk),
Norfolk Island, 106, 108–109
Norn, 35, 45–52, 133
Norse
 East, 133, 152
 West, 49, 51, 133–134, 152
 West, insular, 133
Norse, Old, 12, 17, 25, 31, 46–49, 133, 160, 162, 164–165
North America, 11, 68, 73
 New England, 11
North Atlantic world, 46
North Dakota, 12
North East of Scotland, 31
North Sea, 31, 36, 158

Northern Isles, 48–50
Norway, 46, 151–152, 154, 160
Norwegian, 47, 49, 51–52, 72, 133, 142–143, 151, 153–154, 158, 159, 165, 173, 176
 Bokmål, 154, 160
 eastern dialects, 152–154
 Nynorsk, 51, 133, 154, 159
 western dialects, 90, 132–134, 152–154
Nova Scotia, 53, 124

Occitan, 39
Odda, 151–153, 165
Ojibwa, 11
Old Saxon, 132
Orkney, 46, 48–50, 133
Ostyak. *See* Khanty
Ottoman Empire, 139

Pacific Ocean, 60–61, 65, 70, 97, 107, 149
Pacific varieties of pidgins and creoles, 60, 63–65
Paisley, 49
Papua New Guinea, 60, 62, 75, 83, 90
Paramaribo, 98
partly restructured vernaculars, 106
Party of Fear, 14
Pearl River Delta, 63
Peloponnese, 148
peonage, 71, 73, 121
Permian region, 139
Persian Empire, 148
Peru, 39
Peterborough Chronicle, 162
physics
 Einsteinian, 131
 Newtonian, 131
Pictish, 31–32
pidgin development, 74, 76
pidgin genesis, 75–76
pidgin, expanded, 80, 82
pidgin, stable, 78
pidgincreoles, 79–80, 175
pidginisation, 70, 74, 76, 84, 95
pidgins, 24–25, 29, 39, 55–60, 63–65, 67, 69–81, 83–85, 87–91, 95–96, 104–107, 109, 111, 118, 126, 131, 147, 149, 168–169, 171, 174–175
Pijin (Solomon Islands), 62–63, 70, 75

Pitcairn Island, 106-109, 155, 179
Pitkern. *See* English, Pitcairn (and Norfolk) Island Vernacular, English, Pitcairn (and Norfolk) Island Vernacular, PEnglish, Pitcain (and Norfok) Island Vernacular, English, Pitcairn (and Norfolk) Island Vernacular, English, Pitcairn (and Norfolk) Island Vernacular, English, Pitcairn (and Norfolk) Island Vernacular, English, Pitcairn (and Norfolk) Island
plantation phase, 68, 73, 82-83, 86, 89, 93, 120-121, 124, 168
Polish, 13
polygenesis, 75-76
Polynesian languages, 2
Poplack, Shana, 123-124
Portugal, 75, 117
Portuguese, 63-65, 67, 75-76, 88, 100-101, 103, 175
  Brazilian Vernacular, 127
post-colonial, 81-82
post-creole continuum, 36, 81-82, 86, 97, 102, 112, 123, 149-150, 168, 170, 174
post-pidgin continuum, 82
Potato Famine, Irish, 40
Prince Albert, 31
prosetylisation, 66, 78, 113
Protestant Reformation, 26
proto-language, 138, 140
psycholinguistics, 40, 170
punctuated equilibrium model, 135
Punjab
  Pakistani, 150

Quebec, 167
Quechua, 39
Queen Victoria, 31

racism, 39, 58, 74-75, 82, 94, 121, 131, 167
racism, linguistic, 57
rationalisation, linguistic, 55-56, 58, 78, 147-148, 164, 169, 173-175
Reformed Church (Dutch), 115-116
relexification, 75, 175
Réunion, 83, 86, 126-127
Rhenish Fan, 134
Rhine, River, 6-7, 13
Rhone, River, 39
rhoticisation, 68, 100, 157
rhoticity, 63, 156, 169
Riga, 26
Romaine, Suzanne, 60, 62
Roman Empire, 7-8, 13, 133, 140, 143, 173
Roman script, 12, 132, 160
Romance languages, 8, 65, 75, 95, 116, 136, 142-144, 176
  Balkan, 136
Romani, 22, 24, 136
Romania, 136
Romanian, 136-137
Romansh, 23
Romanticism, 39
Roper Kriol, 96
Royal Navy, 72, 107
Russenorsk, 72
Russia, 18, 21, 138
Russian, 13, 17, 70, 73, 142, 177

Sabir, 75
Saint Helena, 113
Sámi, 139
Samoyedic languages, 138, 140
Sango, 76
Sanskrit, 23
Sapir, Edouard, 58, 156, 172, 194
Saramaccan, 66-69, 83, 86, 89, 93, 99, 101-102, 104
Sarmatian, 8
Saskatchewan, 12
Sasse, Hans Jurgen, 33-35, 38-39, 42, 45, 53
Sasse, Hans Jürgen, 16
Sauer, River, 7
Scandinavia, 18
Scandinavian languages, 44, 47-48, 136, 158-160, 162-164
Schmid, Monika, 40-42, 54, 194
Schreier, Daniel, 110-113, 166
Scotland, 2-3, 10, 13, 16, 32-33, 35-36, 45-46, 49, 102, 120, 157
  eastern, 158
  North East, 3-4, 50
  West, 3
Scots, 1, 3-4, 10-11, 16, 31, 33, 35-36, 45-52, 58, 68, 102, 119-120, 156-157, 165
  Black Isle, 49
  Caithness, 2
  Insular, 48
  Middle, 4
  North-East, 2
  Orkney, 46, 48
  Shetland, 45-46, 48-53
  West Central, 2, 11, 15, 46, 49
Sea Islands, 67, 121
Second Germanic Consonant Shift, 134
second language, 1, 26, 41-43, 45, 68, 79, 83, 87, 95-97, 103, 108, 113, 115, 117, 124, 149, 165, 170, 175, 178
segregation, 82, 121, 123
semi-creole, 106, 175
semi-creoles, 106, 126-127, 147, 149
semi-speaker, 38, 40
semi-speakers, 35, 37-38, 42-43, 175
Semitic languages, 129, 138, 145
Serbian, 136
servitude, indentured, 117
Shetland, 35, 45-51, 68, 86, 133
Siberia, 138-140
Siegel, Jeff, 57, 60, 70-71, 79, 84-86, 88, 90, 95-97, 100, 149, 151, 165
simplification, 35, 57-58, 94, 107, 114, 116
Singapore, 127
Singlish, 127
Slave trade, 117
slavery, 8, 39, 55, 57-58, 65-66, 68-71, 73-74, 82, 86-87, 89-90, 93-95, 99-101, 103, 110, 113, 117-118, 120-126, 149, 167-168
Slavonic languages, 13-14, 17, 27, 30, 136-137, 142

Slovenia, 34
Slovenian, 33–34
sociolinguistics, 3–4, 9–10, 15, 23, 29, 32–33, 37, 39–40, 53, 56, 72, 74, 79, 81–83, 97–98, 100, 104, 113, 121, 123, 147, 169–170, 175
Solomon Islands, 62, 70, 75
Sorbian, 142
South Africa, 5, 59, 110, 114–115, 118
South America, 66, 98
South Carolina, 67–68, 121, 168
Spanish, 39, 53, 69, 101, 136
  Caribbean vernaculars, 127
Sprachbund. *See* Language Areas
Sranan, 67, 99–104, 147
St Helena, 110–113
stabilisation, pidgin, 74
Stammbaum. *See* linguistic famiy tree
Standard Average European, 142
standard variety, 8, 51, 58, 81–82, 93–94, 109–111, 114, 119, 133–134, 143, 154, 159, 168, 170, 178
Stavanger, 151
substratum, 10–13, 16, 24, 29, 74, 80, 85–91, 96, 100, 124, 175
superstratum, 10–11, 13, 16, 22, 29, 74, 86, 175
Suriname, 66–67, 75, 83, 86, 89, 93–94, 98–103
Sutherland, 36–37
Sutherland, Duke of, 36
swamping, 4, 158
Sweden, 18, 53, 152
Swedish, 47, 49, 133, 152, 160, 176
  Standard, 133
Switzerland, 23, 134
Sydney, 155
synthetic typology, 25, 115, 137, 176–178

Taa, 59
taboo avoidance, 51
Tahitian, 72, 107, 110
Tallinn
  Reval, 26
Tamil, 128
target language, 15, 24, 34–35, 41, 43, 45, 53, 88, 108–109
Tartu
  Dorpat, 26
Telugu, 128–129
Texas, 102, 122
Thessaloniki, 136
third language, 41
Thomason, Sarah G., 9, 12–13, 15, 17, 21–25, 136
Thomason's levels of contact, 12, 22
Tibetan, 23
Tok Pisin, 29, 62, 75, 79, 81, 83, 97, 104, 121
tone, lexical, 57, 90, 92, 148, 176
Transeurasian languages, 141
transition period
  English, 161–162
Trier, 6–9
Tristan da Cunha, 112–113, 155
Trondheim, 151
Trudgill, Peter, 58, 156–158, 160, 165–166
Tungusic languages, 140–141
Turkey, 7–8, 42, 148
Turkic languages, 8, 20, 25, 130, 139–140
Turkish, 19–20, 23, 42, 129–130, 136–137, 177
Tyne, River, 157
typology, linguistic, 19–21, 23–25, 56, 58, 72, 76, 140, 144, 158, 176, 178
Tyssedal, 151–153, 165

Ugric languages, 138–140
uniformitarianism, 55–56, 80, 82–83, 86, 90–98, 100, 104–105, 125–127, 170–171, 174, 178
United States of America, 5, 12, 14, 16, 24, 35, 41, 62, 68, 70–71, 76, 120–121, 123, 156, 164, 172
  Deep South, 102, 108, 110, 120–121, 124–125
  Midwest, 109
  North, 121
  West, 121
Universal Grammar, 84, 174
universals, linguistic, 55
unofrmitarianism, 57
Ural mountains, 139
Uralic languages, 138–140, 145
Urdu, 128–129

Vanuatu, 75
varieties, 'new', 56, 102, 154
Vepsian, 139
Vietnamese, 58, 171, 177
Viking age, 12, 25
Virginia, 121, 167
Visby, 158
Vlach. *See* Arumanian
Vogul. *See* Mansi
Volga, River, 30, 139–140

Wales, 62
Warren, Meralda, 108
Weinreich, Uriel, 98
Welsh, 31
West Africa, 75
West African languages, 57, 67, 69, 90, 100, 176
Winford, Donald, 10, 23–25, 121
Winford's categories, 23–24

Yiddish, 24, 35, 134
Yorkshire, 49, 156
Yoruba, 168
Yugoslavia, 34
Yukaghir languages, 140